Work, Postmodernism and Organization

Organization, Theory and Society

The *Organization, Theory and Society* series publishes leading-edge books reflecting the newest and most significant developments in contemporary organization studies. Each book will adopt an interdisciplinary perspective, which draws on dialogue among scholars concerned with organization from a range of perspectives.

Series editors

Mike Reed, University of Lancaster
Hari Tsoukas, Athens Laboratory of Business Administration

Work, Postmodernism and Organization

A critical introduction

Philip Hancock and Melissa Tyler

SAGE Publications
London • Thousand Oaks • New Delhi

© Philip Hancock and Melissa Tyler 2001

First published 2001

SAGE Publications Ltd
6 Bonhill Street
London EC2A 4PU

SAGE Publications Inc.
2455 Teller Road
Thousand Oaks, California 91320

SAGE Publications India Pvt Ltd
32, M-Block Market
Greater Kailash – I
New Delhi 110 048

British Library Cataloguing in Publication data

A catalogue record for this book is
available from the British Library

ISBN 0 7619 5943 2
ISBN 0 7619 5944 0 (pbk)

Library of Congress catalog card number available

Typeset by M Rules
Printed and bound in Great Britain by Athenaeum Press,
Gateshead

Ours is essentially a tragic age, so we refuse to take it tragically. The cataclysm has happened, we are among the ruins, we start to build up new habits, to have new little hopes. It is rather hard work: there is now no smooth road into the future: but we go round, or scramble over the obstacles. We've got to live, no matter how many skies have fallen.

(D. H. Lawrence, 1960 [1928]: 5)

For William

Contents

Acknowledgements

We are very grateful to Rosemary Nixon and to Mike Reed for their interest in the book, especially during its early stages, and to all those at Sage who assisted in its publication. Our special thanks also go to the Division of Sociology and Social Policy at Glasgow Caledonian University who provided financial assistance for teaching relief, and in particular to our colleagues Bill Hughes and Rachel Russell who have been a constant source of insight and encouragement. We would like to acknowledge our students from 'Rethinking Organization' for giving us the opportunity to discuss many of the ideas explored here. We are also particularly grateful to Pamela Abbott, Roger Sapsford, Martin Parker, and many others who have offered constructive comments on much of the material contained here, particularly during the earliest stages of the book's gestation. Finally, we would like to thank those people who have supported us in a whole variety of ways, in particular Paul and Victoria, Veronica and Jeremy, Tim, Wendy, Michael, Abbigayle, Adam and Gemma, Tor, Steve and Wendy, Molly, Olive and last but not least, William. Despite the influence that those cited above have had on the writing of this book, we are, of course, entirely responsible for any factual errors or inaccuracies of interpretation (although if anybody is willing to share the blame we would be more than accommodating).

Finally, while we would like to say that working together on this has been an immensely enjoyable experience for both of us; Bill, Rachel and Murphy know the truth.

Philip Hancock and Melissa Tyler

Introduction

When Scott Lash (1990: ix) observed that 'postmodernism is, patently, no longer trendy', he was, quite naturally, unable to foresee the impact it would have on organization theory.[1] Since the early 1990s it has been difficult to attend any conference, or pick up any serious journal or book concerned with organizational life, without encountering some reference to the themes and theorists that have come to be associated with postmodernism. This is not to deny that often the term 'postmodern' is itself noticeably absent from such discussions. Rather, the issues referred to might be, for example, the impact of post-Fordist flexibility on the organization of the labour process, or perhaps the need to re-evaluate the significance of the cultural or linguistic constitution of organizational life. Yet despite a lack of direct reference to postmodernism or the postmodern, what frequently underpins so much of this work is an apparent desire to challenge the values bequeathed by what has come to be known as the 'project of Enlightenment', that is, the pursuit of social progress through the search for objective knowledge, and the domination of the object world through the application of human reason and the scientific method.

In the context of such a post-Enlightenment project, then, post-Fordism might be understood not just as a different way of organizing work, but as a direct assault on a rigid modernist epistemology exemplified in the search for the 'one-best way' of Taylorism. In a similar vein, the increasing fascination with, say, corporate culture could be taken to suggest not only a contemporary stage in the development of managerial strategies of intervention, but also a fundamental reformulation of the concept of organization, one that departs from the rigid ontology of organization as structure, and that replaces it with a far more fluid conception of organization as process.

This is not to suggest that it is only those who have sought to champion the postmodern cause who have contributed to this growing body of ideas and literature. With perhaps even greater frequency, the term 'postmodernist' has been employed as a means to criticize or undermine those who claim to provide a novel and illuminating understanding of what it means to 'be' or 'study' an organization. As such, the term has, in certain quarters, become little more than one of blanket abuse frequently directed at those who are seen to deviate from one orthodoxy or another. Certainly, however the subject of postmodernism is approached, one cannot escape the fact that it is a term, if not a coherent body of ideas, that raises both questions and answers as well as passions and, more often than not, blood pressures.

In this book, we are not seeking either to celebrate or simply to dismiss postmodernism. Rather, our aim is to map out for those new to postmodernism, or to the work that has sought to synthesize it with organization theory, what has been written and said about it. This is not to claim that our cartographic endeavours are in any way neutral or objective. For, in writing this book, we have developed our own critical perspective on postmodernism, one that has to a greater or lesser extent informed every chapter. Furthermore, we came to this project with a set of values and beliefs about the value of organization theory already in place. Broadly speaking we hold to the view that, however unfashionable it may be, as a branch of social science organization theory must be not only critical in the formal sense of the term, but also radical. That is, we believe in the continuing role it should play in exposing and challenging the existence of organizational power relations that serve to fetter both individual autonomy and collective responsibility. As such, it is by this yardstick that we measure what we consider to be the value of postmodernism, not only to organization theory, but also to social and political thought more generally.

Nevertheless, while it is relatively easy to make such grand and noble claims, when it comes to the practical consideration of postmodernism the reality is somewhat less straightforward. In many respects, part of our fascination with postmodernism is a result not so much of what it has to say, but of what it omits. With ambiguity and ambivalence the watchwords of the postmodern commentary, the term leads to a seemingly endless disassembling or deconstruction of the taken-for-granted assumptions of modern science and the very grounds upon which any critical evaluation can be undertaken. As Jean Baudrillard, for many the postmodernist par excellence, has noted, the term is intrinsically lacking in meaning: '. . . it's an expression, a word which people use but which explains nothing. It's not even a concept. It's nothing at all' (1993: 21). From this perspective, to mount a critical appraisal of postmodernism is akin to tilting at windmills. For whatever we criticize is, in the end, our own creation; perhaps little more than a straw target, the product of our own attempts to impose order and meaning on to what some would rather celebrate as chaos and disorder. Within this context, then, our critique may be decried as having little or no validity, well not of any universal stature anyway. Indeed, perhaps we don't even have the right to expect that anybody else will understand what we have written in the same way as we do, let alone agree with us.

With such a seemingly hopeless fate awaiting our own efforts, then, it is perhaps no wonder that for others who are working on the radical periphery of organization theory, postmodernism is, if not somewhat offensive, then certainly exasperating. Its epistemological and ethical relativism seems to leave little sustainable ground for making even the most basic knowledge claims, let alone for developing a radical political critique of organizational power structures. It may be possible, as we have attempted here, to write a critical book about postmodernism and organization theory, but is it possible to 'write' critical postmodern organization theory? While, for example, Gibson Burrell's *Pandemonium* (1997) represents something of an attempt to do just that, its rejection of a linear narrative and its emphasis on a reflexive style of writing as professed deviations from the formal expectations of 'modernist' academic formality, are, at best, limited. As for others who have attempted to write on the relationship between postmodernism and critical organization theory, they have either tended to take a relatively hostile view (Alvesson and Deetz, 1996; Thompson, 1993; Tsoukas, 1992) and thus have been able to ignore the postmodern critique of modern standards of rationality and argumentation or, alternatively, have celebrated its theoretical insights (Bergquist, 1993; Boje et al., 1996; Hatch, 1997) without actually trying to 'be' postmodern.

Clearly, whatever this book is, it is not a postmodern book. Its content and style, like those mentioned above, tends to follow traditional academic conventions and, while acknowledging the need for reflexivity, certainly does not shy away from its authorial voice — one that offers up a very particular interpretation of the material covered. What it tries to be, however, is a relatively lucid and critical introduction to the evolving relationship between postmodern theory and the practice and theorization of work organizations. Of course, in doing so, it identifies merely what we, the authors, think are the important issues raised by this relationship, while also providing us with space to explore what may be an alternative way of understanding certain aspects of it.

Having said all that, this remains a book written, primarily, for students of organization theory, be they based in university business schools, Sociology departments or perhaps outside mainstream academia. We have, therefore, endeavoured to provide as least some semblance of structure and progression to the following pages, in an attempt not to lose too many readers along the way. Structurally, the book is divided into three parts. The first, 'Postmodernism and Organization Theory', charts the literature that has sought to make common cause between the ideas associated with postmodernism and the theoretical analysis of organizations, aiming to distinguish between what can be understood as an attempt to theorize organizational postmodernization, and that which aims to devise a form of postmodernized organization theory. The second part of the book, 'Postmodern Ideas and Organizational Themes', explores several substantive areas of theoretical and managerial activity that, we suggest, are characteristic of an incorporation of a postmodern sensibility into the practices, and study, of organization. What we mean by this is that they all seem to share a concern with the valorization of previously marginalized dimensions of organizational life, those deemed to exist in a conceptual space peripheral to the objective, and therefore 'serious', interests of organization theory. In the final part of the book, we reflect critically on what this seems to suggest, to us at least, about the relationship between work, post-modernism and organization.

The opening chapter introduces what Bertens (1995) has referred to as the 'idea of the postmodern', exploring the work of a number of theorists who have come to be associated with the postmodern turn in the social sciences, including Jean-François Lyotard, Michel Foucault, Jacques Derrida and Jean Baudrillard. This chapter is primarily designed for those less familiar with the language, theories of society and approach to knowledge that have come to be associated with postmodernism. As such, it also seeks to contextualize a set of frequently recurring terms, often encountered in the literature on postmodernism in the form of conceptual dualisms such as reality/representation, differentiation/de-differentiation and so on, in an attempt to ensure sufficient familiarity with them as we progress on to the subsequent chapters. Clearly, for those of you already more than accustomed to the language and theories associated with post-modernism, this chapter is probably superfluous to your requirements and can be bypassed accordingly.

Chapter 2 concerns itself with the work of those who consider the extent to which various social, cultural, economic and political changes in recent decades have meant that work organizations have been increasingly undergoing what can be termed a process of *organizational postmoderniza-tion*. Here we argue that, overall, debates about what a postmodern organization might look like have tended to be stifled by the apparent paradox of pursuing such an endeavour within the theoretical parameters established by postmodernism. Drawing on literature that has attempted to describe and explain the changing nature of contemporary organizations, we chart a passage through the post-industrial thesis (Bell, 1973), taking in accounts of the 'information' or 'network' age (Castells, 1989, 1996) and ending with contemporary debates surrounding the relationship between post-Fordism and the possible postmodernization of work organizations. In doing so, we seek to critically consider the theoretical legacy of the postmodernization thesis, locating it within a series of broader socio-economic developments, distinct from, yet ultimately related to, the emergence of postmodernism.

The third chapter of this part engages with the implications of post-modern theory or, more accurately what is termed 'meta-theory',[2] for the theorization of work organizations. Despite the apparent paradox of developing a postmodern theory of what is frequently deemed to be a quintessentially modernist process, that of the formal and systematic organization of work, a range of considered attempts to develop a post-modern approach to understanding organizations have emerged over the last twelve years or so that problematize the ontological, epistemological and methodological assumptions of traditional organization theory. What has tended to characterize such endeavours has been the means by which they have thrown into sharp relief the idea that organizations exist as independent entities, distinct from the actions of those who comprise and/or perceive them. This critique has therefore attempted to shift the analytical focus of organization theory from 'the organization of production to the production of organization' (Cooper and Burrell, 1988). Following on from our consideration of this material, we attempt to reflect critically on some of the potential limitations of postmodern meta-theory for the theorization of organizations; not least of these, we argue, the political implications of postmodernism for the pursuit of radical organizational change.

Following a brief summary of the material covered in the first part of the book, the second proceeds with the first of the more substantive chapters. Here, we explore the increased significance that has been placed on the theorization of organizations as cultural forms, and on the ways in which management activity appears to have become increasingly geared towards the nurturing of prescriptive cultural identities among organizational employees. In doing so, we identify not only several specific ways of approaching this issue, but also provide a critical reading of the relationship between the emancipatory claims of postmodern meta-theory and the ways in which these claims can be seen to be 'put into practice', so to speak, through the development of managerial strategies for the management of organizational culture.

The fifth chapter focuses on the increasing significance of the emotional life of work organizations, taking as our starting point Fineman's (1993) contention that emotion is so intrinsic to the very process of organization that work organizations can best be understood as 'emotional arenas'. How, why and with what implications this is the case are questions which we address in this chapter with reference, for example, to the increasing importance of emotional labour, especially within the expanding service sector, and the possible post-emotionalization of the workplace and of work itself. In doing so, we suggest that, as with the idea of organizational culture, emotion has emerged as another site of managerial intervention, illustrating a further example of the gradual colonization by management strategists of employee affectivity in the pursuit of greater organizational efficiency.

This critical theme is further developed in Chapter 6, which explores the proposition that contemporary work organizations provide a context for both the expression and control of sexuality. Here we examine the apparently dialectical nature of 'organization sexuality' (Hearn and Parkin, 1987), moving into a consideration of the various ways in which sexuality and organizational life have come to interrelate in the contemporary era of the so-called postmodernized organization. This leads to a focus on the tension between sexuality as a potential site for creative resistance to the imperatives of a narrow organizational instrumentality and as a medium through which organizational employees are further seduced by the value sets established by an incorporation of postmodern themes into contemporary managerial technologies of control and governance.

After a brief summary of the material covered thus far, the third part of the book, consisting solely of our final chapter, involves a critical reflection on its central concerns – namely, the relationship between the ideas that have come to be associated with postmodernism and work organizations. It departs from what has been the largely review-based nature of the majority of the previous chapters, and tries to formulate an alternative means of conceptualizing what seems to be happening within organizations and organization theory, in response to the challenges of postmodernism. This is based on the idea that what lies at the heart of postmodernism, as both a meta-theory and a project of organizational change, is the drive to liberate the repressed and marginalized aspects of modernity, be it in the cause of an emancipatory social science or the ability to exploit, in a more complete and efficient manner, the human potential for material and cultural productivity. To illustrate this, we concentrate on a theoretical discussion of employee subjectivity, which we conceive of as a process rather than as either a static or entirely indeterminate state of being; as both constituted and arrested within contemporary work organizations. Drawing on the tradition of Critical Theory, and grounded in a philosophy of inter-subjectivity, we suggest that what postmodernism represents, as a means of intervening in the world, is a partial transcendence of the restrictions that modernist modes of organizing have placed on human autonomy. However, employing what we consider to be a dialectical understanding of the world, we also observe how this may also represent a potential intensification of the asymmetrical relations of power and control that have accompanied the history of human material and cultural development. In doing so, what we hope to provide is an alternative conceptualization of the relationship between postmodernism, in all its guises, and the pursuit of an organization theory that is attuned to inequitable relations of power and control within organizations, while welcoming developments within the field, developments that, we would hope, provide a conceptual space for the liberation of previously marginalized aspects of human experience, both within and without the specific parameters of the work organization.

In closing this brief introduction, it should perhaps be noted that while the general themes and ideas contained here are undoubtedly the outcome of an almost un-recountable series of discussions, arguments and experiences shared by the authors, it is also the result of a fairly modernist division of labour in terms of its production. The first part was designed and written by Philip Hancock, including the final summary, while the chapters and final summary comprising part two were the work of Melissa Tyler. The final part of the book, it is probably fair to say, was far more of a joint venture, with many of the ideas developed in it remaining the source of some, albeit minor, disagreement and disputation.

Notes

1 We use the term 'organization theory', rather than say 'organization analysis', or 'organization studies', as favoured by Clegg et al. (1996) and also Parker (2000a), due to what we feel is its closer resonance with the largely theoretical concerns of the book.
2 See Chapter 1 for an explanation of our use of this term.

PART 1

Postmodernism and
Organization Theory

1

The Idea of the Postmodern

It is strong and fashionable. Over and above this, it is not altogether
clear what the devil it is. In fact, clarity is not conspicuous amongst its
marked attributes. (Gellner, 1992: 22)

Postmodernism is a theory, a contemporary practice and a condition of
the contemporary era. In short we live and breathe it. (Sardar, 1998: 27)

What Hans Bertens (1995: 3) has referred to as the 'idea of the postmodern',
remains one of the most contested and, as Bertens himself describes it,
'exasperating' ideas currently circulating within the contemporary social
sciences. This exasperation is helped little by the emergence of two parallel tendencies. On the one hand, almost every commentator on the subject
seems to offer his or her own particular definition or conceptualization. On
the other, many writers, whose ideas have generally been associated with
the postmodern canon, have frequently been at pains to eschew the term
and any identification of their work with it. Nevertheless, what Bertens
also suggests is that postmodernism is an idea with a history, a history
within which a number of common propositions about the nature of contemporary industrialized societies, and the ideas that we hold about them,
have evolved.

Taking this as our starting point, in this opening chapter we provide a relatively brief introduction to some of these common propositions in order to
contextualize our subsequent consideration of the impact of postmodernism

on contemporary organization theory. In some respects, this has been made easier for us by the fact that attempts by those who study organizations to engage with the implications of postmodernism have generally tended to focus fairly specifically on the writing of a limited number of individuals. These are most notably Jean-François Lyotard, Michel Foucault, Jacques Derrida and Jean Baudrillard. As we noted however, such individuals have not always identified either themselves or their ideas with postmodernism as such. Nevertheless, they have come to be regarded as providing the intellectual framework for postmodern thought and have, in turn, significantly influenced the incorporation of the idea of the postmodern into the domain of organization theory.

Commencing with an introductory discussion of the concepts of *modernization*, *modernism* and *modernity*,[1] particularly in relation to Cooper and Burrell's (1988) conceptual bifurcation of what they term systemic and critical modernism, the chapter then proceeds to a critical overview of a number of the key ideas associated with several leading postmodern meta-theorists. We use the term 'meta-theory' here to denote theoretical activity which, rather than aiming to theorize about particular social forms or specific cultural phenomena, is directed towards the activity of theorizing about theory itself (Morrow and Brown, 1994). As such, it is something of an umbrella term covering issues of ontology (the study of the nature of the world), epistemology (the study of knowledge), and normative theory (the study of how the world ought to be). Because these are all themes that postmodern discourse tends to integrate, the term 'meta-theory' seems – to us at least – to be a particularly useful one.

We then turn our attention, in the penultimate section of the chapter, to a related but distinct body of writing. One that has, on the whole, sought to develop not so much a postmodern meta-theory, but rather a social scientific analysis of contemporary western societies, which posits a process of socio-cultural postmodernization. Here we consider the work of a range of contemporary cultural theorists such as Baudrillard (1981, 1990), Harvey (1989), Jameson (1991) and Lash (1990) who have, in various ways, explored the imperatives underpinning, and the implications of, the emergence of postmodernity as a relatively novel set of cultural and, indeed, organizational phenomena. In the concluding section we reflect critically on this material in an attempt to evaluate its implications for the practice of organization theory.

The Enlightenment: cradle of the modern

As Cahoone has noted, 'any discussion of postmodernism assumes a great deal of knowledge about modernism or modernity, or the modern world, or how it has been interpreted' (1996: ix). Certainly for us, any attempt to provide an overview of the ideas and practices that have come to be termed 'postmodern' requires at least a cursory exploration of that which postmodernism claims to have transcended, rejected or replaced, namely *the modern*. In some ways, however, it was only with the advent of the idea of the postmodern that many social scientists began to reflect seriously on the experience of modernity.[2] Prior to this, the modern was something that had been largely taken for granted. To be modern was to be concerned with the issues of the present, while looking towards the promise of progress in the future. In what has perhaps been one of the most influential and reflexive descriptions of what it is to live in the modern world, Marshall Berman declared:

> There is a mode of vital experience – experience of space and time, of the self and others, of life's possibilities and perils – that is shared by men and women all over the world today. I will call this body of experience 'modernity'. To be modern is to find ourselves in an environment that promises us adventure, power, joy, growth, transformation of ourselves and the world and, at the same time, threatens to destroy everything we have, everything we know, everything we are. (1983: 15)

While vulnerable to a number of criticisms, not least that such a generalization ignores a range of factors which may well ensure that the possibility of 'adventure, power, joy, growth, [and] transformation' is far from a universally shared experience, this is a powerful and evocative image of what it perhaps means to be modern. Yet where does this mode of experience originate? What demarcates it from the pre modern, and why should we now consider that we have, in some way, transcended it?

While still contested both historically and philosophically, it is now broadly agreed upon that the modern age, as we have come to understand it, took shape sometime around the mid-eighteenth century.[3] This was the culmination of a period of intense intellectual activity, one which had taken place across Europe over a 150-year period from the mid-seventeenth century onwards, and which has since come to be known as the European Enlightenment.[4] Based on Robert Hollinger's (1994: 7) concise summary, what has come to be known as the *Enlightenment project* can be condensed into the following principal ideas:

1   To be human means to be bound by universal, rational and moral principles that bind all human beings into a universal humanity and which provide guidance on conduct and judgement.
2   Only a society based on science and universal values is truly free and rational.
3   Knowledge is constituted by a set of beliefs that all human beings can assent to rationally; that is, on the basis of a universally valid set of methodological assumptions.
4   The more we know about ourselves and the world we inhabit, the better human life will become, because ignorance is the cause of unhappiness and immorality.

Underpinning these beliefs in the nature of reality and our potential for knowledge of it was the philosophical disposition that we know today as *humanism*; a belief in the faculty of human reason and agency as the keys to unlocking, and bringing under the domain of a unified humanity, all the mysteries of the natural and social universe. In short, the Enlightenment principles outlined above reflect a confidence in the ability of human reason to provide an understanding of the world, and faith in the ability of human beings to use this understanding subsequently to improve it. Before this could be achieved, however, humanity had to cast off the restrictions of religious authority. As Smart has put it, for the philosophers of the Enlightenment,[5] history was no longer seen as 'synonymous with God working his purpose out' (1992: 8). Rather, liberty of thought was, as Cassirer has noted, the defining feature of the Enlightenment vision:

> Instead of confining philosophy within the limits of a systematic doctrinal structure, instead of tying it to definite, immutable axioms and deductions from them, the Enlightenment wants philosophy to move freely and in this immanent activity to discover the fundamental form of reality, the form of all natural and spiritual being. (1951: vii)

Thus, to the proponents of this new intellectual order, human reason was to be allowed free reign, not only to understand the world more fully, but also to make it a better place for humanity to reside. Increasingly integral to this was a belief in the need to promote the approach and methods of the natural sciences. It was believed that through the tool of science, humanity would be able to tame the natural universe, to understand nature and so bring it under human dominion. Thus, reason, science and human progress became inexorably intertwined as knowledge came to be seen as the key to the creation of a secular version of heaven on earth.

As Cassirer suggests above, however, this is not to imply that the thinkers of the Enlightenment rejected wholesale the principle of a natural order of things. While the autonomy of the subject and the faculty of reason were central to their thinking, such autonomy was understood to be based upon a belief in the ability of reason to know and to control the natural world, rather than to create anew. The purpose of the natural sciences, in Enlightenment terms, was thus conceived of as being to search for the 'true' laws of nature, and not to invent such laws. The same can also be said of the social and political philosophies of the age. As Wagner notes, the philosophical systems which emerged in and through the Enlightenment may have rejected the imposition of religiously-grounded limits to thought and action but they continued to accept '. . . the idea of the *recognition* of worldly values and rules, existing before and beyond the individual, to be discovered, known and followed by human beings' (Wagner, 1994: 8 *original emphasis*). As such, there existed a tension at the birth of the modern world, a tension between the freedom of the individual and a belief in the rightful place of the human being within a pre-determined order of things.

Despite, or perhaps because of, this tension, the ideas that emerged from the Enlightenment ushered in a whole host of new ways of thinking about the world and humanity's relationship to it. The most obvious expression of the Enlightenment drive to knowledge was the aforementioned rise of the natural sciences and the advances in technology that derived from it. It was these rapid developments in science and technology that, combined with the expansion of capitalism as an increasingly global economic system, were to provide, at least in part, the driving force behind the modernization of the western world. Within a relatively short period (some two hundred years or so), the expansion of industrial capitalism radically transformed the face of western societies. By the mid-nineteenth century, levels of material production reached heights never before dreamt of, instigating a host of political, social and cultural changes in western societies which have come to be known collectively as the process of *modernization*. Transportation and communication systems became increasingly sophisticated and accessible. Populations became more urban and mobile, as huge towns and cities began to develop. Cash-driven markets began to take over as the primary mechanism for exchanging goods and services, and modes of social and economic organization began to develop which have come to be regarded as quintessentially modern.

This is not to suggest, however, that the modernization process was driven solely by material imperatives. Rather, a dialectical relationship can be identified between the material and ideational dimensions of modernity, that is, between modernization as a social process and modernism as an intellectual movement. The economic and social changes associated with modernization did not occur in isolation, but were shaped by *modernism* as a particular view of the social world, a view that was rooted in the Enlightenment project outlined above and was grounded, perhaps above all, in an unfaltering faith in the power of rational thought. From a modernist perspective, everything that exists in the world as an objective reality – including truth, beauty and morality, for instance – can be understood rationally. Not only does this understanding of the world render material and cultural progress inevitable, it also provides a basis for controlling and directing such progress.

The modernization process, combined with the philosophical and cultural ideas of modernism, therefore also played a vital role in shaping the subjective experience of humanity, and this was reflected in its expression in the form of art and other cultural products which further reinforced the modernist *geist*, or *spirit*. Modernist art, as it established itself in the nineteenth century, provides us with a useful example of the extent to which, as artists struggled to meet the challenges posed by new technologies such as cinema and photography, as well as to represent both the perceived joys and horrors of the modern age, diverse styles and approaches flourished. While some embraced the promises of science and technology and sought to exemplify the new spirit of progress through the medium of design, others challenged what they saw as the increasing cultural dominance of the natural sciences, and sought to express the subjective alienation felt by many in the face of a constant process of upheaval and change characteristic of the experience of modernity. Modernism was thus, from its birth, a creature of tension and contradiction.

This was also more than evident in the emergent social sciences of the nineteenth century, themselves born of the expansion of a modern drive for knowledge and understanding and equally constitutive of the emerging modernist culture. Sociology, in particular, was a discipline born of attempts to chart and understand the social implications of modernization and, as such, contributed greatly to the intellectual and cultural discourse of modernism. For Karl Marx, one of the great figures of modern social science and philosophy, the driving force behind modernity was the expansion of industrial capitalism. For Marx, it was in capitalism – as a mode of production and exchange – that answers to questions emanating from the nature of the modern world could be found. As he noted:

> The bourgeois [the owners of capital] cannot exist without constantly revolutionizing the instruments of production, and thereby the relations of production, and with them the whole relations of society. . . . Constant revolutionizing of production, uninterrupted disturbance of all social conditions, everlasting uncertainty and agitation, distinguish the bourgeois epoch from all earlier ones. (Marx and Engels, 1986 [1848]: 37)

For Marx, then, capitalism not only dictated the socio-economic terrain of society, but also served to define the subjective experience of modern life. It was a world in which 'all that is solid melts into air' (Marx and Engels, 1986 [1848]: 37), a world in which the dynamic of capitalism brought all that was once certain into question and all that was once stable into flux and upheaval. Sharing the same cultural sensibility as the radical artists of modernism, Marx understood modernity as the experience of contradiction and change, of the unholy combinations of certainty and uncertainty, stability and transience.

Marx was not, however, the only modern social scientist to recognize and seek to understand the changes that were taking place around him. For Emile Durkheim (1964 [1893]), perhaps the first professional sociologist, the defining feature of the modern age was a process of increasing economic, social and cultural differentiation. In Durkheim's view, modernization was a process that offered the hope of great progress and cultural development, but which also led to a sense of dislocation or uprootedness for those caught in its wake. As Marx had recognized previously, the driving force of modernity originated, for Durkheim, also in industrial capitalism's requirement for an increasingly specialized division of labour.

This was a view also shared, in part, by the third of the discipline of sociology's 'founding fathers', Max Weber. For Weber (1964 [1925]), the modernization of all dimensions of society had to be understood in terms of the mutation and spread of a particular form of rationality, one characterized by a prioritization of efficiency of method over the consideration of ends, and exemplified in the spread of a bureaucratic system of adminis-tration as the dominant mode of social organization. In Weber's view, this system was one that championed the impersonal and the efficient at the expense of human spirituality and creativity, disenchanting and dehu-manizing the individual as a consequence.

Another important example of a thinker who was both a great influence on Weber and perhaps more than any individual of his time, sensitive to the unstable and Janus nature of modernization in all its forms, was the German philosopher, Freidrich Nietzsche. While often contradictory in his declarations and, as such, subsequently misinterpreted through history, Nietzsche's (1989 [1887], 1990a [1886]) great concern was with what he believed to be the decadent and nihilistic path that modernity was leading humanity towards. The Enlightenment's blind faith in reason, or so Nietzsche thought, had in fact undermined the basis for all belief, had laid bare the metaphysical, and therefore unsustainable nature of those values that had, up until then, kept the passions and desires of humanity in check. In response, Nietzsche declared that the time had come to undertake what he terms on numerous occasions a 'revaluation of all values' (Nietzsche, 1990b [1895]: 197), championing a new moral and cultural sensibility that embraced the carnal nobility of that which had been marginalized by the discourses of modernity, and that rejected the proposed linear relation-ship between reason and progress. Hughes has interpreted this dimension of Nietzsche's writings by declaring:

> What do we do in a crisis of reason? What do we do when we think the mind incapable of guiding individual acts and social processes? What do we do when we consider that all concepts are simply deceptive rationalization? We turn to the body, to the passions and interests for clues to the meaning of being and becom-ing. (1996: 33–4)

Nietzsche therefore, while concerned with the same tensions of moder-nity as his social scientific contemporaries, rejected the possibility of a rational resolution to them. As such, his writings provided a unique con-tribution to the reflexive critique of modernity, one that was not however to have its most significant impact for some time to come.

In contrast, while Marx, Durkheim and Weber all recognized that the pace of change and the newly emerging social structures of modernity were tainted by a set of potentially negative consequences for the human subject – in terms of alienation, anomie and disenchantment – they, unlike Nietzsche, maintained throughout their accounts a faith in the power of reason and human agency to expose the underlying dynamics of modern-ization. Each of them was committed to the potential of modern ideas to offer a path of progress that would transcend its potentially dehumanizing consequences. For Marx, this was to be realized in the proletarian revolu-tion, for Durkheim in the emergence of a new mode of organic social solidarity and, for Weber, in a somewhat more tentative vein, in the possi-ble re-emergence of a charismatic political order.

In this sense at least, then, Marx, Durkheim and Weber in particular were all children of the Enlightenment, whose work sought both to chart the deeper causes of social change and, at one and the same time, to actively direct it in the service of human progress. Their ideas were not simply abstract reflections on the nature of knowledge or reality, but an integral aspect of the modernist age in which knowledge, reason and action were intimately connected, an age in which detractors such as Nietzsche notwithstanding, it was generally believed that despite the tensions and contradictions engendered by modernization, the truth would still set us free.

Systemic and critical modernism

Reflecting on the tensions inherent within modernity, and the relationship between modernity and organizations, Cooper and Burrell (1988: 95) have developed a useful distinction between what they term the 'systemic' and 'critical' dimensions of modernist thought. *Systemic modernism* represents the values and methods embedded within the rise to prominence of the natural sciences, combined with the deployment of formal rationality to identify and resolve problems of order and control. This is contrasted with *critical modernism*, which Cooper and Burrell locate within the radical tradition that evolved from the Enlightenment critique of religious authority and the concomitant belief in the faculty of reason to expose man-made (*sic*) restrictions upon individual autonomy. Thus, with its origins in Kant's (1991 [1784]: 9) evocation *aude sapere* or 'dare to reason', critical modernism represents the reflexive and emancipatory dimension of modernist thought.

Systemic modernism, on the other hand, is understood to be underpinned by the philosophical system of positivism, originating in the work of Comte and perhaps developed most fully in the work of the Vienna Circle (see Bryant, 1985), which emphasizes the universal applicability of the logic of the natural sciences to all aspects of knowledge production, and a belief in intellectual and social progress deriving from this. However, while systemic modernism is often critical of 'reactionary', non-scientific forms of thought, due to its emphasis on an immutable notion of reality as the foundation for all human activity, it has also come to be associated with a conservative approach to understanding the social world (see Adorno et al., 1976 [1969]; Cooper and Burrell, 1988; Marcuse, 1983). As Marcuse notes in this regard, for positivists such as Comte, 'society now was taken as a more or less definite complex of facts governed by more or less general laws – a sphere to be treated like any other field of scientific investigation' (1983: 340). The term 'systemic modernism' signifies, then, a belief in the objectivity of society, in the neutrality of science and, perhaps above all, a commitment to the promise of social progress through the harnessing of nature and the extension of technology.

Hence, while systemic modernism celebrates the constitutive power of human reason and the potential of science to free humanity from tradition and the dominance of nature, critical modernism has tended to refuse to accept uncritically science's professed neutrality and the equation of reason with progress and freedom. Rather, it has emphasized instead the extent to which the principles of science have been instrumentally appropriated by a systemic impetus concerned primarily with the domination of nature, including human nature, and the crude identification of technological progress with human emancipation. From this perspective, the modern world, while characterized under systemic modernism by the pre-eminence of rationality, is deemed fundamentally irrational in that the conception of reason that has come to predominate is both narrow in its conception and inimical to the realization of humanity's capacity for critical self-reflection and autonomous action.

Yet this apparent divergence does not indicate a final and complete schism between the two traditions. As Cooper and Burrell (1988: 97) note, both systemic and critical perspectives hold to a number of shared convictions that could be described as quintessentially modernist. Both approaches maintain a strong faith in the idea that reason provides not only the key to unlocking the nature of reality, but that reality itself must be constituted in a manner congruent with reason. While this may be self-evident in the creed of systemic modernism, it also remains essential to the idea of critique that is so central to its critical variant. This is due to the idea that the activity of critique, as envisaged within the Enlightenment tradition outlined above, and which provides the philosophical *raison d'être* for critical modernism, is premised upon the idea that rational critique can be deployed to identify irrationality within the human world and, as such, bring the world back into line with its authentically rational nature.[6] Both traditions also maintain a humanist belief in the constitutive power of the human subject, that is, a subject which is able to bring under control, in the service of its own authenticated interests, both its natural and social environments. Be it the natural scientist splitting the atom to provide a source of energy, or the social revolutionary re-organizing society to ensure an equal distribution of resources, both are credited with purposeful agency in a world in which humanity, within the restrictions of nature at least, reigns supreme.

To sum up so far, then, it would appear that it is this shared faith in a universalistic conception of reason, and in the power of human agency to bring under its domain the vicissitudes and tensions of modern life, which not only unifies modernism in its various guises, but which also, as we shall see, provides the critical focus of what can broadly be termed postmodern meta-theory.

The rise of postmodern meta-theory

While the idea that a qualitatively distinct way of thinking and living is emerging, one that somehow marks a break with the past three hundred years or so, gained momentum in the mid-1950s, the earliest sightings of the term postmodernism seem to have been in the late-nineteenth century when it was used to describe new modes of artistic expression, which were deemed, at the time, to be 'more modern and avant-garde than French impressionist painting' (Best and Kellner, 1991: 5). As Cahoone (1996) notes, the term also appeared in 1917 when the German philosopher Rudolf Pannwitz, drawing on Nietzsche, described contemporary culture as 'nihilistic', and again in the early 1930s when the term appeared in the work of Federico de Onis who used it to denote a move away from a modernist sensibility in literary criticism. It was not until the 1960s, however, that the term came to refer to anything like a self-conscious artistic movement when, as noted by Featherstone (1988: 203), it was adopted by a range of New York artists and writers to describe a reaction to what they saw as the 'exhaustion' of the radical aspirations of avant-garde modernism, exemplified by its incorporation into the cultural mainstream.

As this particular sensibility spread and refined itself throughout the early 1970s, when postmodernism came to denote a reaction to a modernist aesthetic in architecture, it led Jencks (1996: 470) to make his now somewhat infamous assertion that the symbolic demise of the modernist vision took place at around 3.32 p.m. on 15 July 1972 in St Louis, Missouri. This was the time when the Pruitt–Igoe housing development, a model example of the 'intelligent planning of abstract space', was demolished, having degenerated into what was considered to be a violent and uninhabitable ghetto. It was, Jencks claimed, a perfect example of how modern architecture, as the heir to Enlightenment rationality, had ultimately proven to be as irrational as the philosophy from which it drew its inspiration. Jencks conceived postmodernism, then, as having not only embraced the critical modernist critique of the technicist and instrumentalist values of its systemic counterpart, but also as having moved beyond the proposition that reason and human progress were mutually interdependent. The postmodern, as he saw it, was more than simply an attempt to re-inaugurate the reflexive and critical dimension of the modern spirit. Rather, it represented a transcendence of the very principles that lay at the core of modernity. In many respects, then, Jencks's view epitomizes what might be characterized as a mode of post-Enlightenment meta-theoretical reflection that has sought to challenge, and in some cases undermine, the foundation of western thought as it has existed for around three hundred years.

As a meta-theory, postmodernism rejects the modernist perception that so-called realities – truth, beauty and morality, for instance – have an objective existence beyond how we represent them. As Best and Kellner have put it, the modernist assumption of a fixed, immutable, absolute truth is 'precisely the conception skillfully undermined by postmodern critique' (1997: 236). In other words, postmodernism emphasizes that the social world does not exist, awaiting discovery. Rather, what we take to be the social world is actually nothing more than our conception of it. While, because of particular configurations of power, knowledge, subjectivity and language, certain models of reality are privileged, ultimately one version of reality, beauty or morality is equally as 'true' as any other. From this perspective, the Enlightenment drive to create a 'better' world is, at best, misguided and, at worst, tyrannical, based as it is on only one particular perspective or mode of rationality. Postmodernism, then, asks fundamental questions of modernist attempts to understand and shape the social world, attempts which have come to be associated particularly with the work of social scientists such as Marx, Weber and Durkheim.

If these three represent the holy trinity of modern sociology, the same can perhaps be said of the trio of French theorists – Jean-François Lyotard, Michel Foucault and Jacques Derrida – in relation to the development of postmodern meta-theory. This is not to suggest that a number of significant contributions to the development of postmodernism as an intellectual endeavour have not emerged elsewhere. Figures such as Richard Rorty (1989) in the USA and Gianni Vattimo (1992) in Italy, for example, have offered a number of novel and significant insights to its development. Similarly, the work of feminist theorists such as Judith Butler (1990a, 1993) in the USA, and particularly of the new French feminists such as Hélène Cixous (1986), Luce Irigaray (1985, 1990) and Julia Kristeva (1980), has contributed significantly to contemporary debates on the idea of the postmodern trio. However, both in terms of their general influence on the development of postmodern meta theory, and their particular influence on the impact postmodern thought has had on the recent development of organization theory, Lyotard, Foucault and Derrida remain the essential postmodern. While each of them have, at one time or another, sought to disassociate themselves from the postmodern canon that has flourished in the wake of their writings, it is virtually impossible to consider any aspect of postmodern philosophy or meta-theory without encountering at least one of these names and their associated ideas.

That said, it is perhaps more accurate to describe all three of them more as post-structuralist than postmodern thinkers. Post-structuralism, while difficult to encapsulate in a few sentences, can best be understood as a broadly philosophical approach to the relationship between the human subject and structural forces such as culture, language and tradition. Deriving from its predecessor structuralism,[7] post-structuralism considers the world that we inhabit, including the subjective experience of that world, to be the outcome and product of language. This position, then, ultimately seems to lead to an inability to talk of anything like an essential or immutable reality existing outside the language that we use to describe it. As such our descriptions about the world, our moral judgements or political beliefs are reduced to the status of stories of the world as we see it, premised upon our linguistically constituted apprehension of the world. Post-structuralism can be described, then, as providing a philosophical basis for the postmodern critique of the absolute claims to knowledge that, as we have seen, provides the basis for a modernist worldview. Thus, while it would take another book to unravel the relationship between post-structuralism and postmodernism, it is fair to say that the interrelationship between post-structuralism and postmodernism is an intimate one, one shaped not least by a preoccupation with the relationship between language, subjectivity and knowledge, a concern exemplified in the work of Jean-François Lyotard.

Knowledge and The Postmodern Condition

Originally published in 1979, it was the 1984 English translation of Lyotard's short essay, *The Postmodern Condition: A Report on Knowledge*, which popularized the term postmodernism within philosophy and the social sciences and identified Lyotard, for many, as the leading meta-theorist of postmodernism. It is here that Lyotard expounded his view that underpinning modernism, as an intellectual and cultural phenomenon, was a collection of what he termed *metanarratives* (Lyotard, 1984: xxiv). He used this term to describe any form of narrative deployed to legitimate claims to knowledge or action. The most influential of these, for Lyotard, were the positivist version of natural science and the speculative tradition in German idealism that reached its zenith in the historical materialism of Marx. Yet, for Lyotard, it is the very history of modernity that has exposed such metanarratives as nothing more than convenient fictions. Marxism, in Lyotard's view, for example, has failed spectacularly to provide the progress and emancipation it has promised for so long. Even natural scientists, themselves reliant upon a metanarrative of objectivity and progress, are no longer able to defend the metaphysical realism of their claims to scientific knowledge as the harbinger of emancipation and progress.

For Lyotard, then, the recognition that overarching stories of truth, progress and eventual emancipation are nothing more than historical narratives constitutes postmodernism as a mode of knowledge. A mode of knowledge which is represented by Lyotard as 'an incredulity towards metanarratives' (Lyotard, 1984: xxiv), and as a search for new modes of representing knowledge and truth in a world devoid of any firm ontological, epistemological or ethical foundations and, drawing on the work of Bell (1973), driven by the economic and organizational imperatives of a new socio-economic post-industrialism. This combination of an incredulity towards metanarratives and recognition of the contingency of all claims to knowledge is what, for Lyotard (1984), constitutes the postmodern condition.

Lyotard welcomed the demise of metanarratives and the emergence of a plurality of epistemologies. He championed a heterogeneity of knowledge claims and, indeed, celebrated a diversity of narratives as the basis for a postmodern science which would respect the relative incommensurability of what he termed *language games*[8] (Lyotard, 1984: 10). In this sense,

Lyotard argued that we must learn to acknowledge and respect the legitimacy of a range of linguistically embedded modes of understanding. As he
put it,

> consensus does violence to the heterogeneity of language games. And invention
> is always born of dissension. Postmodern knowledge is not simply a tool of the
> authorities; it refines our sensitivity to differences and reinforces our ability to
> tolerate the incommensurable. (1984: xxv)

Lyotard thus rejected what he perceived to be the universalizing and
totalizing ambitions of Enlightenment philosophy, especially in terms of
its belief in the desirability of consensus underpinning a democratic politics. In this respect, it could be argued that Lyotard expresses an
anti-democratic sentiment, one that views the tyranny of the majority as
every bit as undesirable as the tyranny of the few. He saw conflict, or the
playing out of language games, as the key to a dynamic culture based on
a celebration of diverse modes of understanding and experiencing the
world. In contrast to what he perceived as the essentially modernist pursuit of consensus, Lyotard thus professed a form of postmodern politics
which rested on a rejection of the quest for systematic order across all
spheres of knowledge. In a critique reminiscent of Weber, he argued that
such scientific domination would result in a society in which all values
and actions were to be judged solely in terms of a principle of 'maximum
performance' (Lyotard, 1984: xxiv). Consequently, he felt that the only
alternative to the ascendance of such a preformatted, scientific world
view, one based purely on the principle of efficiency and utility, was a
pluralistic politics of difference.

While Lyotard's later work sought to move beyond the centrality of the
language game, the basic thrust of his thinking remained the same. Of
note, however, was his subsequent rejection of the idea, developed most
notably in his 1988 text *The Differend*, that language is something that can
simply be 'used', in other words, subjected to the intentions of a free and
autonomous individual. Rather, he argued, language actually constitutes
the self-understanding and social positioning of the subject. For Lyotard
(1988), an individual's sense of self is the product of various linguistic
structures, which provide the building blocks from which subjectivity
emerges. In this sense, Lyotard touches upon another particularly important theme that appears to resurface in a number of contemporary
post-structuralist accounts of the postmodern, namely, the so-called *death
of the subject*.

Before considering this theme in more depth in the following section, a
number of criticisms that Lyotard's work has been subjected to should be
noted. Perhaps the most striking problem identified in Lyotard's account
is his attempted theorization of the postmodern condition and of the
material conditions underpinning its emergence. For, in deploying a range
of concepts associated with a number of developments in the productive
relations of western societies,[9] Lyotard accepts, apparently uncritically,

what seems to represent the sort of generalization that he is at pains to attack. While this may in itself be forgivable, offering as he is a treatise on the possibility of a postmodern mode of knowledge rather than on some process of social or economic postmodernization, the causal relationship he establishes between the latter and the former remains problematic in his account. In our view, this is largely because Lyotard apparently continues to rely upon a highly modernist narrative of social evolution to explain his own version of postmodernity. As Best and Kellner note in this regard:

> Rejecting grand narratives, . . . simply covers over the theoretical problem of providing a narrative of the contemporary historical situation and points to the undertheorized nature of Lyotard's account of the postmodern condition. (1991: 173)

Also, it is difficult to recognize anything particularly postmodern about the political position that emerges from Lyotard's emphasis on respect for the multiplicity of language games. While we undoubtedly continue to inhabit a world in which disenfranchised social groups are consistently denied a voice or the means to address their inferior socio-economic conditions, Lyotard's appeal for an acceptance of pluralism seems to offer little except the chance to enter a cultural marketplace in which socio-economic power remains the currency of the day. In this sense at least, rather than incredulity towards metanarratives, Lyotard's account seems to read more like the final victory of classic liberalism. Further, as Kumar (1995: 135) notes, the cost we may have to pay for the end of ideological fanaticism could in fact be too high, robbing us, as it might, of the passion and cultural creativity 'that comes of the struggle of ideologies'.

Despite such criticisms, there has been a fairly favourable response towards the underlying message to be found in Lyotard's writing, especially within theories centring on the idea of radical democracy (see, for example, Laclau and Mouffe, 1985). More generally, his pluralistic vision of a new politics can be seen to reflect many of the changes that have actually taken place in the arena of radical political thought since the early 1980s. Disillusionment with traditional political parties and the growth, often albeit transitory, of single-issue pressure groups, united around issues such as environmental protection, anti-racism or lesbian and gay rights, all reflect the kind of respect for difference that Lyotard would have championed. Furthermore, his appeal for the need to embrace a more eclectic notion of science, one free to draw upon a number of differing or contesting traditions, has also had a significant impact upon social science research and practice, reinvigorating the critical spirit within certain quarters of the field and contributing to the preparedness of those outside its orbit to question the hegemonic status of the natural sciences.

Power/knowledge and subjectivity

While Lyotard's work perhaps represents the closest thing to a coherent exegesis on the nature of postmodern knowledge, it is the extensive work of Michel Foucault that seems to have, thus far at least, exerted most influence on the postmodern turn in the social sciences. The origins of Foucault's own version of the assault on the nature of modern knowledge can be found in the Marxist structuralism of his mentor, Louis Althusser (1969), and also, more specifically, in the linguistic structuralism of Ferdinand de Saussure (1974) and Roland Barthes (1973). For Foucault, however, the primary structural matrix is to be found specifically in the relationship between knowledge and power and its socio-cultural mediation in the form of *discourse*. A *discourse*, an integrated set of ideas or conceptual schema, is not simply verbal in Foucault's work; it also includes various practices determining the context and constitution of reality. Hence, discourse in this sense refers to those unwritten rules which frame what can and cannot be said about any given phenomenon. In this respect, Foucault raised discourse to a primary position in terms of not only what we can say about the world, but also how we can know it. Foucault did not conceive of language, in the form of discourse, as a neutral tool of representation, but as the mechanism through which our sense of what exists in the world is constituted. Emphasizing the relative nature of truth, he rejected the Enlightenment belief in the neutrality of knowledge and the transparency of language and, in turn, sought to uncover how various historically-situated 'truths', or *epistemes* (Foucault, 1970), came into being and served to legitimate certain modes of social power.

Modernity, in Foucault's thought, is characterized by the victory of a regime of power/knowledge that acquires its legitimization through the Enlightenment-inspired discourses of universal reason, subjective autonomy and historical progress. In contrast to the critical tradition associated, most notably, with Marxism, what Foucault's work does *not* do is identify the exercise of power with any particular social class or group. Power is, in Foucault's terms, 'everywhere' (Foucault, 1977a, 1977b) embedded within all forms of social relations and discursive situations. As such, power is represented in Foucault's writing not as a stable quantity, but rather as a fluid phenomenon which comes into being only in and through action. Nor does Foucault view power as purely repressive in the traditional sense. Rather, power, for him, is equally creative and productive:

> What makes power hold good, what makes it accepted, is simply the fact that it doesn't only weigh upon us as a force that says no, but that it traverses and produces things, it induces pleasure, forms knowledge, produces discourse. It needs to be considered as a productive network that runs through the whole social body, much more than as a negative instance whose function is repression. (1980: 119)

Of particular interest in this respect are Foucault's ideas regarding the role of power in the constitution of the individual subject. In a similar vein to Lyotard, the autonomous individual is presented by Foucault as the outcome of a uniquely modern discourse, one that functions through various technologies of power that simultaneously construct and demarcate the individual as that which Foucault termed the 'subject/object' of knowledge. For Foucault, the rise of modern institutions such as the asylum, the prison and even the factory has produced, through the acquisition and deployment of regimes of power/knowledge, a range of objectified categories of subjectivity. These have, in turn, provided templates through which the idea of what it is to be an individual subject has been internalized. Foucault therefore rejected the humanist ideas, outlined earlier, that equate self-conscious subjectivity with autonomy and freedom, arguing instead for the need to deconstruct the idea of the subject, which he viewed as an historically contingent outcome of discursively ordered relations of power/knowledge.

This aspect of his work in particular brings Foucault close, in many ways, to the political position of Lyotard. Deprived of any neutral conception of knowledge, one that is not deeply enmeshed in relations of power, Foucault's work alludes to the need for micro-political strategies of resistance. This is made possible by his contention that despite the omnipresent nature of power, there remains space for resistance precisely at the very points where power is exercised. Thus, Foucault argued that there exists space for individuals to 'recreate themselves' in opposition to dominant discursive representations. This particular aspect of his thinking is made possible, however, only by a shift in his later work away from a concern with relations of domination, towards more of an emphasis on the individual's potential for self-invention. In this latter approach, he declared that any new and radical political project must acknowledge the fact that 'we have to promote new forms of subjectivity through the refusal of this kind of individuality which has been imposed on us for centuries' (cited in Best and Kellner, 1991: 63). This dimension of Foucault's account of subjectivity and power/knowledge opens up a whole range of issues that appears to be deeply problematic, however.

Apart from the criticisms raised previously with regard to Lyotard's conception of the need for localized politics based on the playing out of language games, which can equally be directed at Foucault's own conception of a micro-politics of resistance, there exists the deeper question of Foucault's ontology. Particularly problematic, it could be argued, is his ontology of the subject. As has been noted above, central to his diagnosis of the modern subject is its status as the outcome of discursive relations of power/knowledge. As such, how can the subject, itself represented as little more than an historically contingent outcome of power in all its manifestations, engage in any form of self-creation without reinforcing those power relations against which such activity is supposedly directed? In Foucault's analysis (as in Lyotard's later work), the purposeful subject has, it would seem, largely gone missing. Furthermore, as power is understood not to reside in any particular site or social structure, but to exist relationally, in a

state of constant re-negotiation, the question of 'who is the subject?' is compounded by that of 'against whom does the subject direct its resistance?'.
Indeed, when faced with this very question Foucault's own reply was less
than convincing; that, at best, we must consider the exercise of power to be
a 'war of all against all' (Foucault, 1980: 208).

Ironically, we could say, much of Foucault's historically-based analysis
does indeed, despite his insistence on a non-hierarchical and highly diffuse
concept of power, portray a set of incredibly hierarchical institutions which
act as technologies of power. Thus, while Foucault undoubtedly sensitizes
us to the idea of power as something which pervades social relations and
that subjectivity, contra the Enlightenment view, is not something that is
simply present as a universal quality, the problems inherent in his analysis
provide a basis for further discussion as the following chapters unfold.

Deconstruction: a postmodern method?

While Foucault's particular brand of postmodernism focused primarily
upon the ways in which language, in the form of discourse, functions as a
medium of power, it is in the work of Jacques Derrida that the concern with
language can be seen to take on a far more methodological flavour.[10] While
complex in the extreme, Derrida's work has proven to be a particularly
influential approach to the analysis of the ways in which language structures
our understanding of ourselves and the world we inhabit, an approach he
termed *deconstruction* (Derrida, 1976: 24). In its simplest formulation, deconstruction can be taken to refer to a methodological strategy which seeks to
uncover layers of hidden meaning in a text that have been denied or suppressed.[11] The term 'text', in this respect, does not refer simply to a written
form of communication, however. Rather, texts are something we all produce and reproduce constantly in our everyday social relations, be they
spoken, written or embedded in the construction of material artifacts.

At the heart of Derrida's deconstructive approach is his critique of what
he perceives to be the totalitarian impulse of the Enlightenment pursuit to
bring all that exists in the world under the domain of a representative
language, a pursuit he refers to as *logocentrism* (Derrida, 1976: 3).
Logocentrism is the search for a rational language that is able to know and
represent the world and all its aspects perfectly and accurately. Its totalitarian dimension, for Derrida at least, lies primarily in its tendency to
marginalize or dismiss all that does not neatly comply with its particular
linguistic representations, a tendency that, throughout history, has all too
frequently been manifested in the form of authoritarian institutions. Thus
logocentrism has, in its search for the truth of absolute representation, subsumed difference and oppressed that which it designates as its alien Other.
For Derrida, western civilization has been built upon such a systematic
assault on alien cultures and ways of life, typically in the name of reason
and progress.

In response to logocentrism, deconstruction posits the idea that the mechanism by which this process of marginalization and the ordering of truth occurs is through establishing systems of binary opposition. Oppositional linguistic dualisms, such as rational/irrational, culture/nature and good/bad are not, however, construed as equal partners as they are in, say, the semiological structuralism of Saussure. Rather, they exist, for Derrida, in a series of hierarchical relationships with the first term normally occupying a superior position. Derrida defines the relationship between such oppositional terms using the neologism *différance* (Derrida, 1976: 23). This refers to the realization that in any statement, oppositional terms differ from each other (for instance, the difference between rationality and irrationality is constructed through oppositional usage), and at the same time, a hierarchical relationship is maintained by the deferral of one term to the other (in the positing of rationality over irrationality, for instance). It is this latter point which is perhaps the key to understanding Derrida's approach to deconstruction. For the fact that at any given time one term must defer to its oppositional Other, means that the two terms are constantly in a state of interdependence. The presence of one is dependent upon the absence or 'absent-presence' of the Other, such as in the case of good and evil, whereby to understand the nature of one, we must constantly relate it to the absent term in order to grasp its meaning. That is, to do good, we must understand that our act is not evil for without that comparison the term becomes meaningless. Put simply, deconstruction represents an attempt to demonstrate the absent-presence of this oppositional Other, to show that what we say or write is in itself not expressive simply of what is present, but also of what is absent. Thus, deconstruction seeks to reveal the interdependence of apparently dichotomous terms and their meaning relative to their textual context; that is, within the linguistic power relations which structure dichotomous terms hierarchically. In Derrida's own words, a deconstructive reading

> must always aim at a certain relationship, unperceived by the writer, between what he commands and what he does not command of the patterns of a language that he uses. . . . [It] attempts to make the not-seen accessible to sight. (1976: 158, 163)

Meaning, then, is never fixed or stable, whatever the intention of the author of a text. For Derrida, language is a system of relations that are dynamic, in that all meanings we ascribe to the world are dependent not only on what we believe to be present but also on what is absent. Thus, any act of interpretation must refer not only to what the author of a text intends, but also to what is absent from his or her intention. This insight leads, once again, to Derrida's further rejection of the idea of the definitive authority of the intentional agent or subject. The subject is decentred; it is conceived as the outcome of relations of *différance*. As author of its own biography, the subject thus becomes the ideological fiction of modernity and its logocentric philosophy, one that depends upon the formation of hierarchical dualisms which repress and deny the presence of the absent

Other. No meaning can, therefore, ever be definitive, but is merely an outcome of a particular interpretation.

His critique of the repressive nature of the hierarchical structures of western philosophy also leads Derrida to a political stance which is similar to that encountered in the work of Lyotard and Foucault. While he is reticent to attach himself to any firm political project, his support for various radical causes could be taken to be indicative of the radical potential of a politics of deconstruction, which seeks to expose the subjugation of the Other in all spheres of human life. Derrida has even attempted a limited reconciliation with Marxism, positing deconstruction as a radicalization of the Marxist 'spirit' (Derrida, 1994).

What Derridean deconstruction does not offer, however, is a systematic political programme. Rather, it represents what Seidman (1998) has described as a 'politics of subversion'. Once again, we are faced here with an indubitable tension between the call for a politics of social critique and the lack of any apparent foundation from whence this can be mobilized. Having sought to undermine the possibility of certitude, to unmask the repressive nature of philosophical logocentrism, and to identify the undecideability of meaning, it begs the question 'on what normative foundations can political critique be defended?'. Furthermore, is it legitimate when discussing political and social problems to refer to reality as nothing more than a 'text'? While it might be legitimate to acknowledge the indeterminacy of meaning within the literary universe (although this, in itself, is highly contentious), social discourse, it could be argued, is embedded within the constraints and boundaries established by 'real' political practices and economic relations. Indeed, Derrida himself appears acutely aware of the suffering that such factors cause millions of people across the globe. It would seem that the deconstructionist rejection of a realist ontology, combined with a concomitant suspicion of the metanarratives of truth and emancipation in Derrida's work, is, as Kumar (1995: 131) notes, so 'relentlessly subversive that it subverts itself'. A problem particularly evident when postmodernism is translated into the pursuit of a radical politics of change, which Lyotard, Foucault and Derrida have all championed in one form or another.

From postmodernism to postmodernity

So far we have sought to address, through the work of three of its leading theorists, the idea of the postmodern as a series of meta-theoretical propositions. The ideas of postmodernism have been defined, in large part, in opposition to the philosophical ideas bequeathed by the Enlightenment and include, most notably, a rejection of the possibility of a representational and universal truth, and of the essentially unified nature of the knowing subject, combined with a decline in the legitimacy or credibility of meta-narratives that link the progress of knowledge with human emancipation.

Instead, postmodernism has emphasized the centrality of epistemological heterogeneity, the valorization of cultural and political difference, and the ways in which the idea of the rational, autonomous subject is itself the outcome of a conjunction of historically specific discursive formations.

While relatively extensive in its exposition of a postmodern alternative to the philosophical worldview associated with the Enlightenment, the work of those postmodern theorists considered so far has nevertheless lacked any coherent attempt to develop an analysis of contemporary sociocultural conditions in relation to a process of postmodernization. Of course, it is perhaps not surprising that those who adhere to the principles of a postmodern approach to questions of knowledge find it difficult to consider the extent to which we are now experiencing the postmodern as a 'new social formation' (Bertens, 1995: 209). After all, such an approach would itself rely on the possibility of mobilizing the kind of totalizing socio-cultural analysis that postmodern thought appears to reject. Indeed, the idea of a condition of postmodernity would, it could be argued, have to be the creation of a particularly modernist way of looking at the world, relying, as it does, on the ability to discern holistic regularities and causal relations between the cultural, economic and intellectual realms of social life. Any account of postmodernity, then, would involve synthesizing diverse aspects of the social world into a more or less totalizing analysis of the contemporary condition.

On the whole, where such attempts have been made, therefore, they have tended to occur largely outside of the work of postmodern meta-theorists and to be located in the writing of those who can perhaps be described more accurately as theorists of postmodernity (Featherstone, 1991; Harvey, 1989; Jameson, 1991; Lash, 1990), who tend to emphasize the extent to which postmodernity can best be understood as a socio-cultural phenomenon. While remaining deeply sceptical about the more outlandish claims of postmodern meta-theory, such theorists have sought to understand the rise of a postmodern sensibility largely in relation to a parallel shift in the sociocultural and economic relations of contemporary western capitalism. Perhaps the most notorious among these is Jean Baudrillard, who has, over the last thirty years or so, produced a series of ideas that, if not necessarily definitive of the possible characteristics of a postmodern society, outline what he sees as being its primary features while, at the same time, claiming to reject the totalizing conventions of modernist social science.

The hyper-reality of postmodernity

The seemingly ever-present ghost of Marx has provided the backdrop for many of the ideas that have emerged within the postmodern genre representing, for Lyotard in particular, one of the great metanarratives of modernity. It is in the work of Baudrillard, however, that Marxism provides the clearest theoretical starting point for an analysis of postmodernity. Drawing on Marx's account of the primacy of commodity relations under capitalism, Baudrillard has argued that it is no longer the exchange value of commodities *per se* that underpins socio-cultural and economic relations, but rather the symbolic value that we attach to such commodities. Through what Baudrillard terms their *sign value* commodities provide the basis for socio-economic and, indeed, cultural exchange (Baudrillard, 1981). In a similar vein to Derrida, Baudrillard views signs as having broken away from any referent relationship to objects in the real world and, for that matter, to any fixed internal relationship between what they signify and what they mean. Thus, for Baudrillard, it is no longer the exchange value of the object that ascribes its value, but rather its value as a sign in relation to other signs. We no longer consume objects either for their use or for their exchange value, but rather for what they signify or say about us, or the kind of person we would want to be seen as.

The domination of the sign within contemporary society has led to a situation, Baudrillard (1983a, 1983b) argues, in which an implosion has occurred, one that has eradicated previously held distinctions between originality and representation, truth and fiction. This had led to a process that Baudrillard refers to as *simulation*, whereby simulated models of the real replace the real itself. As Baudrillard puts it, 'it is no longer a question of imitation, nor of replication, nor even of parody. It is rather a question of substituting signs of the real for the real itself' (1988a: 167). Baudrillard refers to perfect simulations that are more real than reality itself as *simulacru*; copies without an original to which they can be compared or designated as replica. In turn, these generate a state of *hyper-reality*, (Baudrillard, 1993: 146) whereby the simulation supplants the real and which, in turn, establishes the template for further simulations so that the idea of the real or original no longer has any bearing on the way we perceive the relationship between reality and representation. Hyper-reality, then, means that

> you can never really go back to the source, you can never interrogate an event, a character, a discourse about its degree of original reality. That's what I call hyper-reality. Fundamentally, it's a domain where you can no longer interrogate the reality or unreality, the truth or falsity of something. (Baudrillard, 1993: 146).

A notable example of hyper-reality can be identified in idealized images of femininity or masculinity frequently portrayed in the mass media. These are more than simply representations of the ideal body because, in 'reality', nobody (*sic*) is 'really' this perfect. Rather, such images are simulations, based upon established *codes* which people then strive to emulate as perfect examples of a non-existent reality. Baudrillard, in turn, theorizes the emergence of hyper-reality in terms of a process he terms *implosion*. As Best and Kellner (1991) note, this does not simply refer to an implosion or collapse of the boundaries between the real and the hyper-real, the original and the simulation, but between all dualistic modes of understanding and organizing in everyday life. High and low culture, politics and entertainment, work and leisure are all de-differentiated. Implosion therefore implies a reversal of the differentiating tendencies of modernity identified particularly by Durkheim that we outlined earlier in this chapter. Baudrillard's analysis of post-modernity, then, while clearly (and some would say, somewhat ironically) an attempt to present a totalizing analysis of the condition of contemporary western societies, reflects a number of the themes we have encountered in our discussion of postmodernism thus far. Like Lyotard, Baudrillard grounds his diagnosis of postmodernism in the collapse of any certain basis for claims to truth or knowledge.

However, unlike the work of postmodern meta-theorists encountered so far, Baudrillard's analysis of postmodernity is far less imbued with any form of radical political agenda. Indeed, hyper-reality seems to leave little scope for meaningful political engagement of any kind, with society reduced to a 'silent majority' (Baudrillard, 1988a) of mindless consumers who, in Baudrillard's account at least, have been enchanted by the signs and images of the mass media. Baudrillard's own version of the death of the subject thesis results, therefore, in his positing the social world as beyond the possibility of human intervention (Baudrillard, 1990). The only political strategy left for Baudrillard is for the subject to make the conscious decision to become more 'object-like' and, in doing so, jettison those attrib-utes of agency and meaning that are deemed obsolete. The last meaningful act, or 'fatal strategy' (Baudrillard, 1988a: 185) on the part of the subject, then, is to renounce all meaningful acts and to relinquish the motivation to pursue any purposeful activity.

It is perhaps not surprising, then, that considering the somewhat nihilistic conclusion reached in Baudrillard's account of postmodernity, his work has encountered extensive criticism from several quarters. Many of these criticisms are simply variations of those we have considered thus far in relation to postmodernism as a meta-theory. However, his apparent willingness to provide what he considers to be an empirically defensible representation of the social and cultural configurations of a postmodern world has left Baudrillard vulnerable to charges of methodological inep-titude and empirical misrepresentation. For example, in relation to the material contained in his travelogue *America* (1988b), Best and Kellner critically observe how Baudrillard 'hangs out in southern California and concludes that the United States is a "realized utopia". He fails to see, however, the homeless, the poor, racism and sexism, people dying of AIDS, oppressed immigrants . . . ' (1991: 138). Yet, as they go on to note, such gross empirical oversights would be tolerable if Baudrillard acknowledged the epistemological consequences of his diagnosis of the condition of knowledge in a postmodernized world and, as such, pro-fessed to be offering nothing more than a very particular interpretation or 'story'. However, this does not appear to be the case, for Baudrillard seeks continually to express what he considers to be the 'truth' about contemporary society, a truth that he appears to claim is itself universal. In this sense at least, Best and Kellner note how, in their opinion, 'Baudrillard represents totalizing thought at its worst' (1991: 140).

Nevertheless, despite the apparent limitations of Baudrillard's theory of postmodernity, or at least the limitations of its credibility, there can be no doubt that in many ways his work exemplifies the postmodern cultural spirit. His style is eclectic, his attention to academic standards of citation and argumentation questionable,[12] and his observations frequently verge on the intellectually offensive. It may be, therefore, that it is not what Baudrillard says, but how he says it (and the fact that he achieves considerable recognition for it) that reveals so much about the condition of postmodernity.

While Baudrillard's account of postmodernity may be somewhat unpalatable for some, there can be no doubt that it raises a number of themes and issues that have had a considerable impact upon the ways in which social scientists and philosophers think about the social world. In particular, his work on the increasing significance played by the mass media on the way we perceive the world around us, his writing on the apparent implosion of social and cultural categories, and his ideas on the emergence of simulated modes of experiencing the world all resonate with a number of contemporary concerns within the social sciences, to which we now turn our attention. In the penultimate section of this chapter, we consider these themes as they have been presented in the work of a number of contemporary social and cultural theorists who have conceptualized the changes that societies of the industrialized world are currently facing as 'postmodernity'.

Postmodern culture: de-differentiation, space and capital

For some theorists of postmodernity, new modes of technology, processes of globalization and a concomitant shifting cultural sensibility have imploded into a state of postmodernity that marks a significant empirical shift away from the socio-cultural contours of the modern epoch. Featherstone (1991) in particular views postmodernism as a largely hedonistic cultural phenomenon shaped by consumerism as the pursuit of pleasure. For Featherstone, postmodern culture provides an opportunity to engage with a multiplicity of identities and cultural experiences.[13] A not dissimilar approach is taken by Lash (1990), for whom postmodernity can best be understood as a process of *de-differentiation* through which boundaries between what were previously taken to be distinct and separate cultural and intellectual spheres are collapsed. Echoing Baudrillard's (1983a, 1983b) conception of social and cultural implosion outlined above, this process of de-differentiation is understood as a shift from a modern to a postmodern 'figural' configuration (Lash, 1990: ix) whereby previous distinctions of taste and value are no longer tenable.

Theorists such as Jameson (1991) and Harvey (1989) have, in turn, developed highly influential and, it could be argued, more critical analyses of postmodernism inspired largely by a Marxist reading of such developments. In such accounts, postmodernity tends to be conceptualized as a series of cultural and intellectual forms representing what Jameson terms 'the cultural logic of late capitalism'.[14] For Jameson (1991: 1), *late capitalism* refers to a stage of capitalism driven largely by electronic technologies of production and distribution, and the concomitant emphasis this places on the need to increase rates of consumption so as to avoid economic crises deriving from overproduction. It is this imperative which he views as the driving force of cultural de-differentiation and the pursuit of an essentially hedonistic culture, materialized in the desire to consume the products of late capitalism. Thus, for Jameson, the postmodernization of culture and the rise of a postmodern intellect, are both epiphenomena of a structural shift in the forces and relations of capitalist production. Consumer culture is thus seen to function as the focal point for the construction of individual identities, providing some, albeit transitory, sense of stability and location for the fragmented postmodern subject. That 'we are what we consume' is the logic of a postmodern society for Featherstone and Jameson alike. For Jameson, however, while consumerism provides a point of social integration, it also denies the subject any critical vantage point from which they can view their relationship to the broader make-up of socio-economic relations.

David Harvey's (1989) analysis of the 'condition of postmodernity', provides a similar, if somewhat more extensively materialist, account of postmodernity. Harvey identifies *postmodernization* as a shift from the rigid practices of Fordism to the flexible modes of production and exchange characteristic of a post-Fordist mode of economic organization (see Chapter 2). Emerging from this is what he terms a process of 'time–space compression' (Harvey, 1989: 284), which, for Harvey, describes the cultural impact of the expansion of new technologies of exchange and production, as well as the rapid computerization of international finance markets. As Harvey describes it:

> with accelerations in turnover times in production, exchange and consumption. . . . Past experiences get compressed into some overwhelming present. . . . Everything, from novel writing and philosophizing to the experience of labouring or making a home, has to face the challenge of accelerating turnover time and the rapid write-off of traditional and historically acquired values. (1989: 291)

Both Jameson and Harvey, therefore, critically analyse the possible configurations of postmodernity as a cultural and social response to developments in contemporary capitalism. As such, they reject what they see as the more outlandish claims that postmodernism in some way represents an exclusively novel mode of social organization. Rather, while both appear willing to accept the idea of the postmodern as a socio-cultural phenomenon, they consider it to represent more of a *re-configuration* of essentially modernist values and forms of socio-cultural life necessitated by technologically-driven changes in the nature of capitalism.

In a similar, if more sceptical vein, Anthony Giddens (1990) and Ulrich Beck (1992) have argued that while a range of important socio-economic changes are taking place, especially in relation to the changing relationship between time and space, and the increasingly significant role of reflexivity in defining the contours of contemporary culture, to describe the age we are entering as postmodern may be somewhat premature. Instead, they argue that while modernity is currently undergoing a period of transition, this can be best characterized as a period of *late or reflexive modernity*, one in which we are coming to terms with the changes alluded to above. Furthermore, implicit within this argument is the belief that postmodernity will not, and indeed cannot, be achieved unless humanity is able to overcome the very features of the crisis that appear to have established, for other writers, the idea that we are already entering a postmodern age. This in itself can only be achieved, for Beck in particular, through *more* modernization, not less. By this he means the broader and more concerted applications of reason to overcome the legacy of industrialization, to raise the desire for a better world above that of a crude faith in industrial technology and the goods it produces.

A more comprehensive rejection of the idea of the postmodern, in all its manifestations, is to be found in the work of the Marxist critic Alex Callinicos (1989) and the critical social theory of Jürgen Habermas (1987a, 1989, 1993). Habermas, for example, defends what he considers to be the incomplete project of modernity (Habermas, 1993), from those such as Foucault, Lyotard and Derrida, whom he considers to be 'young conservatives', far too eager to reject the emancipatory potential of modernity and its belief in the power of reason to uncover and dispel prejudice and repression. In his definitively titled *Against Postmodernism* (1989), Callinicos dismisses the idea that postmodernism in any way represents a meaningful break with the cultural, economic or organizational imperatives of modernity. While he agrees with the likes of Lash and Featherstone that the last thirty years or so have witnessed the growth of a new social strata of well educated, culturally sophisticated consumers, Callinicos does not equate the popularization of postmodernism simply with the economic and cultural strength of this particular group. Rather, he views it as the direct outcome of the perceived failure of the revolutionary spirit of the late 1960s and the retreat of the intellectuals at the heart of this movement away from any radical political engagement in the face of a consumer capitalism which appears, at least, to have achieved an almost unassailable hegemonic status. For Callinicos, 'the discourse of postmodernism is best seen as the product of a socially mobile intelligentsia in a climate dominated by the retreat of the Western labour movement and the "overconsumptionist" dynamic of capitalism in the Reagan–Thatcher era' (1989: 171).

Thus, while his analysis is essentially similar to those of Harvey and Jameson, for Callinicos, to reject the idea of the postmodern is essentially a political act. Postmodernism, in his analysis, is little more than an ideological system, fabricated by an apolitical intelligentsia, to legitimate their aspirations towards mainstream credibility and acceptance of capitalist hegemony. As such, postmodernism, and theories of postmodernity, represent little more than an ideological distraction from the business of serious social criticism and should be dismissed accordingly.

Conclusion

Despite the force of critique exemplified in Callinicos's denunciation of postmodernism, and the apparent tensions and contradictions in the idea of the postmodern, as we have tried to outline here, the questions it raises and the problems it presents have come to represent an integral dimension of the current social scientific landscape. As we have tried to stress, however, this chapter should in no way be taken to represent anything like an exhaustive overview of the ideas and debates that are currently shaping this particular landscape. Rather, it has sought to outline what we consider to be a number of important contributions which, we hope, will help to provide a framework within which to consider the relationship between the idea of the postmodern and the world of work and its organization in the following chapters. Let us try, then, to sum these up.

First and foremost, postmodernism appears to represent a shift in the intellectual and, broadly cultural, sensibility of the age. Whether manifest in Lyotard's 'incredulity towards meta-narratives', Foucault's equation of power/knowledge or Derrida's notion that there is nothing beyond the 'text', this sensibility renders problematic a range of Enlightenment-derived propositions about the nature of the world, and brings into question the idea that we can either know or intervene meaningfully in its reconstitution. Where such attempts are made they must be viewed reflexively, that is as little more than the outcome of a particular perspective based upon a contingent rather than a universal or ahistorical rationality. This, in turn, has led to the emergence of a particular political conviction that is perhaps best exemplified in the deconstructive approach of Derrida; that a postmodern politics of emancipation must seek to uncover and expose those acts of repression that the logocentric nature of modernist rationality has perpetrated in the name of representation and universality. Language and culture are viewed in this context as the primary site in which the repressed 'others' of western rationality can find a voice which has, up until now, been silenced. These 'others' may include the discourses of feminism, the cultural values of various ethnic identities and those dimensions of being that have been designated as the 'irrational' in human life such as sexuality and emotion.

With reference to the idea of a possible condition of social postmodernization exemplified in the writing of say Baudrillard, Lash and Featherstone, the emphasis here seems to lie on the prioritization of culture over other constitutive aspects of the social whole such as the economy, or indeed the collapse of such boundaries. This emphasis upon culture in turn reflects and reinforces the post-structuralist-inspired conception of the de-centred subject as expressed to a lesser or greater extent in almost all accounts of postmodernism. Rather than culture emerging as the expression of shared norms and ideals constituted through inter-subjective social relations, subjectivity is viewed as the outcome of historically-located cultural discourses, most notably, in the contemporary age, of conspicuous consumption and the value of the sign. Furthermore, what unites all of these approaches is an attempt to reflect on the extent to which the institutions of modernity can endure, if it is the case that many of the very principles underpinning such institutions are no longer tenable.

Yet such philosophical meanderings are not the whole story, as we have seen. Postmodernism has also been understood as a socio cultural response to what has been presented as a set of very real material developments. The growth in information technologies, combined with rapid developments in industrial production and financial exchange, have undoubtedly provided the impetus for a whole range of changes in the ways in which we experience the social world. Indeed, from this perspective, whatever postmodernity may encompass, there is little evidence to suggest that it implies a state of post-capitalism.

Bearing in mind that postmodern meta-theory continues to evolve and debates on the nature of postmodernity as a socio-cultural phenomenon remain subject to critical commentary, we now move to consider, more in keeping with the specific focus of the book, the impact that postmodernism has had upon the field of organization theory over the last twenty years or so. In doing so, we aim to bring together a wide range of material, and to try to make sense not only of how, but also of why, postmodernism and organization theory seem to have emerged as such accommodating bedfellows. Thus, many of the ideas and criticisms we have encountered so far will be re-visited and developed.

Notes

1 For a more extensive discussion of the relationship between modernism, modernization and modernity, see Berman (1983) and Featherstone (1988).

2 It would of course be inaccurate to suggest that a self-reflexive critique of what it is to be *modern* had not already been underway long before this current historical juncture. Intellectuals and writers from Hegel to Sartre, Nietzsche to Kafka have all, in one way or another, engaged with the tensions and contradictions of modernity. However, the point we are making here is that the nature of modernity *itself* was seldom addressed prior to the impact of postmodern ideas.

3 As noted, the emergence of the modern age is a disputed point. Alternative accounts have posited its birth with the seventeenth-century Renaissance while, more controversially, there have been those who have suggested that 'we have never been modern' (Latour, 1993), a point also raised by feminist critiques of the Enlightenment.

4   The first self-conscious engagement with the idea of the Enlightenment is to be found in Kant's essay of 1784 *An Answer to the Question: 'What is Enlightenment?'* (Kant, 1991), in which he viewed the Enlightenment as having offered humanity a way out of its 'immaturity'. That is, it had allowed humanity to discover the faculty of autonomous reason as the proper guide to action and behaviour.

5   For instance, de Condorcet, Diderot, Hume and Kant.

6   For example, Marx's critique of capitalism, it could be argued, rests primarily upon capitalism's growing 'irrationality' in the face of developing socio-economic conditions.

7   See, for example, the structural linguistics of de Saussure (1974) or the Marxist structuralism of Althusser (1969).

8   A term derived from the later work of Wittgenstein (1958).

9   Lyotard refers here specifically to the work of Daniel Bell and his writing on post-industrialism (Bell, 1973).

10   The question of whether deconstruction does in fact represent a methodological approach is, however, a contested one. It seems that what Derrida means by deconstruction differs from what Heidegger (from whom Derrida derives the term) means. With reference to Derrida's use of the term, it may be more appropriate to consider deconstruction as a 'sensibility' – a way of conceiving the world.

11   To describe deconstruction as a methodological approach, Sarup (1993) uses the analogy of the X-raying of paintings which attempts to discover, under the epidermis of the last layer of paint, another hidden picture.

12   Take, for example, this excerpt from the notes on the translation of his 1988 volume of selected writings: 'Baudrillard rarely provides full citations in his own notes. . . . At times Baudrillard's quotations have not been located anywhere in the text he cites' (Baudrillard, 1988a: viii).

13   Also see Lyotard's earlier observation that 'eclecticism is the degree zero of contemporary general culture: one listens to reggae, watches a western, eats McDonald's food for lunch and local cuisine for dinner, wears Paris perfume in Tokyo and 'retro' clothes in Hong Kong; knowledge is a matter for TV games' (1984: 76).

14   A term originating from the Marxist economist Ernest Mandel (1978).

2

Organizational Postmodernization

Organizations are geared to respond to rather than regulate markets. They are seen as frameworks for learning as much as instruments of control. Their hierarchies are flatter and their structures more open. The guerrilla force takes over from the standing army. All this has liberated the centre from the tyranny of the immediate. (Murray, 1989a: 47)

Flexible working, more like the Martini contract; anytime, anyplace, anywhere; but no more money and less holidays into the bargain. If this is a postmodern way of working they can stick it. (Disgruntled university employee responding to the new partnership contract on offer by his institution)

As we embark upon the second millennium of the Christian calendar, it is perhaps inevitable that we should be on the lookout for signs that western societies are about to undergo some kind of momentous change; that the old order is slipping away fast, to be replaced by a brave, or perhaps not so brave, new world, a world in which the technological revolution of the previous two hundred years will finally bear fruit, alleviating old drudgeries and bringing about new, possibly more emancipated modes of social and economic organization. Certainly this was the spirit that began to inform the work of a number of prominent social commentators and sociologists during the late 1960s, heralding the publication of a range of semi-futuristic accounts of a new 'post-industrial' era that would surpass both the achievements and failures of the modern industrial age. At the heart of such accounts there was, more often than not, a belief in the central position that work, and its organization, would play in such historic transformations. New technologies of production and exchange, the re-structuring of the labour force and even a shifting relationship between work and leisure were all cited as the driving forces behind and, in part, the consequences of, this forthcoming socio-economic and cultural revolution.

Yet while, as the final decades of the century ticked away, such historical visions were treated with increasing scepticism, they were replaced by a series of, in many ways, complementary pronouncements on the changing nature of work and the organizational environments in which it takes place. While perhaps somewhat less concerned with the possibility of widescale social transformation, in many ways such ideas posited no less of a vision of revolution in the contemporary workplace. Drawing their inspiration both from the post-industrial visionaries, and what they saw as the emergent new organizational forms of the Pacific Rim economies, and attempts to emulate their cultural practices in the west, such writers proclaimed, if not the impending demise, then the radical modification of the modern work environment. Against the scientific certainties inherited from industrial and management theorists of the early twentieth century, they envisaged a new, flexible and less hierarchical kind of work organization. These workplaces of the future, having transcended the rigidities of the modernist mindset, would be free not only to produce, but also to innovate and create. Harnessing the explosion in information and production technologies, they would have more time and resources to concentrate on the cultural and human needs of their members, until they had reached a stage of development that could indeed be conceived as postmodern.

In the following chapter, we reflect on these related visions of an emergent post-industrial, and eventually for some commentators, post-modernized organizational form. As such, this chapter is not so much concerned with issues of postmodern meta-theory, but rather with the question of what a postmodern organization, if indeed such a thing does or can exist, might look like. This is a distinction which, it should be noted, has also been adopted, particularly in sociology, and most notably in the work of Bauman (1988) who has attempted to differentiate between what he terms a *postmodern sociology* and a *sociology of postmodernism*.[1] The former describes a sociology driven by the assumptions of postmodern meta-theory while the latter represents a concern with studying possible sites of social postmodernization using traditional sociological concepts and approaches. This is a distinction that, in organization theory at least,[2] has also been deployed through the idea that postmodernity can be understood as a periodizing or ontological concept (see Hassard, 1993a), a concept that describes particular structures or practices that have broken, in one form or another, from those of modern organizations, which themselves are seen as distinct from pre-modern modes of organizing.

We begin with a brief consideration of the interrelationship between organization and the broader process of modernization. Here we emphasize the idea that a deep affinity existed between the emergence of the modern world and the process of organization, especially in the domain of production and exchange. We then go on to explore the development of a body of literature which has contributed to the view outlined above that contemporary industrialized societies have started to display tendencies which somehow represent a break from the structures and organizational imperatives associated with the modern organizational form. Ranging from the post-industrial thesis of Bell (1973) through to the flexible specialization and post-Fordist perspectives of the likes of Piore and Sabel (1984) and Murray (1989a, 1989b), we look at how such work laid the foundations and supplied many of the concepts for the more recent emergence of the idea that we are currently witnessing the development of a postmodernized organizational form.

Organization/modernization

In Chapter 1, we described briefly some of the characteristics of a world undergoing a process of modernization, including a rapid expansion in levels of material production, processes of rural migration and urbanization, the impact of faster and more reliable modes of communication and the differentiation of the cultural and intellectual spheres of life. Yet, what was largely omitted from that account was the role that the development of complex organizations played in the process. For, as Stewart Clegg (1990: 25) notes, modernization both as a technical and cultural project, would not have been possible but for the concomitant emergence of complex systems of social and industrial organization. Citing Wolin (1961), Reed (1996a) points out how the growth of complex organizational systems was seen by Saint-Simon, the nineteenth-century French philosopher and social visionary, as providing the technical media through which the Enlightenment vision of a rational society could be realized:

> Organization as power over things – that was the lesson taught by Saint-Simon. The new order would be governed not by men but by 'scientific principles' based on the nature of things and therefore absolutely independent of human will. In this way, organizational society promised the rule of scientific laws rather than men and the eventual disappearance of the political element entirely . . . [organization] is the 'grand device for transforming human irrationalities into rational behaviour'. (Reed, 1996a: 31)

It was this vision of a rational organizational order that, by the early twentieth century, came to be translated into the now classical management theories associated with the likes of Frederick Taylor (1911) and Henri Fayol (1949). Taylor's conception of scientific management, for example, provides a perfect illustration of the attempt to apply the principles of modern scientific thinking to the organization of human activity in general, and wage labour in particular. Taylor's stated aim was to harness the principles and methods of the natural sciences to uncover the single most objective mode of organization, the *one best way* to carry out any task, so as to lead to the maximization of productive efficiency. Once this had been 'discovered' it was then to be enshrined in formalized, written rules and procedures that would then be enforced by an educated managerial stratum which would enjoy the full control of the activities of the labour force.

In turn, the motivation of employees to undertake such regimented labour was to be found in the relatively high levels of financial remuneration that would accompany such practices. This was a strategy itself based on the presumption of the rational character of the individual who would consider the exchange of a degree of individual autonomy for higher levels of income and an improved material lifestyle to be a reasonable one.[3] Thus, in Taylor's vision, science would serve to remove the irrational and emotional dimension of the human element from organizational life, replacing it with formal, rationalistic structures that would ensure maximum efficiency and minimal conflict.

This vision of a completely rationalized approach to the labour process found form in the mechanized assembly-line techniques of Henry Ford. At his car manufacturing plant in Michigan, Ford combined somewhat instrumentally Taylor's prescription – high levels of financial remuneration, the separation of conception from execution, and the organization of the division of labour in accordance with scientifically grounded observations – with the technology of the moving assembly line, to achieve unprecedented levels of manufacturing output. Thus Fordism, as this system of organization which combined Taylor's principles of scientific management with an assembly line mode of production was termed (see Gramsci, 1971), represented what might best be understood as the materialization of the systemic modernist vision of man (sic) and machine working together in perfect harmony. Fordism organized this relationship according to rational principles, arrived at from scientific research, and implemented in accordance with impersonal rules and directives. Its aim was the maximization of output, with the human worker conforming to the role of little more than a rationalized factor of production.

The impact of Fordism was not solely confined to the organization of production, however. Ford himself understood that the mass production of commodities would, if it was to avoid producing a condition of over production and thus economic crisis, require a sustainable culture of mass consumption to accompany it. Thus, integral to Fordism was the need to nurture a culture in which 'ordinary' working men and women would be encouraged to consume the goods provided by a mass production system. Yet while Ford's own attempts to ensure that 'rational' patterns of consumption became the norm among his employees – most notably through the use of an army of social workers based in the Ford Sociology Department, and the widespread encouragement of his employees to save their income for the purchase of their own Ford automobile – had limited impact, the principle came to represent an important part of the rationalization process of organized modernity. As Sabel notes, the principle of maintaining high levels of demand was not lost on the governments of increasingly interventionist western states who,

> increasingly used their fiscal and monetary powers to stabilize the long-term growth of demand. The aim was to induce firms to expand by ensuring markets

for their increased outputs. National and social welfare and unemployment-insurance programmes protected individuals against personal disasters and further stabilized demand by guaranteeing minimum levels of purchasing power for persons with no income. (Sabel, 1994: 102)

As such, Fordism developed well beyond the confines of the work organization into a relatively coherent socio-economic system that linked production, consumption and cultural expectations through a process of socio-economic rationalization (see Gramsci, 1971). Demand management became, as the twentieth century reached its mid-point, a central concern of the increasingly corporatist states of the industrial west.

In this sense, Weber's earlier representation of the bureaucratic mode of administration was perhaps significant, above all else, for its identification of the existence of an elective affinity between the modernization process in general, and the rise and growth of rational modes of organizational administration. For Weber, the bureaucratic mode of organizing, premised as it was on the establishment and recognition of formal procedures and regulations, represented a functional division of labour based on qualification and the impersonality of all decision-making – the pinnacle of rational efficiency (Weber, 1964 [1925]). However, unlike Taylor, Weber's vision went beyond that of economic and organizational efficiency. Despite his subsequent incorporation into the mainstream of organization theory, Weber was deeply ambivalent about the universalizing tendencies of modernity and the eradication of subjectively held value systems, which he saw as exemplified in the standardized and regulated nature of the bureaucratic system. Nevertheless, his 'ideal type' became, for many, the yardstick against which formal organizations should be measured in terms of their tendency towards rational efficiency and, as such, a quantifiable indicator of achieved levels of modernization.

By the mid-twentieth century, however, many of the underlying preconceptions of both scientific management and the bureaucratic model of organizational efficiency were coming under critical scrutiny. Following the Hawthorne studies of the mid-1920s (Mayo, 1933; Roethlisberger and Dickson, 1939), the development of the Human Relations Movement began to challenge the Taylorist notion that the rational economic agent was motivated purely by material gain. Rather, in its place, a Human Relations approach emphasized the social character of work and the importance of interpersonal dynamics in the maintenance of motivation and productivity. During the post-war period, critical studies by the likes of Etzioni (1961) and Blau and Scott (1963) suggested that the organizational tendency towards bureaucracy varied depending upon the configuration of competing interests within the organization. Merton (1949) questioned how the bureaucratic organization, with what he considered to be its tendency towards rigidity and inertia, could optimize its functioning within an economic and political environment characterized by constant change and environmental instability.

Nevertheless, such criticisms were not directed at the logic and structures of the modern organizational form *per se*, but rather represented attempts, largely as the outcome of empirical research, to fine-tune the technologies and mechanisms of management in the pursuit of improved efficiency. As Alvesson and Willmott note, while previous management strategies had been based on the principle of eradicating disruptive irrationalities, such as tradition and sentiment from the organizational domain, in later approaches such as Human Relations, 'sentiment is identified as *an untapped resource* for securing improved levels of commitment and productivity' (1996: 111 *original emphasis*). Organizations, then, were still viewed as essentially rational endeavours designed, as Talcott Parsons (1991) observed, to materialize co-operative relations geared towards the instrumental attainment of specific goals. As such, many of what were considered at the time to be more humanistic developments within the management and structuring of organizational life, such as those associated with Human Relations Theory and Industrial Psychology, have since come to be understood as attempts to further rationalize labour through forms of social engineering (Braverman, 1974) and the extension of the rationalization process into the very 'soul' of the worker (Rose, 1990); processes far from incompatible with the logic of Fordist/bureaucratic organizational principles.

Indeed, by the early 1960s, by combining a labour process based upon the systemic principles of Taylorism with personnel management techniques derived largely from Human Relations and Industrial Psychology, Fordism appeared to have brought about a new era of social stability and economic prosperity (Murray, 1989a). By then it had, or so it seemed, managed successfully to combine production, distribution and consumption into an integrated system, one that was underpinned by Keynesian state economic policy and a culture of mass consumption combined with a popular faith in science and technology. By the end of the decade, however, questions started to be raised about the sustainability of such forms of social and industrial organization in the face of a series of economic and cultural developments, many of which were no longer confined simply to the economies of the west. Falling rates of profit, increasing industrial unrest, changing patterns of consumer demand, the rise of new technologies and the growth of the far eastern economies, most notably that of Japan, increasingly fostered an awareness that change was both necessary and indeed, to some extent, inevitable. This growing mood was picked up on relatively quickly by a number of commentators who set out to try to describe and explain the organizational changes that they saw happening around them, as well as pointing towards what they believed would be future developments in the trajectory of industrialized societies. While not originally presented as a transcendence of modernity as such, these early contributions paved the way for many of the developments that have been labelled 'postmodern' that we consider later in the chapter.

Post-industrialism and the information society

The proposition that the economies of the west were moving towards a qualitatively different mode of social and economic organization than that which had come to be associated with modern industrialism first emerged in the USA during the late 1960s. Initially, this seemed to be based on an optimistic belief in the inevitability of, and opportunity provided by, rising levels of prosperity linked to the emergence of new forms of labour-saving, and therefore more efficient, forms of technology. Popularized most notably in the work of Drucker (1969), Toffler (1970) and Bell (1973), this new paradigm for analysis came to be known as the *post-industrial thesis*, and presented a largely future-oriented account of the impact new communication technologies would have upon dominant modes of social and economic organization. The potential significance of such developments was, it has to be said, far from understated. Toffler, for example, considered this new computer-led revolution to be more significant than the shift from pre-industrial to industrialized societies nearly two hundred years earlier, noting that

> what is occurring now, is in all likelihood, bigger, deeper, and more important than the industrial revolution . . . the present movement represents nothing less than the second great divide in human history, comparable in magnitude only with that first great break in historic continuity, the shift from barbarism to civilization. (1970: 12)

Bell's (1973) analysis, slightly less euphoric in style, viewed the move from an industrial to a post-industrial society as a shift in the axial principles of the industrialized world. Most notable among these was the movement from a social structure based on industrial production to one based upon the primacy of 'theoretical knowledge' (Bell, 1973: 14). Bell claimed that the ascendancy of 'theoretical knowledge' as a commodity was both the result of and the driving force behind a number of major changes in the social and economic relations of modern societies. These included a significant shift from manufacturing to service economies, fuelled by a major expansion in the activities of health, education and government, the consolidation of a new professional and technical middle class, and the growth of what he termed 'intellectual technologies' (Bell, 1973: 14); the capacity to manage, plan and control an increasingly complex social universe through the application of science and rational planning.

While the idea of a post-industrial society was clearly not based upon a rejection of the underlying principles of modern rationality as such, it did seem to point to a changing social landscape, one in which previous modes of organization, centred upon the co-ordination and management of large-scale industrial plants, would be supplanted and replaced by a combination of small-scale, research-driven hi-technology industries and service sector commodities such as education, health and leisure. Integral to such developments, at least in Bell's account, would be a breakdown in the traditional class composition of the labour force, itself a product of industrial modernization. The numerical domination of the industrial working class would therefore be supplanted by the rise of a new techno-cratic middle class, the product of an expansion of further and higher education and the shifting demands of the post-industrial labour market. In turn, this shift would be reflected in a change in the social relations of work itself, which would gravitate towards being based upon interaction between people rather than between people and nature as, he argued, was the case in more traditional, industrial organizations. Thus, for Bell, the tenor and culture of organizational life, as well as its formal structuring around the needs of highly mechanized and standardized processes of manufacturing, would be altered by the larger-scale processes of post-industrialization.

Similar themes have also been developed in works as divergent as Paul Halmos's (1970) prediction of a *personal service society* and Claus Offe's (1985) analysis of what he termed *disorganized capitalism*.[4] For both these men, movement towards a more service-oriented industrial base in west-ern societies was starting to produce an equally transformed workplace ethos. For Halmos, the growth in the professional strata of the western workforce, concerned with the provision of welfare and other 'personal services', was leading to what he considered to be a 'momentous change' (Halmos, 1970: 145) in the culture and ethos of society, that is, one less con-cerned with issues such as profit maximization and more concerned with the quality of service provided to its citizens. For Offe, 'disorganized cap-italism' also reflects, in part, the expansion of the service sector and its impact on western economies. Offe argued that the rational model of industrial organization, based on the principles of efficiency, profit-maxi-mization and adherence to strictly defined procedures was gradually being supplanted by the requirements of an economy founded increasingly on the imperatives of service industries. Service work, he argued, tends to deal with heterogeneous situations and to take place within a controlled environment that cannot be measured simply in terms of profit, but which must be assessed largely by much more intangible criteria such as satis-faction or communal value. Thus, the potential also existed in Offe's view for the emergence of a post-Weberian mode of organizing which would depend less on rationalized, hierarchical structures of authority and control and more on 'calculations based on convention, political discretion or pro-fessional consensus' (Offe, 1985: 138).

By the 1980s, however, the post-industrial thesis had come under sus-tained critique, particularly for its tendency to romanticize the liberatory potential of its posited new class formations (Gorz, 1982; Touraine, 1974) and for over-emphasizing the novelty of the 'new' service and research industries which, it has been argued, have always been central to any industrial regime (Frankel, 1987; Kumar, 1978). It also suffered from the empirical observation that the trajectory of western societies had not appeared to follow that which the post-industrialists had laid out for them.

Western economies still produced manufactured goods, unskilled and semi-skilled labour was still required, albeit increasingly in the tertiary sector of the economy, and work organizations continued to operate in terms of formal bureaucratic principles and management expertise. Yet despite these objections, many of the themes that had emerged as part and parcel of the post-industrial thesis survived in the reformulated vision of the *information society* which went on to develop, in particular, the post-industrial preoccupation with the centrality of knowledge, its production and dissemination.

Once again at the forefront of the popularization of such ideas was Bell (1980a, 1980b), who viewed the expansion of computerized information systems and their merger with communication technologies as the defining feature of a new 'information age'. The popularization of this new vision took on, in the work of Toffler (1981), Stonier (1983) and Naisbitt (1984), an almost messianic tenor, one that promised to lead humanity to a world which is '. . . more sane, more sensible, and sustainable, more decent and more democratic than any we have ever known' (Toffler, 1981: 2–3). Information, then, and its free flow across the globe was offered as a path to human salvation, producing a world free from want, war and suffering (Stonier, 1983); a re-affirmation of the Enlightenment project of emancipation through reason, with reason, in this case, being realized through the expansion of information technology.

Indeed, there can be little doubt that the growing impact of information technologies on the re-structuring of work and its relationship to other aspects of our lives, is undoubtedly one of increasing significance. Advanced computer and communication systems have changed not only the ways in which organizations communicate both internally and externally, but have also altered for many, in the form of say teleworking from home (see Huws et al., 1990), where work is actually carried out and, as such, what it means to be a part of a work organization. Such technological developments have also led, perhaps inevitably, to the emergence of new problems of organizational control and co-ordination, such as managing across distanciated relations of time and space, challenging managers and management educators to shift their thinking in terms of traditional models of employee management. Yet technology has, to a certain degree, also been identified as providing certain solutions to the 'problem' of management in terms of increasingly sophisticated modes of electronic surveillance and control (Dandeker, 1990; Lyon, 1993; Sewell and Wilkinson, 1992a; Zuboff, 1988). Such surveillance not only takes the form of direct visual observation such as through video and CCTV, however. It also involves more indirect forms of control such as computerized stock controls, machine switch-on times and so on, which enable employers to track employee movements and time spent actually working. It is the development of such technologies, designed primarily to exert control over the activities of the individual, which has raised questions about the supposedly liberating benefits of a pending information age, and has raised fears about the increasingly panoptic nature not only of the work-place, but of society at large.[5]

Manuel Castells (1989, 1996), for example, is responsive to the idea that the growth in information and communication technologies will have significant implications for the trajectory of industrialized societies. Yet, he refuses to accept uncritically any proposition that such developments can be separated from the continuation of asymmetrical relations of power. For Castells, even where there are apparent benefits in terms of increased levels of material wealth and living standards, the undesirable consequences of such a shift potentially outweigh the benefits. In *The Rise of the Network Society* (1996), for example, he argues that no matter how impressive technical developments in the field of information technology are, the main problem facing the world is the extent to which developing countries are threatened with even greater levels of exclusion from the global community, incapable as they currently are of matching the technological capabilities of the west. On a more micro-level, Webster and Robbins (1989) have raised concerns that the invasion of every aspect of our daily lives by various forms of computer-driven information technologies can be seen to represent little more than a form of 'social Taylorism'. Our consumer habits are both monitored and regimented in such a way that every aspect of our everyday lives is reduced to the pursuit of efficiency and productivity, be it in how we work, or spend our money, or even spend our leisure time.

Thus, rather than reversing the rationalizing tendencies of industrial modernity, this analysis suggests the possible emergence of an era in which every dimension of our lives is monitored, directed and regulated. Such a criticism brings home, once again, the point made in relation to post-industrialism, that while information technologies may alter the way we do certain things, they do not seem to have altered the underlying economic and political principles according to which contemporary societies function. As Kumar notes:

> The imperatives of profit, power and control seem as predominant now as they have ever been in the history of capitalist industrialism. The difference lies in the greater range and intensity of their applications made possible by the communications revolution, not in any change in the principles themselves. (1995: 154)

Despite the apparent shortcomings of the post-industrial thesis and the idea of an information society, these relative weaknesses have not, it should be noted, served to detract from the influence both strands of thought have had on organization theory. While their bold assertions of social and economic revolution may, in hindsight, appear to have been somewhat exaggerated, it cannot be denied that the expansion of information and communication technologies have had a marked impact upon both the working and social lives of the populations of the industrialized societies and beyond and, as such, on the concerns of organization theory.[6] However, whatever the particular strengths and weaknesses of the post-industrial and information society theses, an alternative account of the direction of economic and organizational change emerged during the 1980s that had an even more profound impact upon the study of contemporary work organizations than post-industrialism.

Neo-Fordism, flexible specialization and post-Fordism

During the early 1980s a range of new conceptual terms – *neo-Fordism*, *flexible specialization* and *post-Fordism* – appeared. Such terms were conceived, or so it would seem, as an attempt to describe the idea that, rather than witnessing the end of industrialism, industrialized societies were undergoing a radical shift in the ways in which production and distribution were organized. As the term suggests, *neo-Fordism* (Aglietta, 1979) was constructed on the back of the idea that the organizational features characteristic of Fordism were no longer appropriate in the face of changing socio-economic conditions, associated particularly with two main developments. First, the apparent inability of the working classes in advanced western economies to consume at the rate and in the quantity required failed to ensure the feasibility of Fordist economies of scale, an inability that was largely due to the incapacity of the economy, despite significant state intervention, to redistribute sufficient levels of income away from capital and towards the labour force itself. Secondly, the Fordist labour process was unable to extract levels of surplus value necessary to counteract declining rates of profit. Thus as Brenner and Glick note:

> Fordism, as a paradigm for organizing the labour process, could henceforth deliver only declining productivity growth because, over the long term, management exhausted the gains that could be secured from an intensification of labour through Taylorist time-and-motion studies, job fragmentation, shopfloor reorganization and the introduction of new machinery on the basis of existing technology. (1991: 97)

For Fordism to survive it needed, therefore, to somehow evolve beyond the limitations placed on it by the organizational principles it had inherited from Taylorism. For Aglietta (1979), this was being attempted by the late 1970s through a range of strategies that he regarded as neo-Fordist, which were intended to ensure that Fordism could adapt to changing social and economic circumstances. These included the transference of production to lower-cost parts of the world economy, such as East Asia, while centralizing research and management functions in the advanced industrialized nations. Also significant was the development of more flexible patterns of production and labour organization, which were intended to reduce costs in areas where the manufacturing process could not be exported.

The related concept of *flexible specialization*, originally developed in the work of Piore and Sabel (Piore and Sabel, 1984; Sabel, 1982, 1994), also located the so-called crisis of Fordism in the inability of a system based on 'mass' production to meet the demands of an increasingly differentiated global marketplace. While Japan, as a case in point, was obtaining an internationally competitive edge through the production of high-quality products and, more importantly, through product diversification, western manufacturers were finding themselves unprepared and ill-equipped to respond to this competitive challenge. The only solution seemed to be for traditional Fordist-based producers to adopt a similar system of 'flexible specialization'. That is, as Piore and Sabel define it,

> . . . a strategy of permanent innovation: accommodation to ceaseless change, rather than effort to control it. This strategy is based on flexible – multi-use – equipment; skilled workers; and the creation, through politics, of an industrial community that restricts the forms of competition to those favouring innovation. (1984: 17)

The introduction of flexible specialization required, however, a full-scale reversal of the rigid structures of the Fordist division of labour. This, in turn, was predicted to result in a reduction in levels of unskilled labour and also in the use of fixed function machinery. At the heart of Piore and Sabel's analysis was the proposition that by adopting such flexible practices, the Fordist tendency to reduce the employee to little more than an appendage of the machine could be reversed, resulting in a 'revival of craft forms' of labour (Piore and Sabel, 1984: 17). They argued that this would, in turn, enable employees to realize their potential for human creativity and imagination. While Sabel (1982) had originally argued that such changes were most appropriately realized through small 'high technology' industries such as those which co-operate through a network system, his more recent work has posited the idea that the same process was not only appropriate to, but was starting to take hold of, more traditional western mass production industries. As such Sabel has argued that, throughout the 1980s, a process of convergence was starting to occur between highly modernist mass production-based organizations and more traditional, retro forms of craft-based production (Sabel, 1994).

In a similar vein, Kern and Schumann (1987, 1989) identified a pattern of development comparable to that suggested by Piore and Sabel, namely the emergence of a multi-skilled workforce and the utilization of more highly specialized production techniques. However, rather than viewing this as a process of pre-industrial craft revival, they saw it largely in terms of a gradual incorporation of manual labour into a new technical profession and the expansion of theoretical knowledge as the primary qualification among the workforce. Thus, forms of labour that were previously marginalized under the Fordist system were now becoming integrated into the industrial labour process, a process which required '. . . a man who is manually gifted and theoretically talented' (Schumann, 1987: 47).

By the late 1980s, however, the ideas of neo-Fordism and flexible specialization had largely been subsumed under the more general concept of post-Fordism, popularized largely through the work of a group of social theorists, economists and political analysts grouped around the analytical journal of the Communist Party of Great Britain, *Marxism Today*. Yet while neo-Fordism had referred to a process of modification of Fordist practices, post-Fordism was used to describe what was seen as an attempt to transcend Fordist modes of economic and social organization, ranging from the management of the labour process, drawing, most notably on Japanese-inspired models of industrial management (Kenney and Florida, 1989; Pascale and Athos, 1981), to relations of consumption and even individual lifestyle (Murray, 1989a, 1989b). Under the banner of 'New Times' (Hall and Jacques, 1989), post-Fordism was presented as a direct confrontation with the principles and practices associated with Fordism. For example, in the UK, the retail industry was identified as one arena within which such flexible, post-Fordist organizational practices were becoming increasingly significant. With an increase in the use of computing systems, for example, producers and retailers were able to carefully match stock to consumer demand and therefore to overcome, at the point of purchase at least, the problem of Fordist overproduction. This also enabled retailers to identify and service what are termed 'niche markets'. By utilizing computerized information technology, in conjunction with increasingly sophisticated market-research strategies, retailers were able to analyse consumption patterns in depth. This enabled them to meet increasingly differentiated markets with differentiated products.

Such niche marketing could only operate effectively, however, if the manufacturing process also fostered the same degree of flexibility. The Japanese car manufacturing giant, Toyota, was particularly singled out as a pioneer in this respect, much as Ford was eighty years before, with two key components of the Toyota post-Fordist strategy being given special attention. These were the introduction of the 'just-in-time' (Hutchins, 1988) system of component supply, and what the exponents of this strategy saw as innovative methods of flexible labour control and organization. The former, aiming to eliminate wasted time and output, abandons the traditional practice of maintaining large in-house stocks of component parts in favour of a system whereby, through the utilization of computer stock control mechanisms and ordering systems, components are ordered from suppliers on the basis of daily production plans. The latter, which Murray (1989a, 1989b) feels to be the most significant transformation underpinning post-Fordism, revolves around the introduction of an increasingly skilled, highly motivated and above all flexible core workforce.

Indeed, various forms of flexibility have come to be regarded as fundamental to post-Fordist organizations. Atkinson (1985) concluded from his UK-based studies of work organizations that four such forms of flexibility can be identified in contemporary organizations. *Numerical flexibility* refers to an organization's ability to meet fluctuating levels of demand through the deployment of casualized or sub-contracted workers who supplement, in times of increased demand, a core of relatively well paid and contractually secure employees. *Functional flexibility* means that the largely core workforce comprises a relatively highly trained, multi-skilled set of employees who are able to perform a number of tasks and roles within the organization regardless of its formal designation. What Atkinson termed '*distancing*' involves the transfer of the responsibility for employment relations into the external market, again through the widespread use of sub-contracting and so on. *Financial flexibility*, as the name suggests, revolves around the use of differing rates of financial reward for skills learnt, tasks performed and so on.

For Atkinson, post-Fordist organizations combine these various modes of flexibility, creating an employment structure based on a core and periphery labour force (Atkinson, 1985: 19). The core workforce, with its qualitatively high levels of skill and expertise, is considered to produce higher-quality products than was possible under Fordist regimes but, more importantly, to provide 'a continuous quality feedback loop'. Continuous training, the establishment of quality circles and the concept of the semi-autonomous team structure have all been implemented in an attempt to harness this vital resource. Of equal significance, in this respect, has been the emergence of new regimes of industrial relations that have aimed to maximize employee commitment and co-operation through 'job for life' security, company pension plans, private health care schemes, single union deals and no-strike agreements. Of course, the existence of such a core is entirely dependent on the existence of the periphery workforce who, employed mainly upon part-time, temporary contacts, can be shed easily and cheaply in times of economic downturn or market contraction.

This emphasis on acquiring employee commitment has also had a significant impact, or so it has been suggested, on how organizational structures of authority and control should be approached to ensure maximum levels of output and efficiency. More often than not, this view has been grounded in the literature that has invoked western managers to adopt the style associated with Japanese management (Ouchi, 1981; Pascale and Athos, 1981).[7] However, considering the problems sometimes associated with the cross-cultural transference of such ideas, others, such as Mulgan (1989) for example, have argued for the need to radically reconceptualize how power within organizations operates. Describing what he terms strong and weak power controls, with the former requiring large amounts of energy relative to the processes which they control, and the latter using proportionately less, Mulgan (1989: 347) argues that post-Fordism is characterized by the ascendancy of the latter over the former. This shift is not only marked by the type of production technology which post-Fordism tends to employ, however, but by the social organization of the workforce. While, for Mulgan, Fordism relied upon strong power controls, with rigidly enforced hierarchies of authority performing tightly defined functions and responsibilities, post-Fordism aims to engender flexibility and innovation through the decentralization of power. This means that there appears to be no 'single point of leadership'; horizontal rather than vertical accountability prevails, as does a thriving of 'fluidity, change and the creative use of chaos' (Mulgan, 1989: 348).

CRITICUS of P.F.

However, many commentators have been less than convinced by the claims of those who champion the emergence of flexible post-Fordist modes of organization (Pollert, 1988a, 1988b; Rustin, 1989; Whitaker, 1992). There remains widespread scepticism as to whether Fordism ever truly dominated organizational production to the extent that the proponents of post-Fordism seem to claim. As Kumar (1995) puts it, the charge in this respect is one of mythologization, of an indiscriminate conflation of Taylorism and Fordism. Also subject to some very forceful criticism has been the claim that flexible post-Fordist approaches are emerging as the dominant mode of organization in contemporary western societies (Clarke, 1990; P. Thompson, 1989, 1993; Williams et al., 1992), and as such that we are witnessing the death of mass production and mass consumption, claims which, it has been argued, simply do not match up to the empirical realities.

Even where modes of workplace organization can be seen to reflect some of the principles and practices that have been associated with the idea of post-Fordism, it has been argued (Clarke, 1990; Tomaney 1990, 1994) that they should be seen, at best, as an attempt to combine so-called flexible working practices imported from Japanese organizational models with an intensification of the principles of Taylorism. Thus the rhetoric of emancipation (see Kenney and Florida, 1989) that has often accompanied attempts to incorporate into work organizations the various modes of flexibility outlined above is rejected as little more than an ideological smokescreen, designed and implemented to obscure attempts to increase levels of labour rationalization. It has also been argued that accounts of post-Fordism tend to gloss over the continued existence of primitive Fordist practices in third-world economies, which not only co-exist with western developments but, in an increasingly globalized economy, make such developments possible. Furthermore, the celebration of the emergence of a core workforce, which enjoys relatively high levels of job security, training and remuneration, has also tended to overlook the extent to which this has depended, at least in part, on a growing periphery of casual and part-time employees who enjoy few of the benefits that are afforded to their core sector counterparts (Harvey, 1989).

Despite such criticisms, however, post-Fordism has continued to provide a paradigmatic framework within which a number of related organizational developments have been addressed. Bob Jessop (1994), for example, has explored the changing configuration of the nation state as a response, in part, to the growth of post-Fordist modes of economic regulation, arguing that what we are currently witnessing is a shift from a welfare state model underpinned by Keynesian macro-economic management to what he terms a 'workfare state'. The latter, he argues, is more concerned with promoting supply-side values such as labour market flexibility and economic competitiveness than the Fordist priorities of demand management and welfare provision. Indeed, even those who have previously criticized the post-Fordist thesis, such as Rustin (1994), have acknowledged the usefulness of the concept in developing a critical account of changes in the organization of public services; in higher education, for example, in which the need to respond to the imposition of market forces has necessitated an embracing of more flexible modes of provision. Furthermore, despite an apparent decline throughout the 1990s in the popularity of post-Fordism as a descriptive or explanatory concept, many of the issues that it has raised remain central to contemporary organization theory. Flexibility, de-differentiation, the role of new technologies and the significance of knowledge work have all continued to influence ongoing debates on issues such as Japanization (Elger and Smith, 1994), Total Quality Management (Knights and McCabe, 1994; Wilkinson and Willmott, 1995) and Business Process Reengineering (Hammer and Champy, 1993; Peppard and Rowland, 1995), where discussion has tended to focus on the introduction of managerial strategies designed to mediate between increased demands for organizational flexibility and product quality, and the requirements for a highly trained and personally motivated core workforce. This latter point is something we look at below, especially in the context of a possible emergence of a 'post-bureaucratic' approach to managing work organizations.

Post-bureaucratic management

As we noted above, an important dimension of the post-Fordist model is the necessary presence, within core sectors at least, of a highly motivated and flexible workforce; motivated such that quality control can be largely delegated to the level of the employee, and flexible in that they are both able and prepared to take on roles and tasks that may fall outside of traditional demarcations and trade expertise. This, in turn, has led to a reappraisal in some quarters of the role that management plays within organizational life, and the appropriateness of established management theory and practice in the face of such developments. Much of the material concerned with such issues resonates with many of the themes already touched on here, for example the dismantling of overly bureaucratic modes of control, a commitment to quality at all levels of the production and distribution process, and a greater attention to the cultural climate of, or within, the organization. As such, there can be no doubt that many of the principles associated with the idea of a *post-bureaucratic* (Heckscher, 1994) mode of organizational management have had a significant impact of the changing face of both organization theory and, though perhaps less so, organizational life itself. Often presented in the guise of totalizing solutions to the competitive ills of contemporary work organizations such as Human Resource Management (HRM), Total Quality Management (TQM), and the exhortations to 'excellence' of the gurus of management thinking, such approaches combine, their proponents claim, accurate diagnoses of the current economic and organizational climate with fresh and innovative solutions to the problems these conditions raise.

Often at the heart (*sic*) of such material has been a call for managers to seek to combine the subjective, and indeed emotional, aspirations of their employees with the strategic goals of the organization, through ensuring that work itself is experienced as a meaningful and personally rewarding activity. As such, this approach can be seen to dispense, at least in part, with the Tayloristic assumption that what makes people work harder is the promise of greater financial remuneration, and extend the professedly humanistic imperatives of the Human Relations Movement. This is a theme particularly evident in writing that has focused on the need for those who are in a position to direct strategies of organizational change to foster strong organizational cultures. According to Peters and Waterman (1982), for example, it is no longer sufficient for managers to seek to secure instrumental compliance from their employees. Rather, they must aim at achieving *cultures of excellence*, cultures in which each and every member of the organization would feel both respected as an individual, and yet personally fulfilled only as part of a team. Thus, a sense of autonomy has to be combined with a team spirit based on shared goals and a commitment to organizational success. To achieve such a level of cultural homogeneity managers would have to learn to move beyond their traditional and rationalistic concerns with the manipulation of objective factors such as production targets, staff turnover levels and input/output ratios and start to take seriously the realm of the subjective experience of work organizations. Words such as community, family and even intimacy have moved from the periphery to the centre of managerial discourse, challenging the over-rationalized model of organizational life as comprising impersonal, objectively defined relations of authority and responsibility. Technologies such as mission statements, corporate images and even organizational practices, such as the formation of quality circles designed to propagate these 'new' values, are all seen to contribute to this new-found sensibility. For the purveyors of 'excellence', then, it is no longer enough for employees simply to commit themselves to the organization; they now have to fall in love with it (Harris, 1996).

While much of what can be taken to represent this turn towards the valorization of the subjective, or indeed affectual, dimension of organizational life still appears to be situated within the pages of prescriptive 'how to' textbooks and pop-management best-sellers, there is increasing evidence to suggest that the rhetoric, if not the practice, of such ideas is increasingly penetrating the everyday pronouncements of managers themselves. For example, Martin Wibberley (1993), a former HRM director at Bosch Cardiff, has written in glowing terms about the benefits of developing a strong statement of corporate values in his attempt to foster a culture unique to that plant, a culture that he saw as a synthesis of German, Welsh and Japanese influences, and which fostered a climate in which 'workers and managers clock in and out together, sport the same overalls, share all facilities' and are described as 'team members' (Wibberley, 1993: 33). At the forefront of this has been the development of organizational strategies for promoting the personnel function as an integral dimension of the overall business strategy particularly in the form of HRM (Boxall, 1994; Foulkes, 1986; Torrington and Hall, 1987). HRM, whatever the reality behind the rhetoric (see Legge, 1995), can be seen as exemplifying the principles of post-bureaucratic management, combining as it does a concern with the 'soft' nurturing of committed, compliant yet self-motivated employees with a 'hard' strategic vision of employees as integral to the overall success of the organization; an ideal exemplified in the following comments on the role of HRM within the UK-based Littlewoods Group:

> the human resource department is a catalyst for achieving enhanced customer relationships and helping employees to make a stronger contribution. In return, HR[M] assists individuals to find a new sense of purpose, structure and enthusiasm in their careers. (Nightingale Multimedia, 1999: 165)

How far one takes such exhortations to be genuinely representative either of changing practices by organizational managers, or an achieved level of greater compliance among employees is questionable, however. Managers, while themselves often supportive of many of the 'core elements' associated with HRM (Poole and Mansfield, 1992), tend to be less willing to describe these in their own terms (see Watson, 1995a). Perhaps more importantly, though, as Warhurst and Thompson observe, whatever the ambitions of such managers

> [i]t is too easy in this area to confuse managerial ambition with outcome. But even where it gets beyond the mission statement, or other change texts, engaging with employees' feelings and values is likely to be the most fragile of all managerial activities. (1998: 11)

Thus, Warhurst and Thompson raise the question of whether, however extensively implemented, the practices associated with post-bureaucratic approaches such as HRM are as able successfully to change employees' subjectively-held values and belief systems as some of their proponents may claim. Indeed, even where compliance can be observed, to what extent does it suggest little more than either a surface act, or indeed the outcome of other more instrumentally-driven motivations? The importance of this question is illustrated, for example, in Bell's (1999) ethnographic study of 'blue collar workers' that has suggested that, in the face of a preoccupation among HRM practitioners with strategies designed to promote greater levels of co-operative endeavour, the financial bottom line continued to be seen as a significant source of individual motivation.

Despite such, albeit salient, criticisms, what is of significance to us here are the ways in which the appearance of such ideas have informed, in their own way, current literature on the emergence of new organizational forms and the possible postmodernization of organizational life. While we shall go on to consider this theme in greater depth in the second part of this book, it is worth noting here two interpretations of such developments. First, there is the proposition that the language and practices of contemporary organizations, associated here with a post-bureaucratic mode of management, represent a genuine reaffirmation of the affective dimensions of organizational life. In seeking to move beyond the rational actor model of the modern subject, they both recognize and, in many ways, discursively constitute an alternative rationality at work within the organizational domain, a rationality that recognizes the contingent and multi-faceted nature of the human condition, freeing it from the constraints of formal (modernist) rationality. As Reed notes in this respect, 'postmodern organizations are seen to rely on much more "emotional" cultures in the sense that they facilitate the personal development of individuals within collectivities based on trust, and the relatively high level of risk taking which this involves' (1992: 229).

Secondly, such approaches, particularly those that focus on a conception of the organization as essentially a cultural phenomenon, reflect the cultural turn within postmodernism more generally. That is, they recognize the essentially symbolic nature of a reality that has been, as Baudrillard might have it, separated from its material roots, and transformed into a 'postmodern' constellation of free-floating signifiers. As such, as Keenoy and Anthony note with particular reference to HRM, they can be seen as albeit purposeful attempts to 'redefine both the meaning of work and the way individual employees relate to their employers' (1992: 234).

Organizational postmodernization

In this section, we turn to consider those writers who have attempted directly to relate the kinds of developments discussed above to the possible emergence of a distinctively postmodernized organizational form. As Dent (1995: 886) has observed, however, relatively few have attempted this particular task. Rather, what has generally been the case is that in many of the accounts of organizational change, such as those considered throughout this chapter, the terms post-Fordist or post-bureaucratic have been preferred.[8] However, what little material exists is notable in the way it draws on themes from a range of literatures in an attempt to identify important commonalities that it suggests could represent what Crook, Pakulski and Waters have referred to as an 'emerging postmodern configuration of production' (1992: 192), one that eschews the formalistic imperatives of modernist organizations in favour of increasingly informal, flexible and culturally-driven means of organizing work.

New organizational forms

One of the earliest attempts at synthesizing many of the ideas we have encountered thus far into an albeit tentative postmodern model of organization was that of Heydebrand (1989). Largely basing his analysis on the available post-industrial and Japanization-orientated literature (Ouchi,

1981; Toffler, 1970; Williamson, 1975), Heydebrand claimed that what he termed *new organizational forms* were starting to emerge throughout the industrialized world. Using terms such as post-industrial, post-bureaucratic and postmodern somewhat interchangeably, he set out to establish a theoretical framework for organizational analysis based on the conceptual category of 'labour' and a series of related variables (Heydebrand, 1989: 325). These variables range from the size of the labour force to the regime of ownership and control, and are what Heydebrand believed would define an ideal-type postmodern organization:

> . . . it would have to be small or be located in small sub-units of larger organizations; its object is typically service or information, if not automated production; its technology is computerized; its division of labor is informal and flexible and its managerial structure is functionally decentralized, eclectic, and participative, overlapping in many ways with non-managerial functions. In short, post-industrial organizations or those emerging from the transition tend to have a post-bureaucratic control structure even though pre-bureaucratic elements such as clanlike personalism, informalism and corporate culture may be used to integrate an otherwise loosely coupled, centrifugal system. (1989: 327)

In Heydebrand's work, then, we find a range of themes that we have encountered previously, brought together under the rubric of postmodernization. The emergence of a postmodern organizational form is particularly evident, for Heydebrand, in what he terms the emergence of a new 'mode of administration' (Heydebrand, 1989: 339). Drawing here on Weber's (1964) distinction between traditional, charismatic and legal–rational modes of authority, he argues that the latter – which Weber had associated with bureaucratic organization throughout the modern period – is undergoing a rapid decline. For Heydebrand, however, this process has been accompanied by the rise of a new mode of administration, one which is based on the technological incorporation of formal rationality into the emerging computer systems that are increasingly central to the control and co-ordination of contemporary work organizations. Thus, arguing that the principles of formal rationality are firmly embedded in the information technologies upon which contemporary organizations are so dependent, Heydebrand identifies the emergence of a more substantive, and therefore less instrumental, rationality. He terms this apparent fusion of substantive and formal rationality 'technocratic rationality' (Heydebrand, 1989: 344) which, he argues, has provided far greater opportunity for the incorporation of increased levels of individual autonomy and less directive managerial practices than was the case in modern organizations. Despite the somewhat optimistic tone of his analysis, however, Heydebrand remains sceptical as to whether such an emerging form of rationality can be emancipatory in any meaningful sense. Indeed, he hints clearly at the idea that the operation of certain 'cultural technologies', as well as electronic ones, are themselves primarily instrumental, despite any protestations made to the contrary:

In its social dimension, therefore technocracy is clearly a form of social engineering that structures work situations by means of intensive training, planning, continuous learning, and the use of various human resource management techniques. (Heydebrand, 1989: 344)

Thus, while Heydebrand acknowledges the emergence of post-bureaucratic organizational forms that he broadly identifies as *postmodern*, he clearly remains wary of any suggestion that they are in any way transcendent of the basic modernist drive towards formal rationality. Rather, his analysis emphasizes that in contemporary organizations, this drive has been incorporated into the very basic structures of the organization, facilitated by the expansion of new information technologies.

While similar views have been expressed by the likes of Cooke (1990), it was not until the publication of Clegg's, *Modern Organizations: Organization Studies in the Postmodern World* (1990) that the idea of a particularly postmodern form of organization was developed in any depth. Reacting to the idea that postmodernity was characterized, as has been suggested by Bauman (1989), by a shift from the primacy of production to consumption, Clegg (1990: 17) set out to demonstrate that it is still the case that, in his own words, 'postmodernity requires management . . . organization does not simply fade away' and that, as such, the organization of production should remain a site of continued analysis. Citing empirical examples of alternative organizational forms, most notably those of French-bread making, elements of the Italian fashion industry and East Asian enterprises as alternatives to the typically bureaucratic form of organization, Clegg offers his own template, centred on Lash's (1988) focus on de-differentiation (outlined in Chapter 1), of the postmodernized organization:

> Where modernist organization was rigid, postmodern organization is flexible. Where modernist consumption was premised on mass forms, postmodernist consumption is premised upon niches. Where modernist organization was premised upon technological determinism, postmodernist organization is premised on technological choices made possible through 'de-dedicated' microelectronic equipment. Where modernist organization and jobs are highly differentiated, demarcated and deskilled, postmodernist organization and jobs are highly de-differentiated, de-demarcated and multi-skilled. (Clegg, 1990: 181)

While this description remains very close to that of Heydebrand, Clegg's analysis rejects any notion of technological or institutional determinism, arguing that the direction taken by new forms of organization will be as much the outcome of local 'struggles for meaning and power' (Clegg, 1990: 235) as of global cultural and technological developments. Organizations, Clegg argues, are therefore in a period of transition, with old structures of control and co-ordination breaking down while being replaced by new, more flexible, more diverse and more technologically-led alternatives. Furthermore, he also argues that organizations remain dependent upon local contingent circumstances and the requirements of local markets.

It should be noted, however, that like Heydebrand, Clegg does not endorse a postmodern model of organization uncritically. He is acutely aware of the implications of an increasing divide emerging between a relatively well paid, secure core workforce and a marginalized periphery, particularly in terms of the expansion of social inequalities and relations of exploitation, concluding as he does that 'postmodern organisation may well function more to define, confine and confirm social limits cemented within the modernist project than to transcend them' (Clegg, 1992: 28).

Another perspective that, while echoing Clegg's localized approach to the identification of postmodern organizations, is critical of any attempt to define the features of a postmodern work organization in the way that Clegg does, is that proffered by Crook, Pakulski and Waters (1992). While attentive to issues of flexibility, post-bureaucracy and the like, their analysis is based on the view that any such attempt to define the postmodern organization simply in terms of a new set of organizational imperatives fails to grasp the nature of postmodernization as a process of de-differentiation which manifests itself across the entire organizational spectrum. Consequently, such attempts, they argue, overlook the very fragmentation that is at the heart of the postmodernization process. As they put it,

> the emerging pattern is an absence of pattern, a chaotic mixture of forms of ownership, varieties of task organization, forms of relationship between owners and workers, and worker responses. In general terms then, economic life is experiencing structurally similar processes of change to those found in other arenas: . . . it depends for its character far more on cultural flows of knowledge and information about preferred modes of organization than on technology itself. (Crook et al., 1992: 192)

From this perspective, then, any attempt to develop a definitive model of the postmodern organization, be it affirmative or critical, serves merely to impose a pre-conceptualized notion of what a postmodern organization should look like on to actual organizational practices.

Despite this observation, however, Dent (1995) has described what he observed in his study of aspects of the re-organization of the National Health Service (NHS) in the UK, namely a combination of functional de-differentiation and a cultural aestheticization of the organization, as a postmodernization of the organizational form. He cites, for example, the efforts of one hospital general manager to introduce what he termed 'soft' organizational communication (Dent, 1995: 889) in an attempt to foster a participative organizational culture that would encourage teamwork and participation across all levels of employment. Dent (1995: 889) then goes on to develop an analogy between this anti-hierarchical approach and postmodern architecture in that it rejects 'sky-scrapers and tower blocks in favour of more small local communities'. This approach was not, however, simply reduced to pronouncements or procedures in Dent's account. For example, the same general manager was concerned with the spatial arrangements of the hospital, ensuring that all consultants were relocated in offices adjacent to himself, thus propagating an informal culture of communication and, he hoped, of trust relations.

Nevertheless, it would be amiss not to acknowledge that what also clearly emerges from this study is that, while it would not be inappropriate to identify such developments as postmodern within the kind of frame of reference developed by Heydebrand and Clegg, as Dent himself notes, this does not *ipso facto* indicate a break with the performative rationality of modernity. For example, he indicates (Dent, 1995: 895) in his conclusion how the general manager's approach to the idea of culture was to use it 'politically' in an attempt to integrate a range of divergent interests and value systems in the face of emerging pressures for greater levels of responsiveness and efficiency. Certainly, whatever else, the autonomy and flexibility bequeathed to the employees of the hospital in question was clearly the outcome, and under the control, of the manager in question.

Critical interventions into 'postmodernization'

Many of the criticisms that have been directed towards the postmodernization thesis within organization theory are essentially the same as those directed at writing on flexible specialization and post-Fordism that we have already encountered. For example, the likes of Reed (1992), Parker (1993) and Thompson (1993) all point to what they consider to be the somewhat unconvincing standard of empirical evidence deployed to support what is, after all, a thesis about empirical change. Parker is particularly unimpressed by what he considers to be little more than 'a new phrase to capture the imagination of the jaded reader [a phrase which] appears to have little empirical foundation and provides no convincing reasons' (1993: 206). Alvesson (1995) also makes the point that there is an apparent lack of conceptual clarity in attempts to define and identify the contours of a post-modernized organization. For Alvesson, it is only the term 'postmodern' itself that lends validity to the idea of a process of organizational post-modernization. That is, the term is invoked to provide a unity between different concepts and practices (be they post-industrial or post-Fordist) which does not exist outside of the academic discourse. Hence, postmodernism, as a descriptive device at least, creates its own object of analysis regardless of its empirical validity. Postmodernism thus becomes a conceptual catch-all which, as Thompson (1993) notes, is based on the principle that if some of an organization's features do not conform with the differentiated, bureaucratized model employed to characterize modernity, it is called 'postmodern'.

However, while such observations may indeed reflect a certain tendency, by academics in particular, to try constantly to identify phenomena which are not only new but potentially indicative of a major historical shift, they may also be guilty of ignoring important and significant changes in both the organizational sphere, and in the broader social domain. As Kumar (1995) has pointed out, how many observers of the new textile factories in the north of England during the nineteenth century believed they heralded an industrial revolution that would eventually alter the face of the entire world? Thus, while the developments outlined here may not, as of yet, confirm an epochal shift from modernity to postmodernity, they may suggest the first stage in an historically significant transformative process. There may be good grounds, then, on which to avoid simply dismissing them as empirically unrepresentative and, rather, to continue to monitor them carefully and to subject them to the levels of critical scrutiny that are currently applied to more traditional modes of organizational practice.

Indeed, the importance of this is illustrated particularly in the observation by Warhurst and Thompson (1998) that even where it can be seen that possibly novel modes of organization may be emerging, say for example in the introduction of training designed to engender greater functional flexibility among employees, more often than not they appear merely to signify a surface change, leaving the underlying rationality of the organization intact. This is clearly an observation that sits uncomfortably with the idea that the kinds of practices and principles we have discussed constitute, as Tixier has argued, 'an objective rationality adapted to the values of creativity, self-expression and participation' (cited in Reed, 1992: 229). For, if we are to take seriously the claims of the champions of postmodernism that by adopting their particular worldview we can create a less hierarchical, pluralistic and potentially free society, then what can we learn from critically scrutinizing those organizational practices that, it has been claimed, bear some of the hallmarks of a process of postmodernization?

Do modes of organizing based on the values of flexibility, multi-skilling, employee-friendly cultures and the like, represent anything other than redefined instrumental technologies designed to extract greater levels of labour from employees than the modern or Fordist practices they are supposed to have supplanted.[9] While apparently premised upon new concerns with issues of empowerment, involvement and the deconstruction of rigid attitudes towards methods of production and organizational hierarchy, is the criticism that, on closer inspection, they represent merely attempts to colonize employee subjectivity and other 'previously unrationalized aspects of the work organization', a convincing one (Willmott, 1995a: 46)? These are questions which, while eliciting no simple answers, in part drive this book, and to which we frequently return. For the time being, though, let us briefly summarize the material so far.

Conclusion

Throughout this chapter, we have considered the idea that contemporary work organizations appear to have been subject to changes that might be equated with a process of postmodernization. Such changes include a range of organizational practices centred upon flexibility, de-differentiation, the breakdown of organizational hierarchies and the adoption of quality procedures based upon greater levels of employee commitment and involvement. We have explored the various elements of the post-industrial and information society theses and have then moved our attention to the neo-Fordist, flexible specialization and post-Fordist models of industrial change, which have been devised to explain such changes.

We have considered the proposition, as expressed by the likes of Heydebrand and Clegg, that such challenges to the principles of Weberian bureaucracy and Fordist modes of organizing indicate the emergence of a postmodern form of organization. According to this proposition, the developments outlined above are taken to be indicative of the existence of so-called new organizational forms, particularly when combined with other factors such as increased managerial concern with those aspects of organizational life which had previously been deemed impervious or simply irrelevant to processes of rational intervention. Such organizational forms are thus understood to have evolved beyond the principles and practices of modernity, yet are also understood to remain empirically observable and conceptually definable.

As we have also noted, though, the idea that any such shift or change in the dominant mode of workplace organization is occurring, has also been the focus of critical attention. First, it is argued that there is, as yet, insufficient empirical evidence to suggest that such movement is occurring, if at all, to a sufficiently widespread extent to indicate a significant process of postmodernization. Secondly, it is also argued that even if such changes are discernible, for example in the case of increased instances of flexible working practices, they represent merely a continuation, or even intensification, of the principles that underpin modern industrialism. As such, while we can label them 'post-Fordist' or even 'postmodernist', this represents merely a semantic technique, an attempt by academics to conjure up new domains of inquiry which appear novel and worthy of renewed attention.

However, we would suggest that this labelling of contemporary organizational forms is more than simply a problem of semantics. It is also a problem of epistemology and ethics. The former refers to how we can identify what is and what is not modern or postmodern. To what extent do particular organizational forms become postmodern simply because we choose to label them as such? The latter raises questions that revolve, for instance, around the extent to which postmodern organizations should be, in some way, less repressive than modernist ones. Having rejected the instrumental rationality of systemic modernism, any organization based on postmodern principles should, in theory at least, offer an environment far more conducive to human development, experimentation and overall freedom than its modernist predecessor. Such a normative position is, of course, quite in line with the ideas of, say, Lyotard or Derrida, who would view the systemic principles underlying modern organizations as something that must be challenged and overturned. If one can still identify practices which are clearly *not* geared towards this eventual end, then either this signifies that they are not truly indicative of a postmodern organization, or that the postmodernist claim to be emancipatory is simply a sham.

However, while we are not ready, at this stage of events anyway, to evaluate such claims too closely, they do provide, at least in part, the impetus for the next stage of our account, in which we explore the challenges that postmodernism has presented to organization theory as a discipline and to the meta-theoretical principles by which it is underpinned. In the following chapter, then, we move away from the idea of a postmodern organization towards that of a postmodern organization theory, in an attempt to continue to chart the impact of postmodernism on the study of work organizations.

Notes

1   See also Parker's (1992) attempt to effect such a distinction through the insertion of a hyphen between the words 'post' and 'modern' (post-modern) to denote a sociological concern with the study of potentially postmodernized organizational forms.
2   Although this distinction was originally described more generally by Featherstone (1988).
3   However, see Chapter 4's discussion of Taska's (1992) view that central to Taylor's motivational strategy was a clear understanding of the significance of the cultural context within which organized labour takes place.
4   A term popularized most notably by Lash and Urry (1987).
5   See Chapter 3 for a discussion of panopticism and surveillance, especially in relation to the work of Michel Foucault.
6   The most notable of these, of course, being the shift in the pattern of industrial employment from manufacturing industries towards the service sector over the last decade (Central Statistical Office, 1998: 22).
7   See Chapter 4 for a more extensive discussion of this material.
8   See, for example, the review of some of this literature in Reed (1992).
9   A recent version of the view that many new organizational technologies represent a clear intensification of the principles of modern instrumental rationality is that of George Ritzer (1993, 1997, 1999) and his 'McDonaldization' thesis.

3

Postmodern Organization Theory

[Postmodern thinking] . . . privileges an ontology of movement, emergence and *becoming* in which the transient and ephemeral nature of what is real is accentuated. (Chia, 1995: 581)

[Postmodernism is] a dangerous, and politically disabling set of ideas for critical organization theorists to adopt. (Parker, 1995: 553)

The latter quarter of the twentieth century witnessed a growing confidence among analysts of organizational life to consider and experiment with a range of what are, within the discipline at least, novel and innovative ways of conceptualizing and studying work organizations. Underpinning this development was a noticeable rejection of what were previously held, and indeed for some, sacrosanct assumptions about the nature of reality and those modes of knowledge production that had previously seemed appropriate to identifying its substance and contours. While it would be too strong a claim to assert that such developments owe their relative popularization purely to the impact of postmodernism, there can be no doubt that postmodern ideas have opened up the conceptual space for new ways of seeing and understanding the organization of work.

Postmodernism has helped to move the study of organizations beyond rigid ontological demarcations between the object and subject of research, and has provoked the investigation of aspects of organizational life previously deemed, at best, peripheral and, at worst, wholly inappropriate for serious social scientific consideration. In doing so, it has opened up a series of debates that continue to be fiercely contested. Issues such as asymmetrical power relations, employee subjectivity, reflexivity and even the ontological status of organizations themselves have all been moved further to the forefront of the research agenda in ways that are, if not always concurrent with the principles of a postmodern approach, certainly informed by the questions that such an approach raises. Shifting our attention away

from the various changes broadly termed organizational postmodernization, in this chapter, then, we consider the ways in which organization
theory has sought to engage with, and indeed appropriate, a number of the
meta-theoretical concerns of postmodernism that we encountered in the
opening chapter. Of course, knowing what we do of postmodernism in all
its various manifestations, it would clearly be inappropriate to suggest
that there is anything like a unified postmodern theory of organizations or
organizing. Nevertheless in the social sciences generally, the rise of postmodernism has resulted in the emergence of a number of closely
interrelated concerns and approaches that we have termed postmodern
meta-theory, the appearance of which is certainly no less evident within
organization theory. Here, as we suggested above, the rejection of representation, the need for reflexivity, and a concern with the relationship
between power, language and the constitution of subjectivity, are all recurring themes.

   We begin this chapter with a brief historical review of a series of developments within organization theory that, we would suggest, paved the
way for the reception of postmodern ideas from the late 1980s onwards. Of
particular note, in this respect, have been attempts, in the face of mainstream positivistic modes of organizational analysis, to bring the sphere of
human subjectivity into the organizational equation. We then chart the
emergence of self-consciously postmodernist approaches to organization
theory, arguing that, while ultimately pursuing different agendas, such
contributions expound similar perspectives on the nature and utility of
postmodern theorizing for the study of organizational life. A number of
general contributions to, and indeed criticisms of, the postmodern turn in
organization theory are then reviewed before a more in-depth critical consideration is given to what we consider to be two of the most influential
aspects of postmodern thought in the field. These are, first, the ongoing
engagement within the discipline with the ideas of Michel Foucault and,
secondly, the conception of critical organization theory as a mode of deconstructive practice inspired largely by the work of Jacques Derrida. The
chapter concludes with a brief overview and raises a number of questions
that we seek to address in the chapters that follow.

The backlash against positivism

While an enthusiasm within certain quarters of organization theory for a
range of ideas associated with postmodern meta-theory is a relatively
recent phenomenon, there exists a clear lineage of intellectual development within the field that undoubtedly provided, if not the foundations for
an acceptance of postmodernism, then certainly grounds for its relatively
sympathetic reception. This can be understood largely in terms of an
increasing discomfort, throughout the 1970s, with the positivist and functionalist assumptions that underpinned the majority of organizational

research and analysis at this time, and followed the revival within the social sciences more generally (Garfinkel, 1967; Goffman, 1959; Schutz, 1967) of an interpretive approach to social research.

An interpretive account of organizations

Reiterating the point we made in the previous chapter, the origins of organization theory can be traced largely to the appropriation of Weber's (1964 [1925]) writings on bureaucracy, as well as to the more managerialist concerns of the likes of Taylor (1911) and Fayol (1949). While Weber was concerned with the development of an interpretive account of the trajectory of modern society and, as such, his work on bureaucratic organizations needs to be understood within this context, his work also provided a distinctively modernist flavour to the emergence of the discipline. By this we mean that it was broadly grounded in a concern with the application of rationality, reason and science to the pursuit of 'truth', in which science remained a tool of both social investigation and social improvement. This latter aspect of modernism is particularly relevant to the work of Taylor and Fayol, who aims set out to apply the methodological principles of the natural sciences to the functional analysis of work organizations. Largely as a consequence of this (in the case of Taylor in particular, through the popularization of Fordist modes of organization), the direct application of a range of philosophical assumptions and methodological procedures associated with the natural sciences came to dominate organization theory.

Consequently, the philosophical propositions of positivism, combined with the systemic imperatives of functionalist analysis, came to be viewed by mainstream organization theorists as the most appropriate means by which the underlying nature of organizational reality could not only be understood, but also managed and directed. In the main, the findings of mainstream organizational research have been deployed traditionally in the pursuit of improved levels of organizational efficiency and effectiveness. Often this has been directed towards the eradication of what were seen as the informal, and therefore irrational, aspects of organizational behaviour, largely through the imposition of rationally formulated rules and regulations. Such rules and regulations were based, to all intents and purposes, on rigorous observation and a belief in the prescriptive power of the scientific method.

This mainstream approach to organization theory was premised, however, not simply upon a positivist epistemology, but also upon a realist ontology, according to which organizations are conceived as objective entities, akin to natural phenomena that are perceived, from this perspective, as existing 'out there' in the real world. As such, the dominant perception in organization theory throughout its history has tended to be that organizations can be observed, measured and modified as deemed necessary. This realist ontology therefore underpinned the development of organization theory, and what Steffy and Grimes (1986) have referred to as its 'empirical-analytical' research agenda, throughout the best part of the twentieth century, manifesting itself in a range of apparently distinct approaches such as the Human Relations Movement (Mayo, 1933; Roethlisberger and Dickson, 1939) and various forms of systems analysis (Miller and Rice, 1967) and contingency theories (Donaldson, 1976, 1996a, 1996b; Pugh and Hickson, 1976; Woodward, 1970).

The late 1960s and early 1970s, however, witnessed the publication of a range of contributions to the development of a less positivistic and onto-logically realist approach to studying organizations. As the likes of Reed (1993) and Clegg and Hardy (1996) have noted, perhaps the most signifi-cant texts on new ways of thinking about the study of work organizations were those published by Weick (1969) in the USA and Silverman (1970) in the UK. Weick's (1969) social psychological approach, grounded in a form of objective idealism, questioned the realist ontology of organizations, claiming that it was the phenomenological process of organizing, rather than the reified category of organization that should provide the central focus for research into the organizational domain. It was not simply orga-nizational members who gave substance to organizations from this perspective, then, but also those who studied them. For in constituting their objects of study as organizations, describing them, quantifying them, they are, at the same time constituting them as objective entities. Silverman (1970), whose work has in hindsight had perhaps a greater long-term influ-ence in the UK, sought to develop what he termed an *action frame of reference* (AFR) approach to the study of organizations.

Drawing on the methodological insights of Weber's interpretive approach and on sociological phenomenology (Berger and Luckmann, 1967; Schutz, 1967), Silverman's analysis largely eschewed the objectivist assumptions underpinning the dominant orthodoxy. His approach, in a similar vein to Weick's, was premised instead upon the idea that organi-zations must be understood as the outcome of meaningful social action. That is, rather than simply existing as reified, objectified phenomena, dis-tinct from the subjective domain of the individual, organizations themselves need to be understood as the product of the meaningful activ-ity of human agents. This perspective involved, in turn, a rejection of the positivistic emphasis upon quantitative methodology and the assertion of a crude subject/object dualism that appeared so central to the modernist conception of science and knowledge, and relied instead on the deploy-ment of a hermeneutically sensitive interpretive research approach to the investigation of organizational life.

This is an agenda that was further emphasized in 'strategic choice theory' (Child, 1985) and in the ethnomethodological perspective derived from Garfinkel (1967) and adopted by Zimmerman (1971, 1973), as well as in the later work of Silverman himself (Silverman and Jones, 1973, 1976). Such developments all represented attempts to transcend the method-ological limitations of positivism, and to understand the ways in which organizational members ascribe meanings to their everyday activities and to organizational life itself. Thus, the focus of organizational research, it was argued from this perspective, needed to move away from the study of organizations as objectified structures which endure over time, and towards the study of micro-level interactions and the everyday ordering of social relations through the subjective mobilization of differing symbolic and cultural resources.

It has to be noted, however, that despite this apparent attempt to break from a number of the central ontological and epistemological principles of positivism, such approaches continued to place a major emphasis on the agency of the autonomous subject both in terms of its 'object' of investigation and the interpretive function of the researchers themselves, as well as frequently maintaining a functionalist interest in the pursuit of increasingly efficient modes of organizational design and management. As such, this divergence from the underlying principles of the dominant modernist orthodoxy was only partial. Nevertheless, this scepticism towards the idea of the universal applicability of the scientific method combined with a rejection of the idea that organizations exist as objective entities were themes which resonate, as we shall see, with more recent developments.

Critical radicalism

The challenge to the positivist orthodoxy within organization theory that took place during the 1970s did not derive, however, purely from the work of those inspired by the interpretive tradition in the social sciences. The implicit functionalism of mainstream organization theory, concealed by claims to value-neutrality, also became a target for those within the discipline who were concerned not so much with organizational regulation, but rather with the possibility of critique and the promotion of radical change both within organizations and in the wider social environment. Kenneth Benson (1977: 1), for example, writing from an explicitly Marxist position, proposed that the orthodox acceptance of 'rational and functional theories and positivist methodology' had undermined the ability of organization theory to offer a critical account of the ways in which organizations fail to meet the standards of rationality they profess. By way of a remedy to this situation, he proposed that any radically-orientated approach should seek to adopt a more *dialectical* mode of analysis, one that would place at centre stage the concept of social process. Such an approach, he argued, would enable organization theory to take account of the constraining effects which organizations have upon the actions of human agents.

While clearly similar in its ideas to the phenomenologically-inspired social constructivism of say Berger and Luckmann (1967), the radical element, or what Benson described as the 'emancipatory' dimension of this approach, lay in its explicit commitment to disclosing those emergent structural manifestations of agency which serve to limit human creativity and autonomy and, as such, offer alternative paths of action which will free people from 'blockages and limitations occasioned by dominance' (Benson,

1977: 18). As such, Benson wanted to place power and control at the centre of organization theory, issues which, he argued, mainstream approaches to organization theory, underpinned by functionalist imperatives, were either unable or unwilling to engage with.

A major contribution to this radicalization of organization theory also came in the shape of the work of Stewart Clegg and David Dunkerley (Clegg, 1987, 1989; Clegg and Dunkerley, 1980), and also Gibson Burrell (1980), each of whom emphasized the theme of power and its centrality to any radical study of organizations. Power was identified broadly in their work with the exercise of domination through institutional structures and formal procedures, a view that contrasted with the mainstream, managerially-driven approach which saw what the radical critics defined as domination more as 'formal, legitimate, functional *authority*' (Hardy and Clegg, 1996: 626 *original emphasis*). As such, the implications of this critical posture towards organizational power also led to a challenge to positivistic modes of inquiry which took as given the dominant configurations of organizational life. Rather than proceeding from the assumption that organizations exist as pre-given entities comprising a natural order of things, this challenge meant that the very *process* of organization began to be questioned theoretically.

In what was, at the time, perhaps one of the most radical propositions in this respect, Burrell (1980) called for the development of a radical theory of organizations that would reject, once and for all, not only the pretensions to value objectivity of the natural scientific model, but also all forms of empirically-driven methodology. Rather, he argued, if a radical approach to questions of organizational power is to be taken, then researchers must endeavour to remain detached from the logic of positivism and its epistemology of empiricism, replacing it with a more contemplative orientation which would favour the practice of abstract theorization about the reality and process of organization as an important aspect of a repressive capitalist totality.

Another approach that was also critical of the mainstream functionalist neglect of questions of organizational power and control, and which also emerged around the mid-1970s, was that which has since come to be referred to as *Labour Process Theory* (LPT). Originating in Harry Braverman's (1974) re-valorization of Marx's conception of the 'labour process', and his study of the continuing adoption of Tayloristic principles of scientific management within work organizations, LPT has established itself as a significant critical force within the field of organization theory (Brighton Labour Process Group, 1977; Knights and Willmott, 1986, 1990; Littler, 1982; P. Thompson, 1989; Thompson and Warhurst, 1998). Braverman's original thesis was based, in part, on the observation that a central feature of the organization of the capitalist labour process was the de-skilling of the labour force, a process which, in turn, served to compound the power of management, as the agents of capital, over the activities of their employees. It was from this founding principle that a labour process-orientated approach to the study of work and its organization emerged which, initially at least, directed its attention to the investigation of both the implementation of strategies of employee de-skilling, as well as resistant practices developed by employees in the face of such managerial activity. As such, its political objectives, namely the exploration and exposure of the struggle between the forces of capital and labour, clearly eschewed the functionalist intentions of managerially-driven, mainstream organization theory. That said, its focus on the structural dimension of organizational control allied it far more closely with the more traditional epistemological outlook of the empirical social sciences than with, say, Burrell's (1980) notion of 'radical organization theory'.

Indeed, Labour Process Theory did not reject science *per se*, but grounded itself within a Marxist notion of science as a potentially liberatory force in the face of structural ideologies that serve to confound and distort the realities of repressive capitalist economic and social relations. What did unite approaches such as LPT and Burrell's proposal for a radical organization theory, however, was the shared conviction that organization theory must move away from a functionalist interest in the regulation of organizational life, towards a focus on how the structuring of work organizations necessarily involves the operationalization of power relations which subjugate what were deemed to be the 'real' human needs of employees to imperatives of organizational efficiency and the pursuit of profit.

Nevertheless, while such approaches represented a challenge to the positivist principle of value-neutrality and the functionalist imperatives that this neutrality was understood to conceal, both LPT and radical organization theory (Burrell, 1980) remained essentially realist in their ontological positions. This was the case in the sense that both approaches continued to view organizations as relatively stable entities that endure through space and time, located within a totality of capitalist social and economic relations.[1] In this respect, a Marxist-inspired approach to organization theory represented, as with its interpretive counterpart, only a partial break from the dominant meta-theoretical combination of functionalist imperatives (which were rejected outright), positivist epistemological assumptions and a realist ontology (which were adapted in line with a Marxist notion of science).

Paradigm diversity

What was perhaps more significant than the actual content of these approaches, however, was that they demonstrated the degree of theoretical diversity which, by the late 1970s, had started to emerge within organization theory. This was a state of affairs brought into stark relief in 1979 with the publication of Burrell and Morgan's *Sociological Paradigms and Organisational Analysis*. Adapting Thomas Kuhn's (1962) concept of the research paradigm,[2] Burrell and Morgan argued that research into organizational life should be understood in terms of its relationship to one of four 'hermetically-sealed' paradigms of sociological inquiry (Willmott, 1990a). These are *functionalist sociology, interpretive sociology, radical human-ism* and *radical structuralism*.[3] Each paradigm, they argued, represents an approach to the study of organizations premised upon 'mutually exclusive views of the social world' (Burrell and Morgan, 1979: x). While a central intention of the authors in developing this paradigmatic model was to make explicit the philosophical presuppositions underpinning various approaches to the study of organizations, of equal importance was their tactical intent to demonstrate the legitimacy of distinct paradigms and, as such, to provide a conceptual space within which what they saw as more radical approaches to organizational analysis than mainstream functional-ism could flourish. As Burrell himself has since acknowledged,

> What Burrell and Morgan's book may have succeeded in doing was to highlight the break-down of the field of organization theory into warring encampments and to demonstrate that functionalist approaches, whilst popular, politically superior and common, were by no means the only possible avenues open to organizational analysis. The text articulated and legitimated to some extent the voices of those who do not share the functionalist orientation. (1996: 648)

However, as Reed (1993) has also suggested, perhaps the most signifi-cant impact of Burrell and Morgan's 'paradigm' model was to establish the idea that divergent approaches to organizational analysis should be acknowledged as incommensurable. As such, they should not be expected to provide the basis for any exchange of ideas or understanding outside of the paradigms themselves. Not only did this lead to the appearance of disciplinary fragmentation within the field, it also provided a source of legitimization for an increasing tendency towards the championing of a form of meta-theoretical relativism in all its dimensions – ontological, epis-temological and ethical – a relativism that for many would come, above all else, to characterize the negative impact of postmodernism on contempo-rary organization theory (Parker, 1995).

This pre-history of postmodern organization theory can therefore be seen, in large part, as a response to an increasing disillusionment among certain quarters of the discipline with what were considered to be the shortcomings of a positivist/functionalist/realist hegemony which had pretty much held sway throughout its development. This disillusionment led, in turn, to a process of fragmentation within the field, and to the recog-nition of a diverse range of approaches to the meta-theoretical foundations of organizational analysis. While none of these developments represented, in themselves, the evolution of a form of postmodern meta-theory, with the benefit of hindsight we can see how the emergence of a greater emphasis on theoretical pluralism, combined with a concern with questions of power and political engagement, did at least prepare the academic soil in which the postmodern seed was able to find sufficient legitimacy and encour-agement to take root.

The postmodern turn in organization theory

While a certain degree of scepticism has been expressed as to the actual extent of diversification that organization theory has experienced since the 1970s (Reed 1993, 1996a), there can be no doubt that by the end of the 1980s the disruptive impact of postmodern meta-theory within the social sciences in general was also starting to make itself felt in the study of organizations. Commonly acknowledged as the first published article to address the possibility of a postmodern organizational theory (Gergen, 1992; Hassard, 1993a, 1993b; Parker, 1992), Cooper and Burrell's, 'Modernism, Postmodernism and Organizational Analysis: An Introduction' (1988) explored the implications for organization theory of the increasing deployment of postmodern meta-theory within the social sciences and, in doing so, set the terms of debate for a number of subsequent publications. In this article, modernism and postmodernism were conceptualized as 'discursive resources', that is, as alternative ways of defining the nature and scope of knowledge and the means by which it could be accessed and disseminated. Modernism, as we outlined in Chapter 1, was characterized predominately by a belief in the desirability and, indeed, inevitability of historical progress and by a faith in the faculty of reason to uncover the nature of the social universe. Postmodernism in contrast, Cooper and Burrell (1988) argued, is underpinned by the highly post-structuralist proposition that the social universe is inherently paradoxical and indeterminate. From this postmodernist perspective, then, the social world obeys no rational guiding principles and follows no pre-determined historical trajectory.

Applying these basic propositions to the domain of organization theory, Cooper and Burrell argued that modernist approaches to the study of organizational life tend to portray organizations simply as extensions of human rationality. In other words, from a modernist perspective, 'organization' as a process, an entity or whatever, is conceived of as an institutionalized realization of a rationally ordered world. In contrast, postmodern organization theory, they argued, offers the potential to understand organization as 'a defensive reaction to the forces of chaos' (Cooper and Burrell, 1988: 91). Hence, for Cooper and Burrell, organizations as both processes and as structural outcomes of organizing processes could be understood as the products of human attempts to impose order on what is an essentially disordered and irrational environment. Consequently, a postmodern organization theory, in their view, would relate to organizations not as natural or immutable phenomena, but as temporary and contingent expressions of a systemic modernist impulse to '[order] social relations according to the model of functional rationality' (Cooper and Burrell, 1988: 96).

As such, Cooper and Burrell (1988) presented postmodernism as a critical tool, one that might be deployed in order to expose the prevailing dominance of an essentially repressive systemic modernism both in the process and analysis of organization. The outcome of this line of thought, for Cooper and Burrell at least, was a postmodern-inspired approach that would seek to analyse critically the informal aspects of organization and the various ways in which informality and irrationality are 'organized out' of the workplace. As such, a postmodern organization theory would expose, they argued, the historical privileging of the formal over the informal, the rational over the irrational, the masculine over the feminine.

A similar line of thinking also emerged in a later piece by Kenneth Gergen (1992), who argued that traditional models of organization must be understood as deriving from a combination of two 'hegemonic bodies of discourse', namely 'romanticism' and 'modernism' (Gergen, 1992: 208). The former refers to the idea that the human subject possesses an essentially authentic nature that can, given the right theoretical tools, be exposed and nurtured. This, he argued, is reflected in various forms of motivational theory such as that developed by Maslow (1943), as well as contemporary models of Japanese management which stress notions of organizational community and 'belongingness'. Modernism, in contrast, maintains a faith in the explanatory and transformative powers of observation and reason, combined with a faith in progress and universal design, and a tendency to employ the 'machine metaphor' in questions of analysis and prescription. Conversely, postmodernism, Gergen argued, draws upon three interrelated propositions about the nature of knowledge. These are:

(i)   The replacement of the real by the representational
(ii)   The understanding of representation as a 'communal artifact'
(iii)   The need for ironic self-reflection. (1992: 213–15)

For Gergen, organization theory should embrace these postmodernist propositions in order to learn to be more flexible and eclectic, primarily because organizations need to survive in what he considered to be an increasingly postmodernized cultural environment. In contrast to the critical potential for understanding organizations which Cooper and Burrell identified, Gergen, adopting a more functionalist approach, argued that cultural postmodernism necessitates a new postmodernized approach to the management of organizations. What is particularly interesting, in this respect, is that while Gergen's analysis of postmodernism is markedly similar to that of Cooper and Burrell, in so far as both accounts call for the need to abandon the search for fixed meanings and relations of representation, their underlying political ambitions are quite distinct. While in Cooper and Burrell's (1988) paper, the political agenda revolved very much around the development of a radical critique of organizational power, Gergen's (1992) aim was rather to provide a theoretical perspective that would enable management to survive in a postmodern cultural climate, giving intellectual credence to pluralistic and flexible modes of organization that aim, primarily, to meet the demands of a changing business environment. In this sense, Gergen placed considerable emphasis on the potential of postmodernism to provide an intellectual framework within which organizational procedures can be adapted, in order to maintain standards of efficiency and competitiveness in the face of those changes, outlined in Chapter 2, that have come to be associated with a process of organizational postmodernization.

The apparent ease with which Gergen was able to jettison the radical agenda that underpins Cooper and Burrell's engagement with post-modernism, while maintaining a self proclaimed commitment to postmodernism as a radical approach to organizational analysis is not unique, however. Frank Blacker (1992), for example, in an essay published in the same collection as Gergen's, promoted the importance of a post-modern understanding of organization to the successful pursuit of 'change management'. Similar ideas have also emerged in a number of articles (Boje et al., 1996; Gephart Jr et al., 1996) in which the primary concern is how the business world can ensure its organizations are able to thrive in a social environment shaped by postmodern knowledge and cultural expec-tations. Thus, rather than challenging the legitimacy of modern organizational forms, the concern of such work has been more with the question of how organizational enterprises, when faced with a postmodern assault on the old certainties of orthodox organizational theory and prac-tice, can be 'managed' more effectively. This apparently conservative postmodernism, that is, one that adopts a particularly functionalist approach to postmodern meta-theory, is summed up by Gephart Jr, Thatchenkery and Boje when they argued that

> The postmodern paradigm . . . does not seek universal truths or organizing principles but rather seeks local knowledge and insights from which to develop the capacity for reflection and reflexivity in managers and citizens so that chaos can be addressed, accepted and, *when possible, controlled or managed*. (1996: 359 *emphasis added*)

As we noted in Chapter 1, a conservative tendency within postmod-ernism is, of course, not unique to organization theory. That said, the study of organizations has tended to expose what is perhaps postmodernism's greatest weakness, in that its attack on modernist epistemology has reduced its capacity for a normative account of organizations as sites of control and resistance. In this sense, it could be argued that postmod-ernism's rejection of any epistemological foundations upon which an 'ethico-political' critique (Willmott, 1997a) can be established, serves largely to emasculate any radical agenda within organization theory, deny-ing it any sustainable moral position from which an assault on relations of domination can be mounted (Parker, 1993, 1995; Willmott, 1997a).

Indeed, the idea that postmodern epistemology can provide any basis for a politically-engaged organization theory has been questioned by a number of commentators such as Reed (1997) and Thompson (1993), both of whom identify the postmodern fascination with the realm of micro-social relations and localized politics as resulting particularly in a form of intellectual myopia, one that is unable to envision the larger structural forces that underpin relations of organizational power and control. Tim Newton (1996) considered this particular concern in relation to what he termed the problem of 'action' (Newton 1996: 15). Newton reflected on the implications of postmodernism for the foundation on which our claims to political action can be justified and argued that, if we accept a postmodernist view of knowledge, we are forced constantly to address the question '. . . how do we know our representations have any validity when we acknowledge that they are truth effects, not real or absolute positions?' (Newton, 1996: 16). However, while we go on to consider such criticisms in more depth as this chapter unfolds, what we intend to do now is explore a number of attempts to develop a more tentative and, it should be said, less ambitious incorporation of postmodern meta-theory into the ways in which work organizations can be conceptualized and studied.

Tentative models for a postmodern organization theory

As a consequence of the reservations alluded to above, a number of attempts to develop a postmodern organization theory have endeavoured to mediate between the relativizing tendencies of postmodernism and the political aspirations of a critical study of organizational power (Alvesson and Deetz, 1996; Hassard, 1993a, 1993b, 1996; Kilduff and Mehra, 1997; Watson, 1995b). Such attempts at mediating between these two imperatives have tended to develop a bifurcated understanding of postmodernism, exemplified in various allusions to 'hard' and 'soft' (Watson, 1995b), 'affirmative' and 'skeptical' (Kilduff and Mehra, 1997), 'reactionary' and 'resistant' (Alvesson and Deetz, 1996). Hard postmodernism, for example, derives for Watson (1995b: 1) from the relativizing stance of Lyotard's (1984) incredulity towards meta-narratives. Similarly, Kilduff and Mehra (1997), drawing upon Rosenau's (1992) division of postmodern thought into *affirmative* and *sceptical*, argue that the former represents Lyotard's conception of the postmodern condition. For Watson, hard postmodernism constitutes

> . . . a way of looking at the world which rejects attempts to build systematic explanations of history and human activity and which, instead, concentrates on the ways in which human beings go about 'inventing' their worlds, especially through language and cultural innovation. (1995b: 1).

While for Watson this position represents an internally coherent epistemological perspective, he feels it must be rejected if the possibility of a critical social science, one that is able to engage with a 'world out there' in a way which is distinct from the stories people tell about it, is to be maintained. In this sense, he would perhaps concur with Parker that

a 'hard' postmodern epistemology is essentially a way of avoiding responsibility for the implications of organizational analysis[. It is] a distraction from a
rigorous analysis of organizational changes within global capitalism. Such things
are too important to be left to be concealed by an epistemology that can only lead
to extreme ethical-political relativism and an ontology without convincing foundations. (Parker, 1993: 211–12)

Rather than a 'hard' postmodernism, Watson advocates the adoption of
what he terms a 'soft' postmodern approach which, while sensitive to the
constitutive role of language in constructing subjective social reality, does
not abandon wholesale the belief in a world that is external to such linguistic formations. In this sense, Watson builds on a distinction also
championed by Tsoukas (1992: 648), who argues that, in contrast to a 'hard'
postmodernism that underestimates the importance of 'institutions in pat-
terning social life', a 'softer' version indeed constitutes a useful challenge
to the 'cognitive monopoly of an allegedly omniscient subject-centered
rationality' that, in his view, characterizes more traditional approaches to
organization theory. Tsoukas concludes:

A 'soft' version of postmodernism which recognizes the ontological existence of
the social world, however precarious and fluid the latter may be, has a lot to contribute to our understanding of organizations. . . . 'Soft' postmodernists have a
predilection for investigating the chaotic aspects of organizational phenomena,
focusing on subversive processes, instabilities, discontinuities . . . and traditionally ignored 'secondary qualities' . . . of organizations. (1992: 648)

In a similar vein to Tsoukas's (1992: 648) concern for a soft postmodernism
to maintain the need to render organizations 'intelligible via rational enquiry',
what Kilduff and Mehra (1997) term 'skeptical' postmodernism implies a
critical attitude towards taken-for-granted regimes of meaning, but also one
that continues to uphold the need to maintain standards of argumentation
and academic rigour and to establish clear boundaries for legitimate critique.
To this end, sceptical postmodernism implies a postmodern organization
theory which, they argue, should synthesize the best from both modern and
postmodern traditions in a search for localized forms of knowledge and the
existence of paradox, the non-obvious or the counter-intuitive.

This conception of a 'soft' or 'sceptical' postmodernism is not dissimilar
to Hassard's (1993b, 1996) perception that postmodernism can best be
viewed as a 'new paradigm for organizational research' (Hassard, 1993b:
111), in which an epistemological postmodernism, while failing 'to account
for the everyday experiences of social actors' (1993b: 134), can provide the
opportunity for a reflexive analysis and deconstruction of the rationalized, normative idea of the classical Weberian model of the bureaucratic
organization. A similar emphasis characterizes Alvesson and Deetz's conception of a 'postmodernism of resistance' (Alvesson and Deetz, 1996: 193),
which they define primarily as a critical engagement with the stupefying
effects of a systemic modernist discourse.

While conceptually distinct, what each of these respective attempts to outline a 'soft', 'sceptical' or 'resistant' postmodern organization theory, share in common is a concern with several recurring themes. Watson (1995b), Hassard (1993b, 1996), Kilduff and Mehra (1997), and Alvesson and Deetz (1996) all emphasize the role that discourse plays in the constitution of what is taken to be both an external reality and the internal characteristics of human subjectivity. A postmodern organization theory which is 'soft', 'sceptical' and 'resistant' is therefore presented as an endeavour concerned, at least in part, with the exploration of those organizational discourses that offer the possibility of new configurations of identity and the implications they have for structural relations of emancipation and/or domination.

A critical concern with what is referred to as the 'philosophy of presence' (Alvesson and Deetz, 1996) is also a recurring theme. This concept, derived from the writings of Derrida (1976) discussed in Chapter 1, refers to the way in which our understanding of the social world is always shaped by the relationship particular phenomena have to their absent others. This critique of a philosophy of presence thus functions as a basis for the exploration of how the naturalized, taken-for-granted qualities we ascribe to certain phenomena are structured by power relations which are obscured from everyday sight or understanding. It is these power relations that structure our understanding of the world, and which the critique of the philosophy of presence seeks to uncover (Alvesson and Deetz, 1996: 208).

Another, now somewhat familiar, recurring theme in recent attempts to develop a postmodern organization theory is that of the death of the grand- or meta-narrative (Lyotard, 1984). Alvesson and Deetz suggest that their model of a postmodernism of resistance is not so much concerned with the observation that such metanarratives have lost their credibility as descriptors of historical process. Rather, they suggest that what is required is a *qualified* investigation into, and critique of, those metanarratives that can be seen to function as technologies of marginalization, suppressing certain voices within the organizational domain. Consequently, the importance of reflexivity is also emphasized (Hassard, 1993a, 1996; Watson, 1995b), particularly in terms of the need to acknowledge continually that power resides in the very discourses within which organizational theory and research takes place.

Each of these recurring themes suggest, to us at least, the emergence of a tentative agenda for a postmodern organization theory, an agenda that is concerned not so much with making 'correct' observations about the way the world is, as it is with striving towards critical investigation, challenging assumptions and common-sense meanings and promoting experimentation with a range of new research styles and approaches. Nevertheless, it also appears that such attempts remain faced with the challenge of developing a sound philosophical basis for a 'qualified' critique of metanarratives (Alvesson and Deetz, 1996), one that seeks to avoid a relativistic nihilism without reproducing the repressive discourses of a rationalized modernism. In this respect, it seems that the onus remains firmly upon the individual social science practitioner to maintain a state of heightened reflexive awareness. It also seems evident that, in many ways, Watson's 'soft postmodernism' and Hassard's 'new paradigm' represent little in the way of a radical departure from other well-established interpretive or phenomenologically-grounded research strategies within the social sciences. More important perhaps, is that such approaches to the study of organizational life, in their current state of evolution at least, continue to remain sketchy about the basis on which ethico-political critique of contemporary processes and structures organizational can be sustained. In other words, a bifurcation of postmodernism, as an attempt to address some of the implications of the relativizing tendencies of postmodern meta-theory, seems merely to avoid, rather than address head on, some of its more problematic aspects.

This is a problem that is, it must be noted, recognized by Alvesson and Deetz themselves, who reflect on the extent to which the relativizing implications of postmodernism threaten to slide organization theory into an extreme relativism whereby 'the world as understood is not really a fiction in this situation since there is no "real" outside which it portrays falsely or which can be used to correct it' (1996: 210). Hence, despite their apparent acceptance of the critical potential of a postmodernism of resistance, Alvesson and Deetz (1996) in particular remain sceptical that, due to these relativizing tendencies and abstract concerns, postmodernism can actually deliver a defensible basis for a politically-engaged organization theory. To say that social reality is in large part constituted through discourse, and that discourse itself entails certain power relations, is certainly seen as an important aspect of any critical social science, let alone one concerned specifically with work organizations. However, to attempt then to address the antinomies this creates simply in terms of, say, a call for a heightened state of reflexivity, continues to do little to address convincingly the philosophical problems that have been unleashed.

In his attempt to map out the contested terrain on which the various debates on postmodernism are taking place within organization theory, Boje (forthcoming) cross references the bifurcation of postmodern ideas into the affirmative and sceptical positions outlined above, with a distinction (one that is made in much of the literature on postmodernism[4]) between episodic theories of modernity–postmodernity and epistemological theories of modernism and postmodernism. He complicates this by identifying what seems to us to be an increasingly complex and expanding middle ground of theories both within and between these various positions. In the 'affirmative' camp, Boje identifies an episodic focus on a concern with postmodern ways of knowing as offering solutions to organizational problems (Bergquist, 1993) and the assertion, in Hatch's (1997) work for instance, of the existence of postmodern organizational forms. He also locates Cooper and Burrell's (1988) focus on an epistemological postmodernism that we discussed earlier in this chapter in this affirmative position, albeit one that implies that postmodern modes of organization must be understood in relation to modernism (see especially Cooper and Burrell, 1988: 96). In the middle ground between these two episodic and epistemological approaches, Boje locates Hassard's (1993a) conviction, outlined above, that postmodern approaches can realize some of the (unrealized) critical potential of organization theory. Boje locates an epochal concern with the ways in which a transition from Fordism to post-Fordism (discussed in Chapter 2) does not obviate existing frameworks of power, in the work of Clegg (1990) in particular, in a more sceptical, epochal approach to postmodernism.

In terms of an amalgamation of a sceptical postmodernism and a concern with questions of epistemology, Boje cites Parker's (1993: 212) claim that theorizing postmodern organizational forms is a naïve 'distraction from rigorous analysis' as well as Thompson's (1993: 188) aforementioned conviction that a concern with postmodern modes of organization is 'non-sense'. In the middle ground between these two episodic and epistemological sceptical positions, Boje locates Burrell's (1997) concern with the 'dark' and violent underside of organizations. Boje positions his own work which, he argues, is characterized by the conception of post-modernism as a 'potential' that needs to be subjected to deconstruction to prevent modernist appropriation between the affirmative and sceptical perspectives. He argues that, just as there is an infinite range of postmodern perspectives, so there are multiple organizational forms, each of which is a hybrid of pre-modern, modern and postmodern episodes.

In this sense, Boje's work (see, for instance, Boje, 1995) not only claims the (epochal) emergence of postmodern modes of organization, but also emphasizes the epistemological implications (and opportunities) posed by postmodernism for the study of organizations. He has also, however, equally been at pains to point out the exploitative power relations that characterize such organizations and to argue that contemporary modes of organizing can perhaps best be understood (much like Burrell, 1997) in terms of the co-existence of pre-modern, modern and postmodern discourses and imperatives. His account of Disney, in particular, as a story-telling organization emphasizes the blurring of epochal/epistemological, affirmative/sceptical approaches to postmodernism, arguing that as a corporation Disney is an amalgamation of pre-modern, modern and postmodern practices (Boje, 1995; see also Boje and Dennehy, 1993). What Boje's analysis of Burrell's (1997) work, and also his own approach to the relationship between postmodernism and organization, highlight then, is that tentative attempts to develop a postmodern organization theory exist within a whole series of debates that are far from clearly discernible.

It seems, however, that bifurcations of postmodernism into hard/soft, sceptical/affirmative, epochal/epistemological and so on, have very much shaped the various ways in which organization theory has attempted to incorporate, albeit selectively, many of the insights of postmodern meta-theory that we outlined in Chapter 1. Particularly influential, in this respect, has been the work of two of the leading theorists associated with postmodernism discussed there, Michel Foucault and Jacques Derrida. It is to the influence of these two figures that we now turn our attention, in an attempt to elaborate further on the impact of postmodernism on work organizations and their analysis.

Power/knowledge and subjectivity

The influence of Foucault's particular brand of post-structuralist post-modernism on the field of organization theory has been clearly striking (see for example, Burrell, 1988; Clegg, 1994; Knights, 1992, Knights and Vurdubakis, 1994; Knights and Willmott, 1989; McKinlay and Starkey, 1998). While early attempts to introduce Foucauldian thinking into organization theory tended to concentrate on his work on epistemology, focusing on the application of methodological approaches of archaeology and genealogy to critical social analysis (Burrell, 1988; Cooper and Burrell, 1988; Knights, 1992), his greatest impact has undoubtedly been in terms of an increasing fascination with questions of power, language and the constitution of subjectivity. This is not to say that Foucault's methodological concerns, especially those associated with his genealogical approach, are not themselves intimately entwined with his writing on power (see Knights and Morgan, 1991). However, apart from the odd exception, of which Savage's (1998) genealogical study of the emergence of the concept of 'career' during the late-nineteenth century is a notable example, the vast majority of recent work in this area has tended to focus more on the exploration of contemporary regimes of organizational *power/knowledge*.

Central to the deployment of Foucault's power/knowledge matrix in the theorization of organizational relations has been the proposition that power infuses every dimension of social interaction (Foucault, 1980), and is itself constitutive of human subjectivity (Knights, 1992; Knights and Vurdubakis, 1994; Knights and Willmott, 1989). In this regard, as a theoretical perspective, it departs from the modernist conception of the subject as an autonomous, transcendental entity, replacing it with one that is fundamentally contingent on prevailing modes of discourse and the expectations these subsequently generate. Thus, technologies of power and control in the workplace are no longer conceived simply as the means for regulating and directing the subjective aspirations of individual employees, but rather, as the media through which such categories of meaning are generated. As such, what is deemed important here is that these categories are not themselves necessarily experienced as repressive by those subject to them, but rather as the very mechanisms through which a coherent sense of self-identity comes into existence. Power is thus seen to be productive in that it 'produces' the resources, particularly in the form of social practices, through which our sense of self is realized. Yet, as Knights and Willmott (1989) note, ever present is the opportunity for relations of subjugation to assert themselves, particularly within the context of the work organization. In this sense, subjugation is defined as the outcome of a situation whereby 'the freedom of a subject is directed narrowly, and in a self-disciplined fashion, towards participation in practices which are known or understood to provide the individual with a sense of security and belonging' (Knights and Willmott, 1989: 550). Indeed, it is this narrow channelling towards practices that serve to reinforce the individual's secure sense of self, while at the same time constituting the self as productive and consuming, geared primarily to the organizational demands of industrial capitalism and the disciplinary technologies that facilitate it, that has provided much of the focus of contemporary work in this area.

Notable among this work has been Townley's (1993, 1994) critique of Human Resource Management (HRM). For Townley, HRM is to be understood as a *technology of governmentality*, in that it represents a collection of discursive resources and practices through which 'objects are rendered amenable to intervention and regulation by being formulated in a particular conceptual way' (1994: 6). HRM combines a surveillance function which accumulates knowledge about employees through, for example, performance appraisals, thus objectifying them, while at the same time endeavouring to re-constitute their subjective sense of self by promoting, for instance, the ideal of a corporate community. Townley argues that by incorporating Foucauldian thinking into her analysis she is able to expose this objectifying/subjectifying and normalizing process that lies at the heart of HRM and which is directed at the constitution of a disciplined workplace subject. Thus, HRM is seen to operate as a regulatory and ordering technology that is central to the management of organizations and the constitution of a compliant condition of employee subjectivity.

This basic premise, namely that managerial discourses can be understood as representing matrices of power/knowledge directed towards the production of a disciplined workforce, is one that sits at the centre of a number of related examples of Foucauldian-inspired organizational analysis. For example, Steingard and Fitzgibbons's deconstruction of Total Quality Management (TQM) develops a Foucauldian reading of how TQM affects 'the lived experience of people in organizations' (1993: 30) by inducing a subjective identification with, and internalization of, 'quality or else' (1993: 31). Alternatively, Jackson and Carter (1998), while still concerned with questions of governmentality and organizational discipline, have considered the ways in which disciplinary technologies aim not only to maintain or improve productivity, but also to promote what appears to be control for control's sake. What they term the 'dressage' function of organizational discipline produces a subjective performance of compliant behaviour on the part of the employee which, simply as a display of the absence of deviance, is deemed worthy of praise and reward.

Integral to Foucault's writing on power and subjectivity (see Chapter 1), and its incorporation into organizational analysis, then, are the concepts of panoptic surveillance and discipline (Foucault, 1991). Developed from the architectural design for a panoptic prison popularized by Jeremy Bentham, (Bentham, 1995 [1791]),[5] panoptic surveillance is premised upon the idea of a continuous state of maximum visibility. Referring to Bentham's original design, Foucault notes how the underlying principle of the panopticon was to

> induce in the inmate a state of conscious and permanent visibility that assures the automatic functioning of power. So to arrange things that the surveillance is permanent in its effects, even if it is discontinuous in its action; that the perfection of power should tend to render its actual exercise unnecessary; that this architectural apparatus should be a machine for creating and sustaining a power relation independent of the person who exercises it; in short, that the inmates should be caught up in a power situation *of which they themselves are the bearers*. (Foucault, 1977a: 201 *emphasis added*)

Within the design of the panopticon, the central tower functioned as an omnipresent reminder that the inmate could be under surveillance but, with no means of verification, save committing an action which could lead to punishment, inmates had to assume that they were under constant observation. The concept of panoptic power is based therefore on the premise that this assumption is internalized and transformed into a mode of self-control which Foucault terms 'discipline'. In Foucault's work, the physical design of the panopticon thus became a metaphorical device, one that described the principles underlying modern technologies of surveillance and their disciplinary effects.

Zuboff (1988) has applied the concept of panoptic surveillance to her account of the emergence of new information technologies which, while promising to democratize various modes of organizational communication, she argues, also produce a far more effective means by which techniques of panoptic surveillance can be designed and administered. As she notes:

> Information systems that translate, record and display human behavior can provide the computer age version of universal transparency with a degree of illumination that would have exceeded even Bentham's most outlandish fantasies. Such systems can become information panopticons that, freed from the constraints of space and time, do not depend upon the physical arrangement of buildings or the laborious record keeping of industrial administration. (Zuboff, 1988: 322)

Information systems, when viewed from this perspective, facilitate a regime of employee transparency in accordance with the principles of panoptic surveillance. They are able to record not only what is said and done, but also the time spent at, say, a particular workstation by an employee and the rate of output that is achieved, and so on. This can then be operationalized as 'knowledge' that serves to reinforce both asymmetrical relations of managerial power and attempts to strengthen the subjective ties which bind the employee to the organizational ethos. Of course, the principle of panoptic surveillance in the workplace need not necessarily rely upon the operation of information technologies such as computerized data storage or electronic mailing systems. While acknowledging the importance of such technologies in establishing a regime of surveillance and discipline, Sewell and Wilkinson (1992a, 1992b), for example, also point to the ways in which practices associated with workplace TQM regimes, such as 'quality circles' and 'manufacturing cells', engender mutual relations of peer surveillance which, in themselves, function as disciplinary technologies. Tyler and Abbott (1998) have, in a similar vein, noted the role that peer surveillance plays in the internalization of certain aesthetic codes within the airline industry, where relations of power and gender are internalized and manifest as a mutually reinforcing gaze between fellow employees.

While the allure of the Foucauldian preoccupation with regimes of power/knowledge, governmentality and discipline has been enticing, as with any valuable contribution to the knowledge base of the social sciences it has, for many, produced more questions than it has answered. Of significance, in this respect, has been the status of the human subject within matrices of power/knowledge and organizational discipline. Despite the ascribed label of post-structuralist, the extent to which Foucault's insights offer anything more than a modified structuralist orthodoxy, which, like various sociological, and particularly Marxist, variants before it, reduces the human subject to little more than a discursively generated fantasy, or ideological construct (Althusser, 1969), has been the subject of often intense debate and is a theme to which we shall return in our final chapter.

Deconstruction and organizations as 'text'

In recent attempts on the part of organization theory to engage with the work of postmodern meta-theorists, Foucauldian social theory has increasingly shared the stage with an interest in Derridean deconstruction and, in particular, the critical analysis of organization as a form of *text* (Cooper, 1989; Kilduff, 1993; Linstead, 1993; Steingard and Fitzgibbons, 1993). Central to the conception of organization as text (see Chapter 1 for a brief summary of Derrida's concept of 'text') is the Derridean notion of *writing*. For Derrida, writing describes the means by which texts come into being; that is, the way in which 'human agents inscribe organization on their environments' (Cooper, 1989: 484). In this context, then, writing can be understood as a process which is directed towards the imposition of decideability and order on the world, a process that is aimed at domination and control of a fundamentally disordered world (Cooper and Burrell, 1988). What Derrida's insights bring to organization theory, it could therefore be argued, is the understanding that organizations themselves are 'written'. As Cooper notes, they are the outcome of processes of textual interaction that can, and should, be understood as texts in their own right (Cooper, 1989).

Following Derrida, 'organization' can therefore be understood as the outcome of a process through which the world, as we discussed in Chapter 1, is divided into binary oppositions in which one term comes to dominate its opposite. As such, as an analytical method, deconstruction is envisaged as a means by which those dualisms that constitute organization can be overturned, revealing the contradictions and tensions inherent within the process itself, contradictions which the logocentric priorities of writing have sought to conceal. As such, a radical deconstructionist approach to the study of organizations should, it has been argued (Knights, 1997), seek to act as a constant mechanism of de-stabilization, undermining at every opportunity taken-for-granted relations of order and stability through the exposure of the forgotten or marginalized dimensions of language.

For Linstead, writing on organizational ethnography, deconstruction provides this approach with 'a means of revealing the contradictions inherent within texts, a means of exposing their logocentrism, their reliance on the metaphysics of presence, and of revealing the inescapable qualities of differance and supplementarity despite repressive textual strategies' (1993: 57). However, while organizations, for Linstead, can also be read as texts – texts that are constantly written and re-written by their 'authors' – he is also aware of the ways in which such texts can be attributed with albeit temporary and unstable structural qualities which impact upon the constitutive subjectivities of those who are responsible for the act of writing. He thus identifies Derridean deconstruction as a radical approach through which, in particular, the organizational ethnographer can explore the ways in which certain readings of organizational texts become normalized and therefore dominant and, in doing so, seek to destabilize their repressive functioning.

The deconstructive process itself relies upon two conceptually distinct stages which Linstead derives from Cooper (1989). The first is an 'overturning' (Linstead, 1993: 58) of the binary opposition of terms that exist within any organizational discourse such as manager/employee. The second is a process of 'metaphorization' (Linstead, 1993: 58), whereby the interrelatedness of the relevant binary terms is exposed in an attempt to destabilize the fixity of their relationship and to ensure a constant state of movement between them, thus problematizing any notion of a stable state of meaning within the organizational text.

Deconstructive engagement with the organization as text is therefore presented by Linstead as a radical means by which the ethnographer can present his or her reading of the text in such a way as to ensure that what remains of prime analytical interest is the means by which organizational truths are constituted and maintained. In other words, the ethnographer's role is to reveal how organizational 'realities' are formed through the operationalization of certain textual strategies. This goal is pursued by exposing the text's own internal contradictions and by resisting any attempt to allow these contradictions to rest in any final, fixed relationship of meaning through an ongoing process of overturning and metaphorization. Thus, an organizational ethnography based upon a postmodern deconstructive epistemology aims, in Linstead's words, to 'resuscitate the subordinate terms, to elevate them, to amplify the silenced voices in order to problematize the dominant understanding . . . rather than create a new hierarchy' (1993: 69).

Specific attempts to adopt a deconstructive approach to the analysis of organizational life can be identified in the work of Frug (1984), Steingard and Fitzgibbons (1993) and Martin (1990). Frug's deconstruction of bureaucracy emphasizes how the bifurcation of the terms subjectivity and objectivity, and subsequent privileging of objectivity, has served to conceal bureaucratic power and so defended 'bureaucracy against the fear of domination by showing that bureaucratic power is based on objectivity, i.e., "neutrality" and "pursuit of a common purpose"' (cited in Cooper, 1989: 496). However, as Frug also notes, such a closure of the binary relationship of objective and subjective phenomena can only ever be partial as the former term is constantly held in a state of tension with its absent Other, namely subjectivity. In other words, a deconstructive analysis emphasizes that each term is dependent on both the presence and absence of its conceptual Other. Thus, while writing on bureaucracy holds that the two terms are distinct from each other, and maintains therefore that subjectivity can be excluded from bureaucracy so as not to contaminate the objective credentials of the bureaucratic form (Weber, 1964), Frug's deconstructive approach emphasizes that the two concepts can never be distinct.

In a similar vein, Steingard and Fitzgibbons's analysis of TQM aims to 'perform a postmodern analysis of total quality management by exposing some of its unacknowledged theoretical assumptions and by making explicit the unstated philosophical questions hidden behind its seductively instrumental façade' (1993: 28). Here, the term 'total quality management' is deconstructed in an attempt to demonstrate the absent or deferred meanings which supplement the visible terms. They argue, for instance, that the term 'total' serves to deny the existence of other perspectives and so privileges the voice of those who adhere to and promote the concept, namely managers. Similarly, 'quality' is seen to address only the quality or the immediate value of product or service, denying the significance of quality as a subjective phenomenon, for instance in relation to the quality of employees lives, or the quality of the environment. The process of writing, in this case of organizational discourses such as TQM, is exposed as a reflection of relations of power and domination, and as one that seeks to establish a fixed and instrumentally-orientated regime of meaning upon an essentially fluid set of relations.

Drawing largely on contemporary feminist post-structuralism and its engagement with the work of Derrida, Martin (1990) also develops a deconstructive analysis that emphasizes the ways in which apparently well-intentioned organizational practices for alleviating gender inequality can actually serve to reify gender difference. Martin demonstrates this with reference to a deconstruction of an organizational story that was told by the president of a corporation to illustrate what his organization was doing to 'help' women balance the demands of home and work. Her analysis deconstructs and subsequently attempts to reconstruct this story, 'examining what it says, what it does not say, and what it might have said' (1990: 339). She compares organizational responses to a heart bypass operation and a Caesarian birth (timed deliberately so that the woman involved could watch the launch of a new product on a closed-circuit television as she recovered in hospital) in order to reveal the suppression of gender conflict, according to which, she argues, the organization in question was 'written'.

A somewhat different approach is taken by Kilduff (1993) who, rather than subjecting an 'organization as text' to a process of critical deconstruction, develops a deconstructive analysis of a text about organizations and organizing. The text in question is March and Simon's *Organizations* (1958), which, the authors claim, represents not only a highly formalistic and rationally-structured text, but one that is grounded on an implicit belief in making a progressive contribution to the development of the field. Yet, Kilduff notes how, in order to justify this belief, the authors employ a number of textual strategies designed to establish an absence within the field, that their own text can then lay claim to filling. For Kilduff, this strategy undermines its own claim to principles of scientific rigour and objectivity. The text under scrutiny strives to establish that 'an earlier tradition in organization studies', one which they associate with the likes of Taylor and Fayol, worked with a crude model of the 'human organism as a simple machine' (cited in Kilduff, 1993: 17). This model, they argue, characterized all organization studies, in one form or another, prior to their own intervention.

Yet, as Kilduff argues, in doing so the authors of *Organizations* tend to homogenize other models (such as those deriving from the Hawthorne studies) so as to create a space for their own textual intervention. Kilduff goes on to argue that March and Simon's own intervention is itself an attempt to write into organizational theory an equally mechanistic model of human action, one that simply replaces the labouring machine with the computing machine (Kilduff, 1993: 19). The text *Organizations* is therefore exposed, Kilduff argues, as representing nothing like the radical break that it claims for itself. Rather, the appearance of progress is achieved through the 'exclusion and distortion of previous texts' (Kilduff, 1993: 28).

Notwithstanding such attempts to incorporate the insights derived from postmodern meta-theorists such as Foucault and Derrida into the social scientific study of work organizations in each of the respective analyses considered above, the deconstructive role of the theorist remains problematic. Attempting to write a model of stability into the organization or 'text', the theorist is faced with the paradoxical situation whereby a constant process of deferral is necessary to ensure the maintenance of the (illusionary) stability of the deconstructive model. Thus, the act of writing is exposed as one which itself seeks merely to impose order and stability onto the processual nature of organizational life (Frug, 1984). Furthermore, questions of epistemic privilege, such as how to differentiate between the epistemic claims of divergent accounts, tend to remain unaddressed, as does the ethical and political status of the theorist. On this basis, then, deconstruction does beg the question of whether or not a postmodern organizational theory is a possibility, given the meta-theoretical priorities of postmodernism outlined in Chapter 1. It is with this question in mind that we consider, in the following section, the relatively recent development of organization theory as 'deconstructive practice'.

Deconstructive practice and the 'new sensibility'

Drawing on terminology derived from Bernstein (1976), Willmott (1998: 216) addresses what he considers to be the emergence of a 'new [postmodern] sensibility' within organization theory. This, he argues, is characterized by the way in which it combines a postmodern epistemological disposition with a reflexive awareness of the challenges that the idea of the postmodern poses for our understanding of the ontological status of organizations. He emphasizes that this 'new sensibility' draws largely on the writings of Derrida in an attempt to establish a relatively coherent postmodern approach to the practice of organization theory, an approach that develops the idea of the 'organization as text'. This approach emphasizes, on this basis, that the ways in which we conceptualize the organizational form are constitutive of that very reality.

In their contribution to the development of this approach, Cooper and Law (1995: 239) divide what they consider to be the dominant modes of thought in the social sciences into two distinct, yet interdependent, approaches that they term 'distal' and 'proximal'. *Distal thought* conceptualizes organizations as relatively stable entities that have bounded parameters. As such, organizations are understood as 'real', spatially and temporally bounded structures, that are accessible through traditional methodological strategies. *Proximal thinking*, on the other hand, envisages an organizational domain as comprising disparate and often unco-ordinated acts and processes, open-ended in their nature and bound only by temporary and unstable conjunctions. While the former approach emphasizes the ontological fixity of the organization, the latter attributes ontological primacy to the fluidity of the process of organizing. This latter approach forces researchers to confront not only the ways in which their conception of organizations is fundamental to how they frame the nature of the very objects of their investigations, but also how these conceptions are themselves organized by an academic discursive system. Drawing on Derrida's concept of supplementarity, Cooper thus notes how

> . . . statements of that discourse which we call 'organization theory' are supplementary, for they represent the 'organization of organization', that is to say, that as texts *on* organization they themselves are 'organized' according to certain normalized criteria (often called scientific and/or academic) so that it

becomes impossible to disentangle the content of organization studies from the theory or methodology that frames it. By this logic, each statement about system or organization is not merely a piece of information about a particular subject matter but – significantly – the statement produces what it 'denotes'. (1990: 196–7 *original emphasis*)

For Cooper and Law (1995) then, philosophical and methodological priorities, the practice of organizational analysis and the domain of organizational inquiry all exist in an ongoing process of constitution and re-constitution. It is in the work of Chia (1995), however, that this so-called 'new sensibility' has been developed with a more explicit commitment to a particular ontological understanding of the organizational 'form'. In Chia's work, the ontological commitment is to what he terms an *ontology of becoming* (Chia, 1995: 581). Chia argues that modern thought typically conceptualizes the world through the lens of 'being-realism' (Chia, 1996: 33), that is, a belief in the social world as a static state of being, which, as in Cooper and Law's (1995) notion of distal thinking, is understood to be susceptible to direct observation and purposeful modification. For Chia, this can be distinguished from postmodern thinking which realizes the ontological primacy of the processes by which particular states of being come into existence, an ontology that Chia describes as 'becoming-realism' (Chia, 1996: 33). For Chia, then, postmodernism is a 'style of thought', with its own 'set of ontological commitments, intellectual priorities and theoretical preoccupations' (Chia, 1995: 580).

Chia emphasizes, in this respect, the critical potential of a postmodernist 'becoming-realism' which views organizations not only as outcomes of organizing processes, but as processes in themselves. He suggests, therefore, that a critical organization theory, grounded in a postmodernist ontology, needs to focus not just on the process of becoming an organization, a subject or whatever, but rather on phenomena such as subjectivity and organizations *as* processual. In terms of the relationship between organization and subjectivity then, Chia's approach also emphasizes the importance of an analysis, not only of how organizations come into and out of being, but also of how the individual subjects who produce organizations are themselves the outcome of organizing processes.

However, for Chia, this raises a problem, particularly in relation to the call for reflexivity espoused especially by the likes of Watson (1995b), a problem that represents what Chia terms a form of 'meta-reflexivity' (Chia, 1996: 46). This, he claims, goes no further than defending the limited perspective of the researchers themselves, acknowledging as it does the situatedness of those undertaking a particular study, and thus 'undermining' their own claim to knowledge (Chia, 1996: 46). In its place, he proposes that postmodern organizational analysis should pursue a form of 'infra-reflexivity'.[6] This phenomenologically-driven approach to research rests on what he describes as an 'ultra-empiricism' which seeks to recover 'the concreteness of our brute experiences *as they emerge*' (Chia, 1996: 47 *original emphasis*). At the core of this approach sits a principle of symmetry which requires that we abandon 'abstract' concepts that attempt to explain complex social relationships *in toto* and, rather, engage with the phenomena of everyday life, employing only contingent modes of explanation. This approach constitutes what Chia describes as a 'weak' form of organizational analysis which, deconstructive in intent, seeks to understand processes of organizing and how individuals attempt to forge order out of chaos in everyday life. Chia's analysis of postmodernism as a contributor to organization theory therefore returns us to a focus on the 'micro-practices and micro-logics of organizing which are realized through local orchestrations of actions, interactions and interlocking patterns of relationships' (1995: 596). It is these 'micro-practices' which, for Chia, are the means through which order and structure are imposed on the world, the outcome of which are organizations, albeit themselves transient forms. In this respect, Chia's position, along with Cooper's, rests on a number of now familiar postmodern propositions. Among these are, first, the idea that reality is in a constant state of flux and movement, and that 'organization' can thus be seen as a means by which humans attempt to 'write' order on to it. Secondly, both Chia and Cooper emphasize the postmodernist rejection of the Enlightenment conception of an essential subject, and its replacement with a model of subjectivity that is understood to be constituted and re-constituted through discursive processes.

Willmott (1998) refers to as a 'new sensibility' in organizational analysis, represented here by the work of Cooper and Chia, constitutes, in our view at least, perhaps the most coherent and engaging attempt to apply the ontological and epistemological concerns of postmodernism to organization theory, such work is far from being above criticism. Weiskopf and Willmott (1997), in a paper that is generally sympathetic to Chia's endeavours, point for example, to the inherent contradiction within any approach which itself is dependent upon representationalist claims about that which it seeks to deconstruct. As they note, 'in order to engage in a postmodern/reflexive analysis it is, paradoxically, first necessary to *defer* its operation. Otherwise there is no-thing to deconstruct, and no-thing upon which to reflect' (Weiskopf and Willmott, 1997: 6 *original emphasis*). Such a contradiction, they argue, requires practitioners of deconstruction to be willing to acknowledge, primarily, their own implication in the practices they seek to criticize. Weiskopf and Willmott also emphasize the obligation, on the part of those who practise deconstructive analysis, to acknowledge the continuing epistemological value of those traditions that seek to identify the existence of those contingently stable institutions and structures that act to close down or organize processes of 'becoming'.

This point is developed further by Willmott (1998) who, while recognizing the critical potential of Chia's approach that prioritizes proximal over distal thought, suggests that this overturned dualism itself serves to further conceal the lived realities of organizational life. Willmott is concerned, in this respect, that such a prioritization ends up repressing our ability to engage with the structural forces that shape such organizing processes. He argues that this results, potentially, in a highly conservative position which overlooks the ways in which such processes are contained through the functioning of organizing discourses which, once brought into being, endure over time and space.

Another critical response to this emphasis on organizations as processual has drawn on the philosophical position of critical realism (Archer, 1995; Bhaskar, 1979, 1986). For Reed (1997), while the epistemological dimension of critical realism is important, what is of greater significance is its ontological commitment to the actual existence of structural phenomena, while maintaining a belief in the agential capacity of the human actor. As such, he argues that

> by granting both agency and structure their just ontological and analytical desserts, organizational analysis will be much better placed to describe and explain the complex interplay between structural conditioning and social action as it reproduces or transforms the social forms through which struggles over material and symbolic resources are organized. (Reed, 1997: 32)

Thus, Reed appeals to the development of a critical realist organization theory, one that addresses what he considers to be the main philosophical, and indeed political, deficiency in any postmodern-inspired attempt to theorize organizations; namely, the need to address what Kumar (1995) describes as the 'hidden forces' (cited in Reed, 1997: 37) of organizational power and control. Such forces, Reed suggests, continue to impact upon the ability of agents to take control of their everyday organizational lives and to engage in the process of organization. Yet such forces also appear to be marginalized in the respective accounts of Cooper, Law and Chia.

It is also questionable to what extent the work of so-called postmodern organization theorists can be deemed to be particularly novel. A concern with 'process' and a commitment to a micro-analytical approach to organizational behaviour have not, it could be suggested, moved that far beyond the traditions of phenomenology and ethnomethodology considered earlier. Indeed, much of what we have discussed as soft postmodernism, such as in Watson's (1995b) work, appears to represent little more than a form of social constructionism similar to that of Berger and Luckmann (1967) or the dialectical approach championed by Benson (1977), by which he also sought to prioritize the processual nature of organizational life, albeit within a more Marxian framework. Furthermore, it could be argued that in seeking to establish such overarching frameworks for analysis, the likes of Cooper, Law and Chia are themselves equally as guilty of the kinds of totalizing and dualistic analysis they are at pains to discredit? Indeed, in an attempt to maintain the status of a coherent and intellectually justifiable account of the complexity of contemporary organizational life, such an approach tends more towards the modernist values of coherent and representational science than it does the postmodern evocation of fragmentation, plurality and indeterminacy.

Conclusion

Whether or not the new sensibility in organization theory of which Willmott speaks can be wholly and unequivocally described as postmodern is a question that cannot be simply or quickly resolved. Certainly, unlike the postmodernization thesis discussed in Chapter 2, it is not susceptible to simple empirical repudiation. The very fact that a significant number of writers in the field have sought to engage with postmodernism attends sufficiently to the case for its existence. The additional fact that a number of these have chosen to refer to a particular body of emerging ideas in organization theory as 'postmodern' also lends weight to the claim that, in so far as discourse itself represents a material phenomenon, postmodern organization theory is well and truly with us.

Throughout this chapter, however, we have tried to emphasize that many of the values and perspectives associated with postmodernism have emerged from an ongoing concern with the perceived inadequacies of more positivist, functionalist and realist approaches to organization theory. Particularly since the publication of Silverman's (1970) work on organization theory, there has been a growing critique of the tendency of more traditional approaches to marginalize the indeterminacy of organizational life and, particularly, to propagate a politically conservative model of the neutral, ends-orientated organizational enterprise. This critique has encouraged a range of theoretical developments in the field that have, in one way or another, sought to grapple with two concerns in particular. These are, first, the complexities of a domain of inquiry that is seen as inherently dynamic and infused with relations of power and domination and, second, the awareness among researchers of the role their own work plays in the constitution of such organizational realities. Furthermore, it has provided a conceptual space within which researchers have found themselves able to explore previously overlooked aspects of organizational life, particularly the relationship between, say, power and subjectivity. It could be argued, however, that 'soft', 'sceptical' or 'resistant' forms of postmodernism lead us to little more than a kind of uncritical pluralism in which the existence of real disparities in socio-economic power and cultural capital go unchallenged in the name of the rights of multiple voices. The question 'what is a postmodern organization?' is itself seemingly invalidated by the postmodern assertion that, put simply, reality is what you make it.

Equally, however, if taken in the spirit of the kind of postmodern approach to organization theory championed by, say, Cooper and Burrell (1988), postmodernism can be seen to represent an alternative attempt to valorize those dimensions of organizational life traditionally eschewed by the discipline, dimensions which, in themselves, may heighten our understanding of how systemic concerns have previously marginalized the 'otherness' of organizational activity in favour of the easily quantifiable and technically-appreciable manifestations of organizational order.

This is a theme to which we return throughout the second section of the book.

In conclusion then, what we have considered throughout this chapter are a number of different attempts to explore the value of various postmodern themes to the development of organization theory. We have also attempted to reflect on the possible consequences of such attempts relating, most notably, to their epistemological implications and underlying ontological assumptions. In the forthcoming chapters, we attempt to bring together the ideas and theories that we have encountered during the first half of the book in relation to a more thematic consideration of work, postmodernism and organization. In doing so, we explore the impact that the idea of the postmodern has had on three substantive areas of contemporary organization theory – culture, emotion and sexuality – that not only illustrate a range of postmodern approaches and potentially postmodernized organizational practices, but which, at the same time, expose the potential limitations of a postmodern perspective on organizations.

Notes

1   See Burrell (1980: 96) for his own description of the importance of realism in relation to this period of his work.
2   That is, the set of guiding principles which define the worldview, appropriate methods of investigation and communally agreed upon past examples of valid achievement, which guide the practice of researchers in any given field (Blaikie, 1993: 106).
3   See Willmott (1990a) for an example of a critical discussion of this approach.
4   See, in particular, Featherstone (1988), Hassard (1993a, 1993b), Hassard and Parker (1993) and Parker (1992).
5   Bentham's original design for a panopticon consisted of a twelve-sided polygon with a central tower through which a warder could place under constant surveillance the inmates who were to be incarcerated in cells built into the walls of the polygon. While most closely related to a prison, Bentham's design was seen as being applicable to any number of situations in which behavioural control needed to be exercised, such as the school or the factory.
6   A term adopted from Latour (1987).

Overview

As you may recall, in our introduction we made it clear that, while ostensibly a book about postmodernism, this was not intended to be a postmodern book; though exactly what such a book might look like is, of course, open to debate. Indeed, as far as we can tell, with the possible exception of Burrell's aforementioned work, *Pandemonium* (1997), no one, as of yet, has really attempted to produce such a text within organization theory. Not that Burrell ascribes the label of postmodern to his own creation (though both he and the sleeve reviewers do allude to the term). Rather, what he aims to provide is an esoteric journey through the dystopian, or perhaps utopian (one is never quite sure), underside of organizational life, one that exposes the forgotten or deliberately hidden aspects of human 'messiness': sex, pleasure, cruelty, disease and death. As such, this is perhaps more of an anti-modern than postmodern work, the modern identified by a stubborn resistance to the untidiness and carnality of everyday life experiences, experiences that, for Burrell, the sterile rationalism of modernity is unable fully to conceptualize or deal with.

Indeed, as Burrell (1997: 5) himself explains, his is a book 'about those branches of social theory which take the Enlightenment to be a source of misgivings and worry', one that problematizes the claims of modernity and its professed path to progress and freedom. Where it might qualify as postmodern nevertheless, is in its attempt to present itself both as a work of reflexivity (a sense of his uncertainty at what he is doing is never far away) and as one that eschews what Burrell sees as the dangers of linearity in both thought and form. Of course it could be argued that a text flowing in directions, bibliography placed midway within it, suggests simply the work of a natural entertainer with an eye for the novel and perverse. Yet, however one wishes to interpret the nature of Burrell's work, ours, in clear contrast, is a book that is both linear and one that attempts to conform to all standard academic and literary expectations. As such, it professes nothing novel or perverse in either its conception, presentation or direction. We now sum up the material discussed so far.

A glance over the shoulder

So, where have we been so far on our albeit linear journey? Drawing on a number of sources, we attempted, in the opening chapter, to establish what it is that may constitute the idea of the postmodern. Charting its emergence as a critical response to the worldview bequeathed by the philosophical system that emerged during the European Enlightenment, we located its ideas in two particular modes or traditions of analysis. First, we reviewed the proposition that postmodernism can be understood as a form of meta-theory, one that is concerned with breaking down established parameters of what can be known or said about the nature of reality, knowledge and being. Drawing primarily on the work of Lyotard, Foucault and Derrida, we attempted to expose a number of core propositions that sit at the heart of postmodern meta-theory and that can be summarized in terms of:

1   A rejection of the Enlightenment belief in the universality of reason, and the objectivity and neutrality of knowledge resulting, in turn, in a critique of the perceived link between an expansion in human knowledge and historical progress.
2   A positing of the primacy of language as constitutive of what we take to be both an external reality and the internal domain of subjective experience, the latter resulting in the conception of the de-centred subject.
3   Deriving from these, a disposition towards a mode of epistemological perspectivism that considers all knowledge claims as relative to their linguistic and cultural contexts. All claims to knowledge, if such things can indeed be made, thus become contingent and temporary.
4   A normative commitment to a pluralist politics of difference, one that is driven by a belief in the valorization of diversity and the creation of spaces within which previously marginalized voices can be heard.

Having mapped out the contours of what could broadly be taken to be a postmodern meta-theory, we then shifted our emphasis somewhat, going on to consider the concept of social postmodernization, premised largely on the proposition that western societies are currently undergoing a potentially epochal shift away from the dominance of production over consumption towards a set of social relations premised on the de-differentiation of these spheres. While the actual motor of change at work here is a contested one, there is general agreement among the writers concerned, who are basically theorists of postmodernity, that many of the dualisms embedded within modern societies, such as production/consumption, work/leisure, knowledge/belief, reality/representation are all under assault. This in turn, it has been suggested, is resulting in a reconfiguration of a range of social and economic practices, such as a decline in the significance of traditional class-based relations to the primacy of relatively transient and, in many respects, largely hedonistic forms of cultural expression and activity.

Following on from this latter theme, Chapter 2 considered the emergence of the idea that an integral dimension of this proposed postmodernization process has been a series of shifts in the ways in which the sphere of economic production and distribution is organized within industrialized societies. Ranging from a series of future-orientated accounts of a post-industrial age in which the production and exchange of services and information surpasses the need to manufacture material commodities, to the proposition that, while manufacturing has indeed remained significant to the activities of the economic base, the organizational principles on which it is grounded have radically evolved, these accounts led to the proposition that organizations themselves are undergoing a discernable process of postmodernization. As we also observed, however, both the empirical evidence provided to substantiate such claims and the level of conceptual sophistication involved have been viewed by many as less than convincing. Nevertheless, many of the themes invoked in such accounts, including increasing levels of functional de-differentiation, the introduction of less hierarchical management structures and the increasing centrality of culture as a mode of organizational integration, all resonate with many of the themes encountered within the more general literature on postmodernism as well as continuing to feature within a range of empirical accounts of contemporary organizational life.

Finally, in Chapter 3, we considered the somewhat more extensive body of literature that has attempted to apply the insights of postmodern meta-theory to the study of organizations. While rather more diverse and complex than the material considered in Chapter 2, and, as such, less easily reducible to a number of bullet points, the approaches taken can be broadly summarized as follows. First, we considered an attempt to outline a tentative or, as Watson (1995b) would have it, 'soft' postmodern approach to the study of organizations. This rested primarily on the principle that all knowledge claims should be understood as partly constitutive of the object domains of which they speak and that organizations are themselves the outcome of, albeit frequently stabilized, discursive regimes of truth and knowledge. This results in an acknowledgement, first, of the role such a postmodern understanding can play in uncovering the ways in which such regimes provide the bases for certain taken-for-granted organizational practices and, secondly, of the need on the part of those who study organizations to engage reflexively with the ways in which their own knowledge claims contribute to the discursive formation of what are taken to be accepted conceptions of organizational activity. Where such an approach remains 'soft', however, is (i) in its resistance to the idea that all knowledge claims are relative and that, as such, standards of academic argumentation themselves represent mere discursively constituted regimes of power, and (ii) in its belief in the existence of externalized structural forces that can remain resistant to the simple reformulation of linguistic categories.

We also explored in this third chapter a concern with the interrelation-ship between power/knowledge, organization and the constitution of subjectivity. This approach, drawing largely on the insights of Foucault and Derrida, has tended to combine a concern with the appearance of what it considers to be various technologies of power/knowledge within organi-zations, such as HRM, with a broadly deconstructive method that operates as a tool by which such technologies can be exposed and challenged. For those working in this tradition, their main concerns are the ways organi-zations are able to constitute the subjectivity of their employees (at all levels) through the propagation of 'regimes of truth', that is, ways of assert-ing the nature of the world and the individuals' relationships to it that shackle them to a sense of identity that conflates the ontological need for personal security with the instrumental requirements of the organization's drive to maximize employee profitability.

The third, and final approach to a postmodern organization theory that we considered, jettisons the last vestiges of the modern conception of the work organization as an enduring structural phenomenon, viewing them instead as purely processual forms. Here, organization as verb rather than adjective takes centre stage, with Cooper and Law's (1995) concept of prox-imal thought or Chia's (1996) commitment to being-realism providing a framework of understanding. From this perspective, any attempt to under-stand or analyse organizations outside the everyday process of interaction and linguistic activity that defines them (including the organizing dis-courses of organization theory) merely serves to further reify that which such discourses themselves produce. Proximal thinking, as a potentially postmodern way of engaging with the world, including that of organiza-tions, negates the idea that the world comprises sets of structurally coherent and systemically stable 'things', and rather views these as illu-sions that obscure the ways in which, through our own tendency to organize the world, to close down relations of indeterminacy and to impose boundaries on the fluidity of life, we constitute and enforce the very basis of those power relations we may well be seeking to undermine.

But what does it all mean?

In Chapter 3, we made reference to Willmott's (1998) discussion of what he has termed a 'new sensibility' within organization theory. What Willmott was specifically alluding to in this respect was the emergence, within the writings of Cooper and Chia in particular, of what he considers to be an increasingly evident concern with reflexivity, that is, in the problematizing of the 'taken for granted' when talking about and studying organizations. It is within this context, then, that he attempts to articulate the emergence of a sensibility that is shaped by a process of 're-cognizing the Other', with the Other in this instance referring to the 'expression of reflexivity' (Willmott, 1998: 234). Reflexivity, previously subsumed under the dominant discourses associated with scientific objectivity and a realist conception of the world, is thus viewed as having been re-valorized, both by the impetus provided by a cultural disillusionment with the promise of the natural scientific vision *and* the rise of postmodernism *and* its adherents' quests to invert the hierarchical dualisms of modernist thought.

It would seem to us, however, that Willmott's conception of the process of re-cognizing the Other is an appropriate way also of understanding the range of developments we have alluded to in the first part of this book. For what postmodernism has brought to organization theory is an opening up of the range of ways of thinking about that which has previously been subsumed under the hierarchical modes of cognition that the Enlightenment left in its wake. Take, for example, the literature concerned with the notion of an emerging postmodernized mode of organization that we considered primarily in Chapter 2. In it we saw an apparent shift from, for example, the emphasis placed upon the primacy of the value of economy of scale, rigidity and differentiation in the division of labour and a dominance of the model of the instrumentally-motivated employee towards a (re)discovery, and valorization, of a range of Others such as smaller, more flexible units of production, the de-differentiation of functional roles and the cultural context within which employees find 'meaning' in their work.

At the meta-theoretical level, apart from a realization of the reflexive dimension of organizational analysis, a range of theoretical developments associated with postmodernism have equally demonstrated a re-cognition of previously excluded aspects of the lived experience and theoretical analysis of organizational life. Power, for example, a dimension of organizational life that, in mainstream organization theory at least, was for some time conveniently forgotten or legitimated through the concept of authority, has once again been brought to the foreground of much of the work in the field. The problem of the subject, for so long subsumed under the modernist conception of the organization as consisting of a series of objective structures and practices, offers yet another example. This is not to say, of course, that none of these concerns had not been addressed prior to the appearance of postmodernism within organization theory. Yet, they have all contributed to, and benefited from, this re-cognition of the Other that postmodernism has helped to bring into the public forum for consideration and debate.

Where do we go from here?

It would, however, be contrary to the spirit of this book simply to accept the potential contribution of postmodernism uncritically. Throughout the preceding Chapters we have, after all, been at pains to point out a number of criticisms that have been levelled at the postmodern turn within organization theory, as well as postmodernism more generally; criticisms to which we have, in the main, been generally sympathetic. In contrast to either a crude celebration of this apparent re-valorization of the Other, or an equally unsophisticated denouncement of it, what we feel needs to be explored is the dialectical nature of such developments, that is, how the re-cognition of the Other, within both the study and indeed management of organizations, opens up potential spaces for greater freedom and experi-mentation yet, at the same time, can equally elevate into view such spaces for those who may seek to appropriate or colonize them for the instru-mental pursuit of more pervasive modes of control and domination. In the following chapters, then, it is our intention to explore what we consider to be several related areas of interest within organization theory that we believe exemplify the playing out of such possible tensions.

PART 2

4

Organization, Postmodernism
and Culture

The last decade has seen the most concerted attempt to transform organizational culture since the rise of modern, bureaucratic organization. (Tuckman, 1994: 727)

He who has a *why* to live for can bear almost any *how*. (Nietzsche, cited in Peters and Waterman, 1982: 81 *original emphasis*).

Around the late 1970s, the concept of culture began to have a profound impact on the way many of us would come to think and write about work organizations. While not as novel a concern as many would have it, its subsequent ability to occupy the minds of an emergent breed of organization and management theorists has been significant to say the least.

Embraced by two seemingly distinct traditions within the field – on the one hand the emerging generation of management gurus and organizational troubleshooters (Deal and Kennedy, 1982; Ouchi, 1981; Peters and Waterman, 1982), who made their names during the early stages of this period, and, on the other, a more traditional academic community (Alvesson, 1990; Frost et al., 1985; Gagliardi, 1990; Meek, 1989; Pettigrew, 1979; Pondy et al., 1983; Turner, 1986) – culture was viewed by many within both camps as the new Holy Grail, one that would not only provide the key to a deeper understanding of life within organizations, but also unlock the door to unprecedented levels of organizational efficiency and productivity.

Thus, by the mid-1980s, the study of culture had emerged as one of the staple ingredients of both organization theory and management education. This was a state of affairs that led Turner, an early academic champion of the study of organizational culture and symbolism, to note, or perhaps even lament, that the 'little backwater' in which he once paddled 'had now been flooded and swept into the mainstream of debate and discussion'(1986: 102).

Yet why did this apparently sudden interest in the cultural dimension of organizational life occur when it did? In what ways have organization and managerial theorists tried to make sense of it, and how have their efforts shaped or re-shaped our understanding not only of organizations, but also of the relationship between organization, theory and critique? And perhaps more importantly, given the subject of this book, to what extent can we identify a range of postmodern themes within, and postmodern approaches to, the study of culture in organizations? These are questions that we aim to address in this chapter, questions that may hopefully provide a further insight into the relationship that has emerged between work, postmodernism and organization.

We consider, first, in its most general sense, the relationship between culture and organization, and the rise to prominence of this association over the past twenty years or so. We then go on to chart what we view as being four distinct research orientations, within which the convergence of culture and organization has been theorized. These range from what we have termed the corporate-functionalist, through the symbolic-interpretive and fragmentary-postmodernist, to the critical-emancipatory approach. In the penultimate section we then problematize such distinctions and see what lessons may be learned from them, before making a number of concluding observations about the relationship between the idea of the postmodern and the emergence of culture as an increasingly mainstream concern within organization theory.

Culture and organization theory

Raymond Williams (1976), as it has often been noted, considers the concept of culture to be perhaps one of the most contested in the English language. Within the social sciences in particular, this contestation has not been alleviated by the frequent prefixing of the term by a range of adjectives, each of which has been devised, or so it has been claimed, to contextualize more securely its usage and to convey some of the subtleties the term demands. Most notable among these are 'popular', 'mass' and, increasingly, 'media', with proponents of each often seeking to embrace aspects of the others in an attempt to claim a greater level of explanatory sophistication for their own chosen preference (see Fiske, 1989; Kellner, 1995; McRobbie, 1994). A similar situation also exists with regard to the use of the concept in organization theory, particularly in terms of understanding culture within organizations. Here we find several terms deployed, again often inter-changeably, each claiming for itself a subtlety of difference that can alter the meaning ascribed to it in any given context both by the author and the reader. While some, most notably Morgan (1997), have used the broad concept of culture as a metaphor for understanding organizational sys-tems, the two most frequently encountered approaches revolve around the concepts of corporate and organizational culture. While these are some-times used interchangeably, there is now an increasing tendency to make a clear conceptual distinction between the two.

Corporate culture is used largely to describe a set of cultural values, norms and their symbolic manifestations, devised by management and transmit-ted, both formally and informally, to the rest of the workforce (Turner, 1990). Usually this is undertaken with a view to achieving enhanced levels of efficiency and productivity through an intensified cultural identification with the organization and its professed values. Underpinning this partic-ular approach is the belief that the 'strengthening' of corporate culture may enhance organizational performance by securing an augmented com-mitment to the organization (see Schein, 1985). As Willmott (1993: 516) has put it, the abiding concern of corporate culturalism 'is to win the "hearts and minds" of employees; to define their purposes by managing what they think and feel, and not just how they behave', and is seen as crucial to securing 'beyond contract' (Fox, 1974) identification with the organization and its goals.

In contrast, *organizational culture*, is used generally to refer to the more organic nature of organizational life, one that grows or emerges from the lived experience of organizations and which 'emphasizes the creativity of organizational members as culture makers, perhaps resisting or ironically evaluating the dominant culture' (Linstead and Grafton-Small, 1992: 333). Here, the emphasis is placed on shared meaning and the aggregation of cultural values which often transverse sub-cultures, accommodating cul-tural diversity by recognizing a commonality of forms whose precise meaning differs among individual members (Smircich, 1983). This latter concept also emphasizes that the emergence of culture is an essentially cre-ative process (Turner, 1990), and that this creativity is confined not only to the production of culture, but also to cultural consumption and the practice of 'organizational bricolage' (Linstead and Grafton-Small, 1992: 332), or cultural re-signification (see Hebdige, 1979). This means that the concept of organizational culture also recognizes the role played by members of organizations in actively interpreting and reappropriating cultural sym-bols, meanings, artifacts and so on, rather than conceiving of them simply as the passive consumers of corporate culture. In this sense, this contested distinction between corporate and organizational culture also parallels the social sciences' distinction between cultural transmission and reception. Parker (2000a), in his extensive empirical study of the cultural environ-ments of three work organizations problematizes this distinction by combining an interpretive research strategy with a dialectical 'critical hermeneutic' (2000a: 91) that looks at how organizational cultures can be understood as 'fragmented unities' (2000a: 5). He argues that they must be understood as consisting of localized struggles for power and meaning, which are also embedded within 'generalizable "structural pressures"' that both ordinary organizational employees, and those given responsibility for directing organizational culture must respond to and adapt within.

Nevertheless, it is perhaps fair to continue to assert that, generally speaking, corporate culture is understood to be something that organizations *have* and, as such, can be manipulated and refined through astute and planned managerial intervention, while organizational culture is considered to be more descriptive of what an organization fundamentally *is*; that is, the emergent outcome of a group of individuals partaking in shared and, usually, co-operative social relations. Yet this dualism is deceptive in another way, in that what we are identifying as corporate culturalism is essentially predicated on the idea that organizational cultures exist as phenomena that can be studied and assessed in terms of their congruence with a range of external imperatives – most obviously, efficiency and maximized productivity. Thus, organizational cultures provide the building blocks upon which more 'appropriate' corporate cultures can be erected (a theme revisited later in this chapter).

A third and related term that we shall also encounter is that of *organizational symbolism*. While the term is often deployed among academic authors as a synonym for corporate or organizational culture, and has since largely been subsumed particularly under the latter, the specific meaning of the term does require some clarification. Generally, organizational symbolism can be seen to refer to the specific manifestations of communal or individually held values and beliefs, usually in the form of artifacts, verbal utterances or behaviours. While, as Alvesson and Berg note, such symbols may represent the expression of a particular organizational culture, they can equally signify 'more limited phenomena without introducing the totality which culture constitutes into the picture'(1992: 85). Furthermore, as with regard to the concept of 'culture', an interest in organizational symbolism can be seen to be expressive of differing concerns. A theoretical concern with symbolism, for example, may focus on understanding how organizations comprise symbolic expressions of shared, or indeed highly localized, meanings and understandings, held subjectively by some or all of the members of a given organization. Alternatively, akin to the principles often seen to underpin the corporate culture orientation, symbols may be viewed as variables with meanings that can be defined and re-defined, usually by management, in the service of greater levels of organizational coherence and collective endeavour. Finally, a critical combination of the two can produce a more radical approach, one that seeks to uncover how symbols act as carriers of particular ideologies, reinforcing organizational relations of power and domination.

Despite the apparent complexities in defining just what it is we mean by the term culture when applied to the organizational context, the fact that so much of the current literature abounds with 'culture-speak', especially that directed at promoting organizational competitiveness, suggests that it is a phenomenon that is deserving of serious scrutiny, albeit in the face of the knowledge that definitive answers to the questions we may ask are unlikely to be forthcoming.

The turn to culture

One question that seems almost inevitable is 'what is it about this current historical juncture that has proved so favourable to the apparent popularization of the cultural dimension of organization life?' For Parker (2000a: 9, 2000b: 126), the starting point for the contemporary 'cultural turn' within organization theory is to be found in 1979, with a conference that was held at the University of Champaign-Urbana on the topic of organizational culture, and the publication of Pettigrew's (1979) article 'On Studying Organizational Cultures'. These events were quickly followed by the subsequent publication of a series of best-selling and largely managerial-orientated texts on how to transform one's organization by 'managing its culture' (Deal and Kennedy, 1982; Ouchi, 1981; Peters and Waterman, 1982). Yet, as Parker (2000a, 2000b) has also noted, it is a debatable point as to whether this signified the emergence of anything particularly novel. For him, culture, and its importance to organizational design and management can be seen to have been evident at the very birth of modern organizational forms, as well as being evident throughout the evolution of organization theory. Citing Taska (1992), for example, he argues that even in the work of Taylor (1911), which for so many has come to epitomize the modernist prioritization of the manipulation of objective and quantifiable factors of production, a concern with the cultural and therefore subjective dimension of workplace relations was already clearly present. For Taska, this was most evident in Taylor's attempt to promote a convergent culture of interest between management and workers through the eradication of informal communicative networks on the shopfloor and the dissolution of any form of workforce sub-culture. Thus, pre-empting the gurus of management excellence by some seventy years, Taylor appears, in Taska's mind at least, to have recognized the need to promote a 'strong' corporate culture as integral to any endeavour to prescribe the conditions under which a maximization of employee productivity and efficiency could be realized. Nevertheless, despite such reservations about the originality of the recent cultural turn within the discipline, there can be no doubt that, to invoke Parker's (2000a: 1) argument once again, there was a subsequent 'explosion of enthusiasm' for the subject from 1979–80 onwards.

One possible reason for the emergence of *culture* as a more explicit concern for both organization theorists and management practitioners alike at this time was the structural re-configuration of the global marketplace and the concomitant rise to prominence of the economies of the Pacific Rim, especially Japan (Frost et al., 1985; Payne, 1991). Certainly, one outcome of this was a desperate search by the leaders of western industry to identify just what it was about such economies, and the organizations that under-pinned them, that appeared to render them so much more competitive than their western rivals. One possible answer to this question seems to have been that of cultural management. That is to say, it appeared that what was making particularly Japanese corporations so successful was a combination of innovative modes of post-bureaucratic organizing, com-bined with an ability to nurture a far greater level of cultural commitment among their workforces. With regard to the organizational processes that western management sought to emulate, these include many of the prac-tices we have already encountered in our discussion of postmodernized organizational forms in Chapter 2, such as the introduction of de-differen-tiated regimes of flexible specialization, just-in-time stock control systems and a commitment to 'total quality' practices.

Of equal significance, however, was the perceived need to parallel the cultural climate generated by these far eastern competitors. Flexible, total quality-orientated working practices, it was suggested (Mulgan, 1989; Murray, 1989a), equally required a new breed of flexible, yet deeply com-mitted, employees if they were to be successful post-Fordist, or even 'postmodern', organizations. This realization, exemplified in what has been termed the 'excellence literature' of writers such as, among many, Ouchi (1981), Peters and Waterman (1982), Peters (1989), Kanter (1989) and more recently Harris (1996), resulted in the message that for western work organizations to compete successfully in a global marketplace, get-ting its corporate culture 'right' was essential, that is, a corporate culture which valued the apparently unique contribution of each employee while at one and the same time, tied them into a corporate community based on an ethos of excellence, quality and commitment. The modernist experi-ment based on rigidly controlled production processes and labour practices was thus presented as an obsolete approach to the organization of work. Flexibility, diversity and empowerment were to be the new watch-words of the organizations of the future, if indeed western industry was to have any future at all.

Yet while this can be seen to offer one possible link between the per-ceived need to facilitate new modes of production and distribution, perhaps associated with some kind of process of organizational postmod-ernization, with the expansion of a managerial interest in questions of culture, the relationship between the idea of the postmodern and the cul-tural turn in organization theory can be seen to run even deeper. As Willmott puts it:

> This identification of employees with the company and its products exemplifies a de-differentiation of economy and culture – an overcoming of the division between the 'personal life', values and beliefs of employees and the impersonal demands of corporations for greater productivity and quality. (1992: 63)

Thus, the postmodern theme of de-differentiation encountered earlier can be seen to have pervaded the work organization through the strategies of cultural management associated with post-bureaucratization or post-Fordism more generally. The old boundaries and hierarchies of organizational life, on the surface at least, Willmott suggests, are viewed as impediments to organizational growth and competitive performance, with the differentiation principle of modernity no longer seen as appropriate to a changing global environment. Furthermore, Willmott also notes how many of the terms and approaches suggested by such writers, focusing as they do on values and ideas such as 'indeterminacy, play and chance' (Willmott, 1992: 62), also suggest a postmodern-flavoured renunciation of the rational, calculating rhetoric of more traditionally modernist modes of management. An excellent culture is not, this suggests, one that is con-strained by the 'one best way' of Taylorism, but is free to fly and be creative. For example, in books such as Pascale and Athos's *The Art of Japanese Management* (1981) and Peters and Waterman's *In Search of Excellence* (1982), this retreat from formal rationality is, at the very least, implicit in their advocation of the importance of such 'unscientific' efforts as, say, the devel-opment of shared, normative values and the nurturing of organizational idiosyncrasies, a point not lost on the likes of critical sociologists such as Harlow and Hearn, who note how culture 'has been said to add something a little "softer" and "less tangible" to the otherwise hard and rationalistic understanding of organizations' (1995: 180). In this sense, then, the lan-guage of the management guru can, we would suggest, be seen both to reflect and, in part, to constitute the more general cultural sensibilities evi-dent within what appears to be an emerging postmodern *zeitgeist*.

The relative explosion in this largely practitioner-orientated body of lit-erature on organizational culture has also been paralleled, however, by the development of an extensive body of research and writing on the sub-ject within the domain of more traditional academic journals and texts. As Alvesson and Berg (1992) have noted, one possible explanation for this aspect of the popularization of the idea of culture in organizations is an increased market for such ideas among managerial practitioners and, per-haps more importantly, organizations prepared to fund such research in the hope of unearthing ways of exploiting more effectively their own 'cul-tural capital'.[1] Furthermore, the influence of postmodernism and other less mainstream approaches to theory and research have also, it must be acknowledged, provided a form of legitimacy for the emergence of more interpretive approaches to understanding organizational life (see Chapter 3), approaches that have often been championed for offering far greater insights into the deeper workings of organizations, overcoming the ten-dency of traditional approaches to reify organizational life, excluding the human component and the activities of sensemaking that are seen as cen-tral to the ongoing process of organization itself.

In this sense, the increasing concern with questions of organizational cul-ture can also be seen to be reflective of a broader cultural shift within the social sciences *per se*, one that, if not 'strictly' postmodern, has certainly been influenced by the post-Enlightenment critique of various strands of positivism and the turn to a more hermeneutic sensibility arising from the collapse of previously secure boundaries between the social sciences and the humanities. Thus, academic groups such as the Standing Conference on Organizational Symbolism (SCOS) have been at the forefront of introducing new concerns and research approaches to the realm of organization theory, ranging from investigations into issues such as organizational aesthetics to the development of novel and innovative ways of promoting academic exchange and collaboration, all of which have often been accompanied by a more than cursory nod in the direction of various postmodern strands of thinking and practice.

This is not to suggest, however, that anything like a unified approach to the study of culture and symbolism within organizations has emerged during this period, a point illustrated by the fact that a significant proportion of the relevant literature focuses more on the differing approaches to the subject than it does on the study of culture *per se*. Nevertheless, such diversity is in itself perhaps indicative of the relative fragmentation of the field, a state of affairs that suggests a postmodernization process by which the dominance of any single theoretical narrative no longer tenable. Furthermore, such diversity remains important in that it has provided space within which a number of interesting issues, particularly those of culture and its relationship to issues of power and domination within work organizations, have found expression. In the following section, therefore, we intend to explore and consider critically some of these various 'research orientations' to the study of organizational culture, noting along the way not only how they illustrate some of the problems that have arisen from the cultural turn within organization theory, but also how they may suggest further important areas of overlap between the current concern with culture within organizations and the more general influence of postmodern ideas.

Research orientations and organizational culture

In the beginning of this chapter we outlined the popular distinction between the concepts of 'organizational' and 'corporate' culture. While such a bifurcation is undoubtedly a useful means of distinguishing between divergent approaches to the subject of culture within organizations, it does not, however, tell the whole story. For, as we have noted, even in the relatively short period of time within which the issue of culture within organizations has come to the fore, a range of different research orientations and agendas has emerged, each bringing with it its own set of philosophical and even political presuppositions. Smircich (1983), for example, refers to the existence of what she terms 'functionalist' and 'interpretive' approaches, while Golden (1992) expands the list to three with the terms 'homogeneous', 'heterogeneous' and 'ambiguous' which are used to describe the varying approaches. Others, such as Meek (1989) and Martin (1992), have also identified what they consider to be distinctive research orientations to the study of culture and symbolism, along very similar lines.

While interesting in their own right, what is perhaps more important, however, as we have just noted, are the ways in which such approaches demonstrate not only significant levels of overlap, but also some of the tensions that exist between the categories of organizational and corporate culture and the influence of postmodernism on both. In this section, therefore, what we try to do is outline what we think are the main characteristics of these various orientations, while at the same time considering how they have contributed not only to the ways in which culture has been conceptualized within organization theory, but also the tensions they generate in and through the act of defining the realties they purport to study.

Corporate-functionalist

What has broadly been termed the functionalist approach (Smircich, 1983) to understanding culture within organizations, is based on the idea that culture is something that can usually be characterized by a condition of 'consensus, consistency, and clarity' (Martin, 1992: 45). Essentially adherents to this approach hold to a somewhat monolithic view, according to which culture is conceived of as functioning as a unifying force or normative 'glue' that holds together different components of an organization together, and maintains organizational equilibrium. This model of culture is illustrated by Schein, for example, who believes that 'what makes it possible for people to function comfortably with each other and to concentrate on their primary tasks is a high degree of consensus' (1985: 83). He continues, 'if such consensus does not exist, it is questionable whether the group has any culture at all' (1985: 93). This is a view that is also echoed by Jaques's assessment of factory culture as 'its customary and traditional way of thinking and of doing things, which is shared . . . by all its members, and which new members must learn, and partially accept, in order to be accepted into service in the firm' (1951: 251). As such, it would appear that what we are dealing with from a functionalist viewpoint is a conception of culture akin to what we have identified above as 'organizational' culture. That is a genuine expression of shared norms and values that evolve from shared experiences and understandings among employees.

However, despite this initial appearance, what we would argue is that on closer inspection we can see how it has also provided the foundations for the development of what has been identified as corporate culturalism. For as we noted above, this approach is premised on the belief that organizational culture is an objective phenomenon, susceptible to managerial control and change and, as such, culture is something managers must 'learn' about in order to seek to engender the 'right' cultural climate within which productivity and efficiency can flourish (see Pheysey, 1993). By portraying culture as something that 'functions' within the organization as a mechanism of stability and equilibrium, the functionalist approach opens the possibility of seeing culture as something that can be designed and manipulated – usually by managers – through the application of techniques or technologies conducive to what has been determined as the organizational plan or mission.

The clearest and most obvious expression of this fusing of functionalist and corporate culturalist values can be found in the kinds of excellence and culturalist literature we referred to earlier. As Alvesson (1991: 217) notes in this regard, a functionalist approach to the study of culture in organizations tends to proceed 'from an ideology of managerialism' that views culture as a strategic variable and believes that 'strong cultures make for success' by raising corporate consciousness to the importance of creating and sustaining a culture uniquely suited to the managerially-determined goals of the organization. From this combination of functionalism and corporate culturalism, then, 'good' management is about fostering such functionally 'strong' corporate cultures (Denison, 1990). Managers are exhorted to view cultural management as a core activity, as something that must be understood as within their direct remit of intervention and control. This combination of a functional imperative and a culturalist orientation is summed up well by Conner, for example, who in his treatise on managing organizational change boldly emphasizes the message that a 'key element to enhancing resilience and minimizing the chance of *dysfunctional* behaviour is to *actively manage* your organization's culture' (1992: 173 *emphasis added*).

Culture, as both an implicit dimension of organizational life and as a 'strategic variable' (see, for example, Revenaugh, 1994), is therefore conflated into a knowable and manipulable package, open to systematic analysis and control. Thus, much of the 'culturalist' literature focuses specifically on culture as it relates to organizational effectiveness (Kilmann et al., 1985) and corporate performance (Gordon, 1992), to person–organization fit (Sheridan, 1992), and particularly to an organization's financial performance (Denison, 1990). It suggests that culture can, and indeed should, be managed to serve organizational interests, often by minimizing the possibility of dysfunctional activity and promoting more functional behaviours, based on the recognition that 'members become attached to their organizations when they incorporate the characteristics they attribute to their organization into their self-concepts' (Dutton et al., 1994: 241–2). Organizational culture is thus transmogrified into a functionalist corporate culture through 'the desire to bind employees' hearts and minds to the corporate interest' (Kunda, 1991: 220), the aim being to produce a culture that is so 'strong' that the boundaries individuals typically maintain between the organization and themselves tend to collapse, resulting in a condition of 'organizational identification' (Dutton et al., 1994) or 'mutuality' (Walton, 1985). This is a process illustrated well in Hochschild's (1997) account of the ways in which an American corporation that she refers to as Amerco sought to manage its corporate culture:

> Amerco has proved to be a creative engineer of workplace culture, improving the motivation and commitment of its workers and assuring their consent to the company's mix of strategies for success in global competition. The centerpiece of the company's plan, set in place in 1983, was a work system know as Total Quality. Instead of bureaucratic control, simplified jobs, and a many-tiered hierarchy, Amerco began to emphasize autonomous hierarchical structure. The aim of this was to create more knowledgeable and company-identified workers who would be invited to share with its managers a 'common vision' of company goals and to talk over ways to implement it. (Hochschild, 1997: 17)

Yet having raised this issue in this way, as we have pointed out, it is also possible to identify much within the material on corporate culture that also bears a striking resemblance to the language and themes encountered within the broader theoretical literature on postmodernism. Dandridge (1986), for example, combines a call for the diminishing of distinctions between the categories of work and play to be introduced into everyday organizational practices while, at the same time, stressing its '*functional benefits*' for issues of employee performance and productivity. This problematizes, therefore, the idea that one can neatly conflate the concept of corporate culture into a broadly functionalist (modernist) framework if one wishes to understand the distinction between work and play as itself a distinctively modern dualism. For if this is the case, can this not be seen as a distinctively postmodern approach to managing work organizations, breaking down the old, modernist categories and embracing the realm of, if not the irrational, then certainly an alternative rationality? That said, we intend to return to this particular question at a later stage in the chapter, providing as it does the impetus for much of the more critical work that has been carried out on the question of organizational culture, concerned as it is with the possibly negative implications of the functionalist-corporatist paradigm. For now, though, let us turn our attention to the second of the orientations we wish to address, namely the 'symbolic-interpretive'.

Symbolic-interpretive

A symbolic-interpretive orientation to organizational culture posits a very different starting point for its investigations than its corporatist-functionalist counterpart. Rather than treating cultures as somehow given and objective, its adherents view culture as a deeply subjective phenomenon. That is to say, cultures are seen as the expression of their members' lived and inter-subjective experiences of everyday organizational life – 'the product of shared symbols and meanings' as Meek (1989: 463) puts it, symbols and meanings that require description and interpretation rather than attempts to quantify and control them. In many respects this represents an example of the interpretive turn deriving particularly from the work of Silverman (1970), alluded to in Chapter 3, a turn that rejects the more objectivist underpinnings of a systemic corporate-functionalist approach in favour of a heightened sensitivity to the ways in which organization is itself an accomplishment of human agency. Smircich in particular emphasizes this when she argues that a symbolic-interpretive approach

> promotes a view of organizations as expressive forms, manifestations of human consciousness. Organizations are understood and analyzed not mainly in economic or material terms, but in terms of their expressive, ideational, and symbolic aspects. Characterized very broadly, the research agenda stemming from this perspective is to explore the phenomenon of organization as subjective experience. (1983: 347–8).

Drawing on the work of sociologists and anthropologists such as Garfinkel (1967) and Geertz (1973), this approach has led to what Morgan (1997: 141) has referred to as an 'enactment view of culture' that seeks to uncover the processes that 'produce systems of shared meaning'.

An important dimension of this symbolic-interpretive approach, as indeed the name suggests, has been a concern with the study of organizational symbolism (Alvesson and Berg, 1992; Jones, 1996; Turner, 1986, 1990). Symbolism in this respect is viewed as a means by which subjective meanings can be accessed and interpreted – as the windows of the very soul of the organization – permeating every dimension of organizational life.[2] This is a case made particularly strongly by Turner when he declares:

> Every organization is a jungle of symbols – symbolic fields, symbolic acts and symbolic games. All of life, inside or outside of organizations, is symbolic, even the biological process of transmitting heredity information from one generation to another. Communication between individual human beings is a symbolic process, and all culture is predicated upon symbolic interaction. (1992: 62)

This is not to say that, as Alvesson and Berg (1992) point out, all those interested in organizational symbolism necessarily believe in the existence of unified organizational cultures or symbolic orders. Rather, symbolic systems may equally indicate the existence of individual or sub-cultural sets of meanings, ones that often come into conflict with each other, indicating a state of cultural heterogeneity rather than cultural homogeneity.[3] Furthermore, the symbolic-interpretivist approach recognizes the relatively unfinished business that is organization. That is, the idea that sensemaking processes within organizations are ongoing and fluid activities, resistant to simple attempts to impose values that are implicitly external to the life-world of those members who inhabit them. It is this possibility that leads Turner to note how an expanded understanding of the creative role of 'culture makers' within organizations may lead to the possibility 'of moving beyond technical and practical interests to interests which might have an emancipatory quality' (Turner, 1990: 95). It provides, therefore, what may be seen as a critical dimension to the study of everyday organizational realities, a dimension that resists the imposition of imperatives or narrative frameworks considered hostile to the generation of inter-subjective value systems and their symbolic expression.

While admittedly such an approach as this can be seen to break in a number of significant respects from the concerns of a corporate-functionalist orientation, most notably in terms of its ontological commitment to a meaning-constitutive view of organizational reality and its rejection of an objectivist approach to its study, it would be fallacious to suggest that such a break is of a wholesale nature. We say this because, while the symbolic-interpretive approach can be valorized in terms of its less instrumental orientation to questions of organizational culture, this has not prevented the methods and insights associated with it from being incorporated into a more corporate-functionalist agenda. Gagliardi (1986), for example, discusses the process of symbolic management and how it can lead to a more effective promotion of cultural change within organizations. Payne (1991: 28) reminds human resource managers that one of the key tasks in establishing and promoting a 'new' corporate culture is 'the establishment of rites and myths and the building of physical and written artifacts'. Indeed, one only has to glance briefly at the literature associated with strategies of cultural management to see that it abounds with talk of symbolic manipulation, and that it demonstrates a clear insight into the importance of managers being able to interpret accurately the meanings that are given to symbolic and cultural forms by the employees towards whom their activities are directed. The interpretation of cultural symbols is not, then, a necessarily neutral act. Rather, the question of who is doing the interpretation, and to what ends, becomes important. As Alvesson and Berg note in this regard, while a concern with organizational symbolism might be pursued in terms of a dispassionate pursuit of knowledge, it can also

> provide a formula through which the nonconscious in organizational life might be turned into the conscious (of managers) and the field of values and norms comes under the control of management, thereby improving the 'rationality' of managerial action and of what is going on in organizations. (1992: 41)

The potential for a concern with organizational symbolism to be utilized in the service of promoting a greater degree of cultural functionality is not, however, the only continuity it shares with a more corporate-functionalist orientation and, indeed, an apparently modernist approach to the study of organizational culture. For, as is the case with the more general interpretivist turn within organization theory discussed in Chapter 3, there remains embedded within its particular philosophical worldview a continued commitment to a distinctively realist conception of organizations. For while its proponents defend the proposition that social and cultural reality is manifest in and through processes of symbolic exchange, and the meanings individuals ascribe to such symbols, they hold to the idea that such manifestations can be apprehended, and indeed interpreted in some form, so as to provide 'firsthand knowledge' (Jones, 1996: 13) of what is really going on within organizations. That is, from this perspective, symbols are seen to provide an insight into what employees really think and feel and, in turn, into de-mystifying the subjective dimension of organizational life.

Where debates do arise, it is not so much over questions of the ontological stature of the symbolic domain, but rather the methodological strategies by which such a reality may be 'apprehended, transposed and reconstituted' (Jeffcutt, 1993: 27). According to Jeffcutt, this has, in turn, perpetuated a process whereby discourses surrounding organizational symbolism have been transformed into little more than commodities that can be exchanged in the academic- and practitioner-orientated marketplaces. Thus, the often radical intent behind such strategies, radical in that they sought to question the instrumentality of the more corporate-functionalist orientation, can be seen from this perspective to have been at the very least marginalized by the very forces they were initially designed to contest, a situation which, certainly in part, has fuelled the development of an alternative approach to the study of organizational culture and symbolism, one that seeks to resist the persuasive logic of modernist social science and the demands of the academic market.

Fragmentary-postmodernist

As we have observed on more than one occasion now, perhaps one of the defining features of a postmodern sensibility is an overriding concern with the increasing role of culture in shaping and defining the nature of social relations.[4] Indeed, for many, culture has itself been, perhaps irrevocably, postmodernized. Dunn (1991: 119), for example, identifies contemporary culture – shaped by aesthetic plurality, ambiguity, a decline of seriousness and a corresponding elevation of play – as 'a hallmark of postmodern practice'. In this context, then, it is unsurprising that the relationship between the idea of the postmodern, both as a meta-theoretical and a periodizing concept, should have been brought to bear on the study of culture within organizations, exerting a significant influence on how organizational culture has come to be understood.

In many ways, however, the emergence of a postmodern approach to understanding and studying organizational culture is not entirely novel, developing as it does many of its basic propositions through an engagement with what a number of its proponents view as the limitations of the symbolic-interpretive perspective. As we noted above, for Jeffcutt (1993), the issue at stake here is the way in which both the symbolic-interpretive and corporate-functionalist approaches share a commitment to establishing a definitive understanding or 'last-word' on the nature of organizational reality through a process of closure, one that privileges 'particular readings and voices while suppressing and denying alternative articulations' (1993: 38). A genuinely postmodern approach therefore, for Jeffcutt at least, would be one that problematizes such boundaries, that seeks to uncover the organizing processes that valorize particular views over others, and that 'seeks to articulate the polyphonic diversity and transience of our everyday organizational lives' (Jeffcutt, 1993: 47).

For Martin (1992), this approach can perhaps best be understood as one that recognizes the centrality of fragmentation. That is, it acknowledges that while organizational cultures exist as a legitimate object of study, any attempt at final closure, at grasping any such culture in its totality, is doomed to failure. Thus, as an approach, postmodernism rejects the idea that we can ever lay claim to a true or definitive interpretation of what, say, a symbol represents in terms of an essential value system or cultural configuration. Rather, it takes the view that organizations comprise a multiplicity of different values and cultural forms – each of which, in itself, may express a whole series of fragmented meanings and be open to multiple interpretations. Furthermore, through the act of interpretation researchers are themselves active in defining and indeed closing off, in many instances, particular models of organizational reality.

While such radical reflexivity may be viewed as a problem by some (see Chapter 3), for others it represents a major opportunity. Viewing the study of culture as a means to open up and explore entirely new ways of understanding organizations, some organization theorists, inspired by the idea of the postmodern, have argued that it is precisely the unconventionality of a postmodernist approach to studying organizational culture and symbolism that is its greatest virtue (Turner, 1990). Cálas and Smircich (1997) have argued, for example, that in the face of what they see as a dominant body of largely functionalist and corporatist literature on organizational culture, postmodernism offers a basis for a strategy of resistance, one that employs the meta-theoretical insights of postmodernism to undertake a continuous deconstruction of the ways in which organizations and the processes of organizing are represented, and therefore constituted, in and through the dominant literature. Thus, instead of aiming to rally and order its forces, even to a strategy of 'opposition', such an approach should celebrate and embrace flux and indeterminacy rather than seeking to impose order and meaning onto its own activities. Similarly, Manning (1992) considers that the insights afforded by postmodernism offer an opportunity to launch an investigation into the gaps, differences, dilemmas, paradoxes and ambiguities encountered in the everyday experience of work organizations, while Morgan (1993: xvii) invites us to 'imaginize' organizations: 'to become accomplished in using metaphor to find new ways of seeing, understanding, and shaping' organizations.

Deploying such an approach, one that emphasizes the existence of a multiplicity or plurality of 'truths', Boje (1991, 1995) in particular calls for an approach to organization theory that focuses on the linguistic qualities of human organizations. He argues that 'organizations cannot be registered as one story, but instead are a multiplicity, a plurality of stories and story interpretations in struggle with one another' (Boje, 1995: 1001). In his critical analysis of the Walt Disney corporation as a 'storytelling organization', for example, he undertakes a deconstructive analysis of multiple organi-zational discourses in an attempt to reveal marginalized voices and their stories. His use of postmodernist analysis aims, then, to re-situate these excluded stories and voices, and to analyse their relationship to what he views as the dominant legend of an official, happy and profitable Disney.

In this respect, the work of postmodern organizational theorists of cul-ture has also been particularly useful in contributing to bridging the humanities – social sciences divide in organizational analysis, not least by bringing literary categories and aesthetic concerns to bear on organiza-tional issues (Gagliardi, 1990; Strati, 1999), and deconstructing organizations as cultural texts (Kilduff, 1993; see also Martin, 1990; Mumby and Putnam, 1992). This approach, one that suggests the possible emer-gence of a radicalized postmodern study of organizational cultures, challenges the legitimacy of natural scientific methodology and, for exam-ple, encourages the use of novels, plays, poetry and films in the study of organizations. In doing so it emphasizes that, in contrast to the method-ological principles and practices of positivism, various forms of narrative fiction provide 'an indispensable approach to strengthening the connection between organizational analysis as an academic discipline and the subjec-tive experience of organizational membership' (Phillips, 1995: 625).

Adopting such an approach, for example, Goodall (1994) draws on auto-biographical techniques in his exposition of 'organizational detective as cultural ethnographer', by fusing Raymond Chandler-style narrative with ethnographic fieldwork, while Easton and Araujo similarly advocate the treatment of 'written reflections on the process of management, what we are normally pleased to call theory, as literature' (1997: 99). In his post-modernist-inspired account of organization, Jeffcuttx also focuses on 'the interrelationship of organization and text', for instance, in terms of 'prac-titioner tales of quests that seek to achieve corporate success in the face of threats from both within (inefficiency) and without (competition)' (1994: 248), bringing in turn a greater sensitivity to the more poetic side of orga-nizational life.

Nevertheless, while a focus on postmodernism as indicative of a partic-ular orientation to research is our main concern in this section, we must not forget the point that, for many, the importance currently placed on issues of culture by managers and academics alike can also be seen to indicate an evolving process of organizational postmodernization. Particularly, this view tends to emphasize the potentially democratic and liberatory char-acter of the choices that are available to members of postmodern cultures in which 'flexibility and innovation are crucial' (Dent, 1995: 878), or in which new possibilities have opened up for the emergence of new forms of organizational communities in which both the unity and difference of their members is respected and nurtured (Parker, 1998). What such approaches claim, then, to a lesser or greater extent, is that what is now important is the emergence of hitherto unprecedented opportunities for cultural self-deter-mination, lifestyle exploration and ultimately the scope for constructing multiple organizational identities. Such opportunities, they claim, can be realized from the huge number of options available to members of the postmodern organization. Where postmodern practices are seen to be characterized by a shift from differentiation and functional hierarchy to de-differentiation and flexibility, culture is embraced as the bond that can replace the rulebook as the primary mechanism for generating organizational cohesiveness, a cohesiveness, however, that is also viewed as offering far greater scope for the individual employee to pursue a project of greater autonomy and personal self-development as he or she learns to live with, and respond to, continual change as the norm (Bergquist, 1993).

The characteristics of cultural fluidity, flexibility, de-differentiation and indeterminacy are therefore taken as what can be seen as representative, at least in part, of a fragmented postmodernized organizational condition. In this sense, as Dent has put it, 'what is distinct about the current postmodern discourse is the growing tendency to equate ontological uncertainty with organizational flexibility' (1995: 877). Often this is itself celebrated in that it is considered to be more indeterminate, more differentiated, more chaotic, than it is simple, systematic, monological, and hierarchical. It is indicative of a rejection of the systemic, functional and essentially repressive cultural forms of modernity. That is not to suggest, however, that this should be considered a universal phenomenon. Some of those who emphasize the potentially liberating impact of the evolution of a postmodern organizational culture suggest specifically that cultural ambiguity is more apt to be prevalent in certain types of organizational setting, such as in organizations that encourage creativity, in turn demanding high levels of flexibility. Or, more traditionally, those professional occupations that have long respected the need to encourage and facilitate high levels of responsible autonomy among their members. Such organizations are considered to be more open to the kinds of postmodernizing process we have discussed here and in earlier chapters, and are more tolerant and indeed often encouraging of individual idiosyncrasies, non-rationalized aspects of organizational behaviour and the open expression of motivational factors that derive from non-traditional workplace activities.[5]

To what extent, however, does this celebratory rhetoric match the reality of corporate life? Taking, for example, the managerial strategy that has been termed the 'management of diversity' (Chemers et al., 1995) – currently promoted as a new approach to equal opportunities, particularly in the USA (Greensdale, 1991) – this appears at first sight positively to exude certain 'postmodern' cultural values, such as a more positive valuation of difference and cultural plurality. Advocates of 'managing diversity' argue that far from pretending workplace differences do not exist, managers should be trying to manage and value diversity, an approach based largely on a rejection of the liberal-humanist principle of 'equality' which treats 'like as like' (Liff and Wajcman, 1996). Various corresponding organizational and individual benefits are seen to derive from incorporating diverse perspectives and approaches into organizational life which, it is argued, should be nurtured and rewarded rather than suppressed and denied. In this sense, 'managing diversity' could perhaps be understood best as the idea that 'diversity encourages creativity, while repetition anesthetizes it' (Kroll, 1987: 29) – the management equivalent of Lyotard's (1984) end of metanarratives thesis and his call for a more pluralistic politics of difference – through which the totalizing logic of modernist organization is challenged and eventually laid to rest.

On closer inspection, however, the rhetoric of the valorization of difference, albeit within a unified organizational framework, seems to underpin more of a belief that traditionally marginalized groups can bring previously unrealized strengths to a workforce and help organizations maintain their competitive edge. This is a view that leads Starkey (1998: 127), for example, to conclude that 'the managerial skill here is to enquire into and harmonize diversity to overcome the dangers of the possible polarization of different interests'. Thus, the basic premise at play here appears to be that 'rather than being rejected, difference should be managed effectively' (Liff and Wajcman, 1996), representing, as it does, yet another potential resource to be exploited in the service of organizational competitiveness and performativity. The instrumental rationality of modernity is thus, or so it would seem, far from dead.

Despite its apparently emancipatory pretensions, therefore, it could be argued that even where the pluralist ethos of postmodernism is brought to bear on organizations, albeit perhaps implicitly, such as in the discourses surrounding the management of diversity, this does not necessarily signify a break with the functionalist imperatives of corporate culturalism discussed earlier. As such, it would seem that the systemic modernist tendency to reduce culture, be it postmodernized or not, to a strategic variable continues to underpin a range of insights and approaches to the issue, despite the often anti-systemic intent of those deploying them. In the penultimate section of this chapter, however, we want to consider the fourth and final example of the research orientations we have identified, one underpinned by a specifically critical reading of organizational culture and the role it plays in engendering greater levels of employee identification with, and conformity to, managerial expectations and priorities, an orientation we have termed critical-emancipatory.

Critical-emancipatory

While sharing many of the concerns of the less functionalist-orientated perspectives outlined above, what distinguishes the critical-emancipatory approach to the study of organizational or, more specifically, corporate culture, is an explicit concern with the ways in which forms of cultural management can be seen to legitimate unequal relations of power and control within organizations. While its roots lie in the radical approach to organization theory discussed earlier in the work of, say, Braverman (1974) and Burrell (1980), it has also more recently come to be identified with a more post-structuralist and even postmodern orientation, with questions of the relationship between corporate culture and employee subjectivity at the forefront of its concerns. Thus, while the critical-emancipatory approach draws on a number of traditions, it is unified by a normative denunciation of the ways in which corporate culture can be seen to tighten relations of control, through a repressive construction of obfuscatory and reified cultural discourses and forms, and, as Stablein and Nord put it, the ways in which the

> study of systems of meaning in human organizations could inform critical inquiry by revealing the unconscious assumptions and the institutionalized processes that, in Marxist jargon, lead human beings to be controlled by their own creations rather than to control them. (1985: 21)

Generally speaking, then, adherents of this approach share the concern expressed by Turner (1986: 112) that attempts to manage corporate culture 'threaten, potentially, to tamper with the most central aspects of our human-ness' and, as Willmott puts it,

> to situate the development and popularity of ideas and practices – such as those of corporate culturism – in the material and historical contexts of their emergence and application. . . . More specifically, critical analysis explores how, as a medium of domination, the scope and penetration of management control is, in principle, considerably extended by corporate culturism. (1993: 521)

On the basis of this critique, the management of culture in work organizations is generally perceived as a sometimes subtle, sometimes overt attempt to define, shape and monitor not only the work behaviour of employees – the traditional object of managerial control – but also their thoughts and feelings. Corporate culture is understood, then, as 'a form of false consciousness, or, more accurately, as a "consciousness restricting" set of ideas and beliefs, having primarily negative consequences . . . restricting autonomous and critical reflection' (Alvesson, 1991: 208–9). In particular, its adherents seek to avoid the functional determinism implicit in more instrumental orientations, placing a greater emphasis on discussion of the ethical issues involved in the use of symbolic management to increase employee tractability. Ray (1986), for example, is critical of the tendency of those who adopt a highly managerial view of the subject of culture for attempting to subjugate the individual to the collective in such a way as to raise moral objections to corporate culture claims and practices, the aims of which are commercial rather than humanistic. Similarly, Saffold (1988) observes how the issue of whether or not management may have the 'wrong' values and ideology, or that it might be unethical to counteract legitimate resistance to cultural manipulation, is rarely acknowledged in the excellence literature. Kunda (1991) reflects on his experiences in 'Tech', a company strongly committed to corporate culturism by asking the question:

Is it really a 'people-oriented company'? Is it a new type of iron cage? . . . Tech culture is not a prison and its managers are neither jailers nor tyrants in the simple sense of the word, but it does, nevertheless, represent a rather subtle form of domination, a 'culture trap' combining normative pressure with a deli-cate balance of seductiveness and coercion. (1991: 224)

While this approach sometimes seems to be preoccupied with revealing the social distortion of 'true' culture, a concern exemplified, for instance, by the Frankfurt School critique of a culturally-metastasizing instrumental rationality, and particularly by Habermas's (1972, 1984) focus on commu-nicative truth as opposed to what he terms 'systematically distorted communication', it also shares much in common with the postmodernist desire to oppose homogenizing accounts of organizational culture, a con-cern exemplified in the work of Cálas and Smircich. As such, the cultural values espoused by management gurus and the like are often viewed as little more than technologies of power, seeking to reconcile what in reality are highly divergent interests and priorities. While cultural heterogeneity is therefore often taken as the starting point for any such analysis, the pri-mary focus of attention is how the strategies and practices associated with corporate culturism seek to restrict, and indeed colonize, the possibility of such diversity.

One notable example of such an approach is Du Gay and Salaman's (1992: 621) analysis of the 'cult(ure) of the customer' in which they argue that 'by stipulating behavioural standards, installing new technologies of surveillance . . . associated with attempts to define and structure employ-ees' subjective meanings and identities', employers engage in a cultural project which might be likened to the process Laclau (1990: 56) terms 'hege-monic reconstruction'. In other words, the effects of cultural (and organizational) dislocation are understood to require the continuous con-struction of collectivities that rely increasingly on manufactured (organized) cultures. Corporate culturism in its various guises is therefore seen as an attempt to collapse distinctions between the inside and the out-side of organizations, and crucially between work and non-work phenomena such as time and space, to render these distinctions natural or, at least, pre-organizational, and then to reconcile these distinctions artifi-cially, as in the case of references to workplaces as 'communities' or as 'families', for instance.

In this respect, Du Gay and Salaman go on to argue that the governance of contemporary work organizations 'engages in controlled de-control' (1992: 625). In other words, to govern the contemporary work organization is both to 'individualize' and to 'totalize' (Foucault, 1977a, 1977b) through the same practices; or as management gurus Peters and Waterman have put it, 'to be simultaneously loose and tight' (1982: 318). Drawing on the ideas discussed in Chapter 3, therefore, corporate culture can be under-stood to constitute a particular form of 'governmental rationality' (Foucault, 1980), through which technologies of power and technologies of the self are merged imperceptibly, and through which otherwise apparent cultural contradictions, most notably between increasing managerial control and an apparent extension of individual autonomy and responsibility, are mediated.

Willmott's (1992, 1993) attempts to develop a critical understanding of cultural management within organizations has also combined the post-structuralist concern with the ways in which subjectivity is constituted in and through discursive technologies with a more Marxian-orientated form of ideology critique. In particular, he points to the ways in which postmodern motifs such as heterogeneity, flexibility and the indeterminacy of meaning have been incorporated into culturalist modes of control in an attempt to 'induce an internalization of norms and values selected by senior managers' (Alvesson and Willmott, 1996: 32). Casey (1995), in a similar vein, has drawn on her empirical case study of a major US manufacturing plant to argue that, in this instance, management increasingly seeks to introduce what she terms 'designer cultures' in an effort to re-order employees' subjectivity, or 'sense of self', as she puts it (1995: 5), in the face of new modes of production and organization and the effect they have on traditional patterns of workplace social solidarity.

This functionalization of culture as an explicit tool for the re-configuration of employee subjectivity is thus conceptualized in this context as a managerial strategy designed to produce what Barns (1991) has described as 'post-Fordist people', that is, employees whose very sense of self is operationalized within a particular configuration, one intimately in tune with the organizational imperatives that derive from the instrumental demands of new techniques of flexible production and workplace organization. This, for Willmott at least, leads to a critical assessment of the logic underpinning corporate culturalism in terms of it representing what he describes as a form of 'hypermodernism' in which 'a variety of "postmodernist" ploys are mobilized to sustain and extend a fundamentally modernist project' (Willmott, 1992: 58) of constituting 'better' and more efficient employees. Within this formulation, cultural 'strength' is signified by the successful engineering of a closeness of alignment of employees with the normative framework specified by the cultural engineers of the corporation (Willmott, 1993).

However, while Willmott is critical of the postmodern gloss often placed on such activities, his attempted theorization of this process draws heavily on the post-structuralist critical account of the modernist concept of the sovereign, autonomous subject, viewing it as a specifically historical response to the state of angst brought about by the realization of the indeterminate and unstable socio-cultural configuration of modernity. This approach is seen to problematize any simple control-resistance model of the relationship between an instrumental strategy of culture management and the response of employees to it because, rather than appearing as a repressive force, corporate culture is often experienced as offering the foundation upon which a secure sense of self can be grounded. Thus, returning to the insights of Foucault, corporate culture can be seen as an albeit localized force of subjectification, one that promotes the illusion of a secure and valorized sense of self that is, in effect, a 'company' self, one which stands firm in the face of the 'indeterminacy of human existence' (Willmott 1995b: 23). This is a strategy that can be most aptly illustrated by the constant appeal to the values of community, family and clan which pervade the corporate culture literature, values which are exalted, it can be argued, in an attempt to formulate an almost pre-modern form of symbolic identification (Hancock, 1997) in which the individual is able to seek meaningful refuge against the vagaries of a (post)modern world of apparent dissolution and fragmentation.

Here, then, a conception of a highly postmodernized version of organizational culture is understood as inadequate, in itself, to resist the totalizing and rationalistic imperatives of modernist organizational practices. Indeed, it can be seen, in the hands of the gurus of cultural excellence, to offer little more than an ideological gloss to a far more pervasive and repressive mode of instrumental domination. This is one that functions not in the service of human emancipation, but in the reconstitution of the human subject as one dependent upon the very relations of control and exploitation that deny the possibility of a human subjectivity unfettered by external constraint and, as such, free to explore the myriad of possibilities open to it.

Culture, organizations and postmodernism

Having considered a range of influential approaches to the study, and indeed the conceptualization, of culture within the organizational setting, one thing is perhaps clear. That is, as is the case within the social sciences generally, culture, and how to approach the questions it raises, remains a contested field within organization theory. Certainly, it is an issue that can be approached from a number of different perspectives and with a range of varying intents. Perhaps the most significant and pervasive division we have encountered in this respect is between what, in Burrell and Morgan's (1979) terms, could be described as a functionalist/regulation paradigm and a more interpretivist/radical approach, or, to invoke Habermas's (1972) theory of knowledge and human interests, one based on a technical and the other on an emancipatory cognitive interest.

The former combines a belief in the essentially integrationist function of organizational culture with a corporatist ethos that prescribes ways in which culture can be more effectively managed in the service of organizational performance and the maximization of employee motivation. In this formulation, culture is reduced to the status of a strategic variable, susceptible to rational design and manipulation, with a range of calculable outputs deriving from it – a view illustrated well by Payne when he notes that, 'cultures are essentially about the *control* of people's behaviour and beliefs ... a corporation that can *create* a strong culture has employees who *believe* in its products, its customers, its processes' (1991: 27 *emphasis added*). The latter seeks to defend the idea that cultures are something which organizations are, and as such are often diffuse and fragmented. Here the guiding principle is to seek understanding of such cultural formations and how they may reflect underlying values and norms.

This view also tends to lend itself to a radical critique of the kinds of strategy associated with the corporate culture literature, viewing them as attempts to impose homogeneous and instrumentally-orientated value sets on organizational employees. These are strategies that, whatever the rhetoric accompanying them, rarely have the genuine interests of those subjected to them at heart. From this perspective, then, corporate culture is often viewed as a form of 'nascent totalitarianism' (Willmott, 1993: 523), one which occludes genuine possibilities for individual growth and development behind the ideal of organizational community, working together for the common (*sic*) good.

Yet despite the obvious divergence between these two approaches, it would also seem that there is a common element. The idea of the postmodern, as both a socio-cultural configuration and as a meta-theoretical approach, can be seen to have left its mark on both. First and foremost, the general concern with questions of culture, and the study of organizational symbolism, can be seen to reflect the focus by many postmodernists on the 'ideational' (Reed, 1996a, 1996b) or cultural aspects of social relations. This approach, throughout the literature on organizational and indeed corporate culture, can be seen therefore to reflect a deepening understanding of the ways in which reality is as much the outcome of symbolic practices as it is of material configurations. So corporate literature abounds with discussions of how best to formulate and communicate organizational values through myths, symbols and stylistic regimes, now seen as the means by which managers may be able to re-invent the identity of both the organization and its employees. Equally, the academic study of organizational culture and symbolism has sought to embrace research approaches that deviate from more traditional modes of objectivist enquiry and embrace more subjectivist, interpretive ways of reading culture as a phenomenon in its own right. Thus, clearly in tune with the champions of management through culture, postmodern theory has brought to the fore the ways in which symbolism and culture may offer a way of understanding more fully what it is that makes organizations 'tick'.

The turn to culture, in all its manifestations, then, could be seen to suggest a process of postmodernization not only in terms of how organizations are managed, but also in terms of how they are studied. Indeed, it has provided for many the intellectual inspiration and epistemological legitimacy for methods and approaches which, even only twenty years ago, would have appeared at best inappropriate and at worst unscientific.

As we have seen, though, the rise of corporate culturalism and the emergence of postmodern theory has also provided the impetus for a new mode of organizational critique. The values with which postmodernists are so often seen to align themselves, such as heterogeneity, pluralism and the denunciation of instrumental strategies of control, have been turned against the gurus of corporate culture, exposing the fundamentally systemic logic underpinning their own cultural turn. Cálas and Smircich's (1997) aforementioned conception of a postmodernism of resistance is but one example, while other writers have focused on the ways in which the strategies and practices associated with corporate culturalism focus on the process of re-constituting employee subjectivity in line with corporate goals and aspirations. This approach not only draws upon the critical tools bequeathed by postmodern insights into the fluid, and therefore potentially colonizable, nature of subjectivity, but has also led to the development of a mode of critique that challenges the inadequacies of postmodern political rhetoric in the face of inequitable relations of power, which are sustained by political and economic institutions.

Hancock (1999), for example, has developed such a critique, drawing on the work of Baudrillard (1981, 1983a, 1983b, 1990), to argue that many of the cultural strategies associated with postmodernized forms of organizational practice are unlikely to lead to a re-humanization of work, but rather to a situation whereby the subject is reduced to the status of a mere object, a status which deprives the individual of any sense of meaningful (human) agency in the face of apparent domination by external forces of manipulation and control. Equally, Willmott's critical writings, as we have seen, have drawn on the inspiration of the postmodern critique of the bounded subject in his attempt to address the essentially subjugatory nature of the postmodernization of corporate cultural discourse. For him, the rhetoric of diversity within the (organizational) community is seen as a means of producing the illusion of subjectivity, while at the same time closing down alternative avenues along which other possibilities of self-hood can be explored.

From this critical perspective, then, much of what can be identified as 'postmodern', in tenor at least, within the discourses of 'excellence' and corporate culture inevitably bears the signs of commodification – it is homogenized, stylized, indiscriminate, even if, or perhaps especially if, 'it prescribes large doses of hoopla and celebration' (Willmott, 1992: 63).

Conclusion

Throughout this chapter we have sought to bring together, and consider critically, a broad range of approaches to, and issues deriving from, the increasing fascination with culture within organizations. In doing so we have attempted to identify some of the more obvious overlaps and commonalities between them. In addition to this, however, we have also attempted to develop a critical perspective on the ways in which the discourses of postmodernism and postmodernization have impacted on the development and legitimization of many of these ideas within contemporary organization theory. This particular approach has led to the emergence of what we consider to be several interrelated themes.

First, there has been the role that a range of discursive resources, which can be broadly characterized as postmodern in tenor and concern, have contributed to the popularization of an apparently functionalist, and increasingly instrumental, project of corporate governance. Particularly evident in the proposals and prescriptions to be found within the literature on organizational excellence and corporate culture, this approach combines the postmodern principles of plurality, diversity, indeterminacy and even playfulness with an overriding emphasis on the pursuit of employee perfomativity and organizational efficiency. This apparent belief in the 'malleability of culture' (Hancock, 1999: 163) appears, in retrospect, to have provided an interventionist resource through which management attempt to intervene directly in the reconstitution of employee value and belief systems. In this sense, it could be argued that such a postmodernist approach to the management of organizational culture primarily involves an attempt to establish structure out of 'creative chaos'. Symbols, value systems and other cultural phenomena, previously understood as somehow outside the domain of rational intervention, have now come under the close scrutiny of management practitioners and academics alike, providing, or so it would seem, an answer to many of the perceived problems facing work organizations as they confront the demands of an increasingly flexible, de-differentiated and, some might say, postmodernized economic and organizational environment, especially one in which leadership, as Bergquist (1993) suggests, has become the art of being able to make sense of, or to rationalize, cultural phenomena that appear to be random and chaotic.

Secondly, in apparent opposition to this colonization of the language and, what some would see as the radical agenda of postmodernism, a number of alternative approaches have sought to embrace the theoretical openness of postmodern theory in an attempt to valorize a very different conception of organizational culture. First and foremost, this approach tends to reject any attempt to impose an ordered or functionalist 'model' on to the organizational lifeworld. Rather, culture is perceived as something diverse and heterogeneous, inaccessible to simplistic research strategies that are, more often than not, seen as being underpinned by the representationalist legacy of the natural sciences. This approach can, above all else we would argue, be credited with providing the impetus for an expansion not only in the recognition of the interdependent relationship between the researcher and the researched, but also in the range of approaches that have been brought to bear on the exploration of culture and meaning within organizations.

Yet this attempt to develop a critical postmodern study of organizational culture remains problematic for, as we noted in the first half of the book, it is difficult to formulate a truly critical agenda within the language of postmodernism without denying many of the meta-theoretical premises upon which such a critique can be established. Most notably, the denial of any transcendent position from which critique can be exercised, and the apparent adaptation of a form of anthropological relativism, undermines the traditional logic of critical social science. Indeed, as we have seen, this can inadvertently foster a climate within which the continuing functionalist and instrumental imperatives of much of the particularly corporate culturalist literature can be occluded behind the motifs and rhetoric of postmodernism. This, in turn, perhaps suggests the need to further develop a more dialectically-informed approach to the analysis of culture within organizations, one that seeks to provide an immanent critique of the mutual interdependence of a range of discursive resources which offer, at one and the same time, the potential for both greater enslavement to, and greater liberation from, the imperatives of a systemic modernist logic that continues to objectify the human subject as little more than a strategic resource. Drawing on a range of critical traditions within the social sciences, those already working from this particular orientation have sought to problematize the normative underpinnings of corporate culturalism, as well as to question the nature and potential that such an approach has for success in the face of the contradictions that it *itself* generates. How far such a project can develop, of course, is dependent on a range of factors. Not the least of these is the extent to which it is able to engage directly with, and critically evaluate, the impact that the idea of the postmodern has had upon the legitimization of a range of culturalist and, more broadly, governmental strategies within work organizations.

With these issues in mind, in the chapters which follow we explore in some depth the relationship between the contemporary organization of work, the management of culture in terms of a more specific focus on emotion and sexuality respectively, and postmodernism both as a body of meta-theoretical ideas and as a way of describing the contemporary configurations of workplace organization. In doing so, we aim not only to introduce the reader to the content of this material and some of the issues that arise from it, but also to move a step closer towards developing our own thoughts on the nature of this apparent tripartite relationship.

Notes

1   While this is not a direct reference to Bourdieu's (1984) concept of 'cultural capital' as it is traditionally understood, the point it makes is implicitly similar.
2   Adopting this approach, Gherardi (1995), for instance, has emphasized the extent to which organizations can be understood as gendered symbolic orders.
3   See Gherardi's (1995: 20–7) analysis of the dragon logo of the Standing Conference on Organizational Symbolism (SCOS) and its relationship to the diversity of approaches to cultural analysis embraced by SCOS. See also the 'Introduction' to Alvesson and Berg (1992) for a brief discussion of the SCOS dragon and its conception.

4 Illustrated by the cultural turn in a rage of social scientific subjects ranging from sociology to psychology, geography to politics, and, of course, most notably in the rise of cultural studies itself within the social scientific curriculum.

5 Examples of this can be seen in the introduction of a range of involvement schemes, such as the 'no tie' policy operated by Salem Sportswear of Hudson, according to which employees are fined (all fines going to charity, of course) for wearing ties to work, or the encouragement given to employees at Apple computers to use kazoos to register their feelings about speakers at management meetings (cited in Harris, 1996).

5

Organization, Postmodernism and Emotion

You have to have a vision, and you have to care – passionately. (Peters and Austin, 1985: 288)

Specialists without spirit, sensualists without heart; this nullity imagines that it has attained a level of civilization never before achieved. (Goethe, cited in Weber, 1989: 182)

As the 1980s drew to a close, talk abounded of an emerging era in which, in contrast to the 'me' culture of the past decade, a more sensitive and caring approach to life would come to dominate. The twenty-first century was to be one in which the heart, rather than the head, would underpin our attitudes and actions. This more caring, sharing age, one in which we would care about the environment and about the plight of those less fortunate than ourselves, both on a personal and a global scale reflected, in many respects, the more general postmodernization of culture, a culture seen as less rational, less instrumental and less goal-orientated. The ways in which work organizations were to be managed and understood were not, or so it would seem, immune to this cultural ideal. As the 1990s progressed, emotion, and the role it plays within the day-to-day organization of work, began to creep to the forefront of thinking within the field. Both the critical theorists of organization and the gurus of new management styles recognized emotion as a largely unexplored and under-exploited dimension of human behaviour within organizations.

In this chapter, we turn our attention to this burgeoning interest in the organizational significance of emotion. In doing so, we consider the extent to which the role of emotion as a way of theorizing organizations resonates with many of the tones of postmodernism. We also explore the degree to which the self-conscious incorporation of emotion into the management of organizations reflects the possible postmodernization of organizational life, not least in its apparent rejection of the imperatives of instrumental rationality in favour of emotional uncertainty and incalculability (Offe, 1985).

While less susceptible to the kind of structuring into distinctive research orientations employed in the previous chapter, the growth in a concern with the emotional dimension of contemporary organizational life can be seen to reflect a number of distinct perspectives which broadly reflect the parallel divisions between the modern, postmodern and more explicitly critical approaches we have encountered previously. Commencing with a brief overview of the conditions surrounding the emergence of a concern with emotion within organizations, the chapter moves on to an examination of a broadly systemic modernist (Cooper and Burrell, 1988) organization of emotion. Considering, first, both the modernist exclusion of emotion from work organizations according to scientific management, and the containment and control of emotion by a human relations approach to the management of work organizations. We then looks at more contemporary managerial concerns with harnessing emotion in the pursuit of organizational imperatives. Here our focus is on the performative basis of this 'new turn to emotion in recent concerns with the incorporation of emotional intelligence' and 'sentimental value' into work organizations (Cooper, 1998), in the pursuit of 'a passion for excellence' (Peters and Austin, 1985). The role of emotion in contemporary work organizations is then examined, in the second section of this chapter, with particular reference to the relatively recent influence of postmodernist and post-structuralist thought on the analysis of emotion in organizations. It will be argued here that a postmodernist perspective on emotion at work can be identified in both contemporary managerial discourses and organizational analysis.

In the third section of the chapter we then examine more critical analyses, primarily of the performance of emotional labour. Both 'non-performative and de-naturalizing' (Fournier and Grey, 1998), this more critical focus on the role of emotion in work organizations has emerged, as noted above, largely since the late 1970s in the UK and the USA out of attempts to synthesize Marxist-inspired labour process analysis with feminism and organization theory. Here the conception of emotion as a subjective process shaped within material relations draws particularly on Hochschild's (1983) analysis of 'emotional labour' and the commodification of emotion within the contemporary workplace and Fineman's (1993) analysis of organizations as emotional arenas which is premised on the assumption that emotion is always managed – whether it is evoked or suppressed – within the process of organization.

Finally, this chapter concludes with a critical evaluation of the role of emotion in contemporary work organizations and their analysis. Recognizing the value of Meštrović's (1997) thesis on the postemotional society, it will be argued that emotion and its incorporation into organizational life signifies not the termination of modernist organization but rather, 'a differentiated continuation of it' (Hassard, 1993b: 112).

The valorization of organizational emotion

Although the existence of emotion within organization has long since been recognized by organization theorists, it is only relatively recently that sustained, critical attention has been paid to the emotional aspects of work organizations. As Noon and Blyton (1997: 123) note, most studies of emotion in organizations have been published since 1980 and particularly since the publication of Hochschild's seminal work on *The Managed Heart* in 1983. Hochschild's introduction of the concept of 'emotional labour' illuminated an aspect of paid work that is central to the lived experience of many workers, but that had been obscured by dominant theoretical approaches both to the management and to the study of organizations. Conceptualizing some of the distinctive aspects of service work in this way opened up fruitful avenues of investigation and analysis of work organizations in general, and facilitated the ongoing reformulation of both academic and managerial conceptions of work necessary to keep pace with transformations in the nature of work and its organization, and in the economy in general.

In line with the emphasis placed on an expanding tertiary sector to be found within much of the previously reviewed post-industrial and post-Fordist literature (see Chapter 2), it would seem that increasingly 'people's work lives are shaped overwhelmingly by the experience of delivering a service' (Allen and Du Gay, 1994: 255). This increase, over the last two decades or so, in the proportion of jobs in which people are employed specifically to work as front-line, 'customer facing' service providers has meant that increased managerial recognition has been given to 'customer relations', as a vital ingredient of a competitive organization, and particularly to the stage management of those organizational 'moments of truth' (Carlzon, 1987) when customers interact with organizations through interpersonal encounters with service providers. To draw on the body metaphor of social organization deployed by Douglas (1966), service providers can perhaps be understood as operating at the orifices of organizations, where the outside comes in and vice versa, and so where organizations see themselves as particularly vulnerable to both success and failure. This recognition has increased the importance accorded to emotion, and particularly its management, by employees in direct contact with customers – those 'making a difference at the margins' (Peters and Austin, 1985: 45) so to speak. In other words, management has increasingly sought to control the images employees create for customers and the quality of interactions between employees and customers. Consequently, 'a key component of the work performed by many workers has become the presentation of emotions that are specified and desired by their organizations' (Morris and Feldman, 1996: 987).

Furthermore, in terms of the analysis of contemporary work organizations, the increasing attention given to emotion can also be attributed, in part once again, to the impact of postmodern and post-structuralist thought and its drive to re-cognize the Other, in both the management and analysis of contemporary work organizations and, in particular, as Fournier and Grey have put it, to a 'concern with writing in what is written out' (Fournier and Grey, 1998: 10). The result is the relatively recent 'discovery' of organizational themes such as culture, sexuality and emotion, for instance. Despite a tradition of neglect in the history of western thought – one in which the 'disembodied', rational (male) mind has reigned supreme (Bendelow and Williams, 1998) – the role of emotions in social and organizational life has come to be recognized recently, by some at least, as central rather than peripheral to the critical enterprise of understanding organizations. Emotions clearly represent a juncture between organization and the most personal realms of an individual's experience. They also straddle both the cognitive and corporeal aspects of our being and resist the Cartesian mind–body dualism that has dominated western thought until recently, including, for instance, its manifestation in the traditional distinction between manual and non-manual labour, a distinction that emotion and its management appears to transcend. As such, the study of emotions raises vital issues for understanding the formation of the 'self' within organizations and the ways in which this is both inter-subjective and inter-corporeal.

As with the concept of culture, the recognition of emotion as an important factor in any attempt to understand adequately the nature and experience of contemporary work organizations and those of the future, has been a development that has taken a number of turns, particularly in relation to the apparent division between a more practitioner-orientated discourse and a discourse embedded more generally within an academic research tradition. The latter takes as its starting point an attempt to understand more fully the complexities of contemporary organizational life. The spirit of the former is summed up in Peters and Waterman's (1985: 287) book *A Passion for Excellence*, in which they argue that organizational emotions (the feelings, sensations and affective responses to organization) 'must come from the market and the soul simultaneously'. In another example of work by one of these authors (Peters, 1989: 457), managers themselves are called upon to harness their own emotional energies by developing a 'passionate public hatred for bureaucracy'. Here emotion, be it their own or that of their employees, is viewed as yet another important resource that managers must come to recognize, a resource that should be harnessed and, where possible, guided in the service of organizational dynamism and success. For those who might wish to distance themselves from such 'pop-management' invocations, however, the conceptualization and study of emotion within organizations represents a compelling resource not for managing, but for understanding organizations; it is a way of bringing to bear the academic gaze on the ways in which organizations produce and reproduce themselves. For Albrow (1992: 323), for example, organizations can be seen as what he terms 'emotional cauldrons', in which the socio-technical systems that have for so long provided the dominant image of organizational life can be seen as 'channels for the

flow of emotions' (1992: 326). Understanding emotion is thus seen as vital –
as is any consideration of impersonal systems of rules and regulations – for
a fully developed organization theory.

Modernity and the organization of emotion

The relationship between emotion and what can be broadly identified as a
modernist organization theory – in both its systemic and critical modes –
has been, and indeed still is, many would argue, a troubled one. It could be
argued that a quintessentially modernist way of conceiving emotion as
pre-social, irrational, cognitive and physiological, underpinned both the
exclusionary principles of scientific management (Taylor, 1911) and their
execution in Fordist modes of organizing, as well as the incorporation of
emotion into organizations within a Human Relations approach to management. In this context, emotion came to be perceived as a force to be
excluded from the 'public sphere' of social and organizational life in the
former, and to be contained and controlled in the latter. Both of these
essentially systemic approaches to management presented emotion as
necessitating a process of organization, associating emotion with the
largely unconscious forces of passion that were regarded as a threat to the
order of modernity. Actions motivated by emotion were characterized in
scientific management and human relations as irrational, unconscious and
corporeal. This simplistic and unidimensional perspective on emotion
arose from a series of conventional oppositions that underlie modernism,
most notably deriving from the Cartesian division between the mind and
the body.

More recently, however, management practitioners and theorists have
come to recognize that, as Collins has put it, 'emotional propensities are . . .
a prerequisite for a successful interaction' (1981: 1001). Consequently, recent
managerial accounts of the organizational importance of, for example, successful service interaction, place a considerable premium on the role of
emotion and its incorporation into organizational life (Bowen et al., 1989;
Cooper, 1998; Goleman, 1996, 1999; Simpson, 1999). Thus, while early
approaches to the management of emotion could be conceptualized as seeking to subject emotion to the process of organization, more recent
management orientations have been predicated perhaps more on the idea
that the reverse should be the case; that is, that organizations should be subjected to emotionality. Yet what these various managerial approaches share
in common, or so it would seem to us, is a highly modernist conception of
emotion as the antithesis of reason. Indeed, in the juxtaposition of emotion
and reason we can identify perhaps one of the most dichotomous and fundamental trademarks of modernity, namely, the designation of emotion as
an organizational Other. Along with other familiar dualisms which shaped
the experience of modernity, such as mind and body, public and private,
culture and nature, masculine and feminine, for instance, modernism

placed reason and emotion in a relationship in which the former was understood to exist only when the latter was entirely absent and vice versa – a relationship of ontological opposition that constituted one of the most fundamental and enduring features of modern organizations.

The modernist analysis of organizations has tended to perpetuate distinctions between the ordered, controlled and abstract on the one hand, and the disordered, uncontrolled and concrete on the other, with the relegation of emotion to the latter, implicitly discredited, set of ontological categories. Modern organizations, as 'the enemies of affection' (Bauman, 1993), have been hailed since their inception as incarnations of rationality and instruments of rationalization. Bureaucracy – as the typically modern (advanced) mode of organizing, *sine ira et studio* (without hatred or passion) (Albrow, 1992) – is seen to be based on an autonomous, impersonal, procedural rationality that has no place for emotion. What Kanter (1977: 22) refers to as 'the passionless organization', that strives to exclude emotion from its boundaries, does so in the modernist belief that efficiency should not be sullied by the 'irrationality' of personal feelings.

Indeed, Weber builds his analysis of the *geist* of capitalism – 'that attitude which seeks profit rationally and systematically' (Weber, 1989: 64) – on the belief that it is anchored in deeply-held religious and emotional attitudes of affective control; on the exclusion of emotions from organizational life. Modernity, for Weber, is seen as an increasingly bureaucratic order from which the 'spontaneous enjoyment of life . . . as an end in itself' (1989: 53) is ruthlessly expunged, one that 'succeeds in eliminating from official business love, hatred, and all purely personal, irrational, and emotional elements which escape calculation' (1989: 216). The formal rationality of capitalism, then, has no (or very little) space for human feelings and sentiments in Weber's account. Indeed, a rational organization of labour – its routinized, calculated administration within continuously functioning enterprises – can be distinguished from a traditional mode of organization, at least in part, on the basis of a disciplined (unemotional) labour force. For Weber, who saw the rationalization of social life as the trajectory of western history, the exclusion of emotionality from work organizations gave bureaucracy, in large part at least, its advantage over other modes of organization.

This rational exclusion of the emotional dimension of organizational life can also be seen to be valorized in the work of Parsons (1966: 77), who argued that the 'achievement ethic' of western capitalism required 'an impersonality in social relations that entailed the dissolution of the social ties of traditional society'. In contrast to the rationality of western organization, he cited the excessive familialism of China and its value system as 'shot through with particularistic themes' as factors limiting its economic development. In their study of occupational mobility, Lipset and Bendix (1959: 255) argued similarly that instrumentality in social relations must be understood as an asset conducive to mobility. They speak of the upwardly mobile as having 'the capacity to deal with others in an instrumental rather than an emotional fashion'. In modernist perceptions of organization, therefore, rationality is revered as emotions are designated as illegitimate or inappropriate and, in effect, are organized out. Thus, privileging rationality and marginalizing or excluding emotion 'bureaucracy perpetuates the belief that rationality and the control of emotions are not only inseparable but also necessary for effective organizational life' (Putnam and Mumby, 1993: 41).

Returning to Weber, however, it would be incorrect to say that his conception of bureaucratic organizational forms is based on a total exclusion of emotion. As the following passage from *Economy and Society* indicates, Weber's account does allow for emotions within modern organizations in so far as their rational calculation is perceived as an intrinsic aspect of their constitution. It is not emotion *per se* that Weber admits into the organization, then, but rationalized emotion, ensuring

> First, that everything is rationally calculated, especially those seemingly imponderable and irrational, emotional factors – in principle, at least, calculable in the same manner as the yields of coal and iron deposits. Secondly, devotion is normally impersonal, oriented towards a purpose, a common cause, a rationally intended. (Weber, 1978: 1150)[1]

Indeed, the pursuit of bureaucracy represents something of a modernist irony of which Weber himself was well aware. As he argued in the context of modernity, the 'passion for bureaucracy is enough to drive one to despair' (Weber, in Mayer, 1956: 127). Furhter, as Albrow (1992) argues Weber's interpretive sociology allows for a more comprehensive and critical explication of the relationship between rationality and emotion than Weber himself achieved, largely because, as Albrow notes (1992: 327), the emotional ontology of his time heavily emphasized a pre-social, biological conception of emotion. Again, somewhat ironically it took the rationalism of his successors 'to make virtues of these limitations and . . . it is they who have suppressed the emotional dimension in his work in the interests of rationalistic organization' (Albrow, 1992: 327).

Certainly, from the 1930s onwards, management theorists and practitioners had begun to realize that even within the confines of organizational life, 'one cannot commission emotions to order, neither can one send them away' (Bauman, 1993: 7). This represented a significant shift from a view of organizations as based on the exclusion of emotion to an emphasis on the idea that work is meaningful and motivating only if it offers security and opportunities for achievement and self-actualization (Herzberg, 1974; Maslow, 1943). Emotion therefore became 'in', so to speak, in so far as it gained a conditional acceptance as managed and organized affectivity. Emotion, in this form, began to be recognized as being of central importance to the pursuit of organizational performance. It became increasingly emphasized, therefore, that the management of work organizations should be based on 'articulating and incorporating *the logic* of sentiments' (Roethlisberger and Dickson, 1939: 462 *emphasis added*). Elaborating on this incorporation of emotion into organizational life, Barnard (1938: 235) argued that pertinent to the role of the executive are 'feeling', 'judgement', 'sense', 'proportion', 'balance', 'appropriateness'. Participative styles of management, deemed to engender loyalty and commitment and so increase worker satisfaction and productivity, increasingly perceived emotion as an organizational 'human resource' to be managed. In Chapter 2 we discussed, in this respect, that while more 'scientific' management strategies had been based on the eradication of irrational elements such as emotion from organizations, approaches such as Human Relations identified those aspects of organizational life previously designated as irrational and as 'untapped resources' (Alvesson and Willmott, 1996) yet also, of course, as potential problems that required management and organization – to be subject to the intervention of reason. Mayo (1933), for instance, emphasized the importance for productivity of primary, informal relations among workers and developed the concept of the 'informal organization' to include the emotional, non-rational and sentimental aspects of human behaviour in the rational management of organizations.

While the early Human Relations emphasis on informal social factors may appear to diverge from those organizational traits considered important by scientific management, both approaches shared in common a similar conception of the role of management *vis-à-vis* emotionality. Management training was considered a vehicle for learning about ways to master, not unleash, emotional factors counter-productive to the organization. The early Human Relations perception of emotion in organizations therefore may have 'modified the idea of rationality but preserved its flavour' (Kanter, 1977: 22). As Pringle notes in this respect,

> While the human-relations theorists added an informal dimension, they did not challenge the theorising of the formal bureaucratic structures. In some ways they reinforced the idea of managerial rationality: while *workers* might be controlled by sentiment and emotion, *managers* were supposed to be rational, logical and able to control their emotions. The division between reason and emotion was tightened in a way that marked off managers from the rest. (1989a: 87 *original emphasis*)

Thus, if the organizational exclusion of emotion is the strategy we could associate most strongly with the ideal type of Weberian bureaucracy and with early advocates of scientific management, a strategy of (selective) inclusion is perhaps the approach located most firmly within more contemporary modernist-inspired approaches, particularly to the management of organizational personnel.

Several costs to the work organization of what is suppressed emotionally in a Weberian or 'rationalistic' model of organizational exclusion have, since the 1930s, been identified by advocates of self-proclaimed humanistic approaches to management. More recently, these themes have been taken up particularly by the champions of 'new style' or 'soft' management techniques such as Human Resource Management (HRM) and particularly by the peddlers of cultural 'excellence' who have advocated a less 'rationalistic' incorporation of emotionality into organizational life. As Cooper, a US consultant and co-author (with Sawaf) of *Executive EQ* (1998) has put it recently, 'emotion has been rejected for years by executives as the messy, effeminate counterpoint to masculine logic and objectivity, but now it has become the latest business buzzword' (1998: 48). The driving force behind this recent 'turn to emotion', it seems, is a clear performance imperative and the perception that 'emotions, properly managed, can drive trust, loyalty and commitment and many of the greatest productivity gains, innovations and accomplishments of individuals, teams and organizations' (Cooper, 1998: 48). According to Cooper, what he terms 'the emotional counterpart of IQ' – 'the ability to sense, understand and effectively apply the power and acumen of emotions as source of human energy, information, trust, creativity, connection and influence' (1998: 48) – represents that 'really crucial ingredient' for organizational success in the contemporary era, or as Jack Welch, the Chair of General Electric, put it, 'soft stuff with hard results' (cited in Cooper, 1998: 48). For Cooper and Sawaf (1998), the deployment of emotional intelligence at work involves five dimensions: knowing one's emotions; controlling one's emotions; recognizing emotions in others; controlling emotions in others, and self-motivation.

In their 'how to' guide, Cooper and Sawaf provide guidelines for the effective harnessing of EQ to enhance personal and corporate performance simultaneously. Weisinger (1998) has argued, similarly, that while IQ is certainly a factor in the ability to perform well at work, the emotional intelligence quotient is as significant. In his book *Emotional Intelligence at Work* (1998), Weisinger demonstrates, in a similar vein to Cooper and Sawaf, 'how to' master the main characteristics of what he terms 'emotional IQ'. This approach is taken a stage further by Harvard psychologist Daniel Goleman (1996), who argues that EI (Emotional Intelligence) matters more to organizational performance than cognitive abilities or technical skills and impacts particularly, he argues, at the top of the 'leadership pyramid' (Goleman, 1999). Similarly, Thomson, Chair of the UK Marketing and Communication Agency, argues that an organization's most important asset is its 'emotional capital': 'the combination of emotions, feelings, beliefs and values that are held around an organization' (Thomson, 1997: 1). Kandola and Fullerton (1995) have also highlighted the organizational benefits of incorporating emotions into the management of diversity, including improved access to talent, enhanced organizational flexibility, the promotion of team creativity and innovation, improving customer services, the fostering of satisfying work environments, improving morale and job satisfaction, greater productivity and enhanced competitive edge.

Perhaps the most passionate commitment to a celebration of the relative merits of 'Working from the Heart' is demonstrated in the account by Liz Simpson (1999) who, in her (subtitled) 'Practical Guide to Loving What You Do for a Living', argues that 'Heart Work'™ constitutes in itself a mission to co-create a culture – one shaped by 'energy, passion and fun' – in which each individual feels able to bring his or her heart and soul, as well as mind and body, to the workplace. Simpson emphasizes that what has traditionally been under-valued or dismissed as a 'touchy-feely' way of managing both oneself and others, one that has no bearing on the 'bottom line' of business, actually produces warm 'fuzzy feelings' that inspire and guide organizational performance more effectively than 'harder' business logic ever could.

Underpinning the championing of EQ, then, is the perception that 'without an actively engaged heart, excellence is impossible' (Harris, 1996: 18). With this in mind, much of the recent managerial concern with emotion has been focused, in characteristically 'Total Quality' fashion, not only on the management of employees through a strategic emphasis on organizations as emotionally-bound communities, but also on the affective response of customers to organizations. This latter emphasis has been driven largely by a concern with the 'continuous improvement' of customer service (Liljander and Strandvik, 1997; Price and Arnould, 1995), particularly through the 'customization of the service experience' (Bettencourt and Gwinner, 1996). Within this emphasis on 'Total Quality', employees have come to be conceptualized as 'internal customers' (Hochschild, 1997).

Such 'new style' approaches, in effect, share much in common with the early advocates of Human Relations and their concern to conflate what are perceived as artificial (and unprofitable) boundaries between the corporation and the individual. They have emphasized, perhaps most notably, that organizational stability may come at the price of losing those sparks of originality, flexibility and creativity that emotions are seen to ignite. The identification of innovative solutions that might emerge from processes that mediate and negotiate between diverse groups is deemed to be foreclosed in a more traditional approach to organization that prioritizes rationality over emotion. Organizational input that might come from valuing diversity of personal experience is also understood to be denied. Passionate commitment to organizational goals, to co-workers and to the organization itself, and the potential for renegotiating both means and missions (and the commitment this is seen to produce) is also seen to be lost in the un-emotional organization – in an organizational world comprised of 'hostile strangers' (Bologh, 1990).

Also recognized within this concern with the management of emotion, which has been steadily gathering pace since the 1930s, however, are the potential performative dysfunctions of incorporating emotion in an instrumental way, which, for those people who are employed at the front-line so to speak, often involves the use of scripts, for instance. As V.A. Thompson has put it, 'synthetic compassion can be more offensive than none at all' (1976: 115). To avoid such 'synthetic compassion', Ashforth and Humphrey advocate 'job involvement and identification with the role and organization' (1993: 108). An interesting issue, in this respect, is the emphasis that they suggest should be placed on recruiting and selecting individuals predisposed to a service orientation as opposed to socializing and rewarding employees who internalize an empathic approach to service (Chatman, 1991; Schneider, 1987). Similarly, Sutton (1991) has suggested that, to the extent that emotional expression is 'dependent upon enduring dispositional factors', recruitment and selection is preferable to socialization and reward. This perception of emotion as an essential aspect of human nature to be co-opted in the pursuit of organizational imperatives of efficiency and effectiveness (Cooper, 1998: 48) is reflected in the gendered division of emotion labour, which we consider later in this chapter.

As Finemen (1994) has put it, what early scientific approaches to management and the exclusion of 'irrationality' from the parameters of organizational life seem to share with later approaches to the management of emotion as a human resource is a restricted, restrained and even mechanical understanding of emotion as an attribute or an object to be manipulated and managed – to be subjected to rationality. Isaack (1978: 918), for instance, has highlighted the importance of the rational deployment of intuition to effective management performance, insisting that intuitive decision-making processes 'be balanced with logical reasoning'. Agor (1986, 1989) has similarly emphasized the significance of intuition, conceived of as 'a rational and logical brain skill that can be used to help and guide decision making' (1989: 15). His premise is that intuition, incorporating mental, emotional, physical and spiritual dimensions, can be used to enhance decision-making that results in positive organizational outcomes. This rationalization of emotion also appears to be the case in respect of the management of emotional health problems (Sonnenstuhl, 1986), of 'emotional disability' (Czajka and DeNisi, 1988) and of 'emotional exhaustion' (Gaines and Jermier, 1983), or in the management of 'dysfunctional emotions' such as anger, anxiety and depression (Ostell, 1996), in an 'unemotional', rational way.

So far, we have presented what appears to be a series of approaches to, and understandings of, the role that emotions can play in the further refinement of organizational management, that is, the harnessing of (potentially disordered) employee emotion as a means through which greater levels of organizational performativity can be encouraged and nurtured through a critical re-appraisal of the modernist marginalization of the emotive dimension of human agency. Emotion, in this context, continues to appear dangerous, the impetuous Other of modern rationality in dire need of taming, yet with added benefits for those who can rise to this challenge successfully. In apparent contrast to this, however, there has also recently emerged an alternative viewpoint based on the recognition that (apparently) un-managed and dis-organized (genuine) emotions, far from being an inefficient and potentially destructive aspect of organizational life to be rationalized and subject to 'quotients', are fundamental to the process of organization, particularly within a commercial era characterized by intensified competition and a 'have a nice day' culture.

Postmodernism and emotion in organizations

As with the broader concept of culture, the inclusion of emotion into organizational life, or rather the contemporary re-cognition of its centrality, suggests a possible postmodernization of organizations as indicated by a number of features which supposedly reflect a postmodern mode of organization, such as disorganization, untidiness and flexibility. Furthermore, with its intellectual origins located largely in the contemporary post-structuralist critique of modernity, aspects of the postmodernist understanding of emotion in organizations can be identified in contemporary organizational analysis as well as in managerial discourses. Within both contexts we can potentially identify a rejection of emotion as an affective expression or reflection of a core or 'inner' self and a perception of emotion as shaped within power-knowledge; a decentring of the rational human subject, and a perception of subjectivity as the outcome of discourse; a rejection of the notion of a univocal relation between forms of representation (a word, image or a smile, even) and an objective, external world; a perception of liberation from the 'natural' world and a rejection of modernist faith in the recovery of a relationship with nature; a perception of action as 'play' rather than 'agency', and the idea that there is no single actor behind action, but a 'toying' with available roles (Lyotard and Thebaud, 1986). Subjectivity, from this perspective, is 'a process and a paradox having neither beginning nor end' (Linstead and Grafton-Small, 1992: 339). In common with those so-called 'new styles' of management that we focused on in the previous section, more post-structuralist approaches tend to be characterized by a rejection of the Enlightenment notion of 'reason' as the highest of human attributes. In this sense, emotions and their inclusion in organizational life are perceived as potentially liberating, presupposing an 'emancipation of emotions' (Wouters, 1989: 111) and a destabilizing, or dis-organizing, process (Cooper and Burrell, 1988).

Underpinning this broadly postmodern approach to the valorization of emotion is an attempt to locate it as a 'missing link' between modernist dualisms such as nature and culture, public and private, mind and body and so on. Emotion is seen as operating at multiple levels in a way that is never fixed or stable, because the cultural interpretations that shape emotion are themselves never fixed or stable. In contrast to those modernist approaches considered earlier, recent developments in the organizational analysis of emotions inspired by postmodernism propose a relational understanding of emotion, arguing that emotions arise only within relationships and are not an essential aspect of a 'core' self. S. Jackson (1993), for instance, argues that because we only have access to emotions through mediating discourses, language contributes substantially to their cultural construction:

> our subjectivities, including that aspect of them we understand as our emotions, are shaped by social and cultural processes and structures but are not

simply passively accepted by us . . . we actively participate in working ourselves into structures and this in part explains the strength of our subjection to
them. (1993: 212)

Thus, in recent studies of emotion informed largely by the ideas of postmodernism, the focus is very much on the increasing 'informalization'
(Wouters, 1998) of relationships in which emotion arises. Organizations are
understood as complexes of work and play, with work roles allowing for
'playful flexibility' (Wouters, 1989: 117). From this perspective, social
actors are seen to construct their identities in organizations largely through
discursive practices, that is, through the rules, behaviours and systems of
meaning that become 'everyday' occurrences in the experience of emotion.
This more 'sensual', experiential understanding of emotion contrasts with
the modernist approaches outlined earlier, in so far as it is premised upon
a deconstruction of the hierarchical organization of rationality and emotionality and of the Cartesian dualisms on which it is based. Combined
with a feminist approach to organizations (Martin, 1990; Weedon, 1987),
poststructuralist-inspired analyses emphasize for instance that organizational discourses construct the identities of men and women differently so
that the traits associated with masculinity are valued whereas the characteristics defined as feminine are constructed as 'Other'. These can be
summarized as follows: rationality (effective, efficient, organizing, orderly,
strong, neutral, objective, reasonable, cognitive, masculine, public) and
emotionality (ineffective, inefficient, disruptive, chaotic, weak, biased,
subjective, (un)reasonable, passionate, corporeal, affective, feminine, private). As outlined earlier, these latter traits have come to be regarded
recently as supportive of, if not essential to, contemporary organizational
performance, particularly in accounts such as Maddock's (1999) that
emphasize the links between femininity, innovation and flexible, empathetic approaches to management. This appears to be in stark contrast to
modernist discourse, within which emotions were dismissed as private,
irrational, inner sensations, tied to women's 'hysterical' bodies and 'dangerous' desires. The modernist view of emotions discussed earlier is of an
entity to be 'excluded', 'managed' or 'harnessed' by the steady hand of
(male) reason.

However, although driven by a critical re-evaluation, and, indeed, many
would argue a highly essentialist understanding of such reason/emotion,
masculine/feminine dualisms, many of the concerns of a postmodernist
understanding of emotion within organizations are also reminiscent of the
performance imperatives of contemporary managerial strategies. Ashforth
and Humphrey (1993), for instance, argue that emotion in organizations
can, and indeed should, be an enjoyable outcome of a process of identification with both the work role and the organization itself. In a similar
vein, Putnam and Mumby (1993: 52) argue for the evolution of emotionally-bound 'organizational communities', suggesting that the fostering of
organizational communities in which freedom of emotional expression is

not simply tolerated but is actively encouraged is more liberating than turning employees into emotional robots. As they put it, 'emotions play a vital role in organizational life, not simply as forms of labour or the means to instrumental ends but as ways to enhance community and interrelatedness' (1993: 55). In the nurturance of emotionally-bound, organizational communities, Mumby and Putnam (1992: 474) argue that the two concepts of 'rationality' and 'emotionality' should be engaged in play to produce an understanding of organization (and theorization about organizing) that neither term can capture alone, so that the incorporation of emotion into organizations and organizational analysis 'could create a space for as yet unimagined ways of talking about and doing organizing'.

Based on their critique of Simon's (1976, 1989) work on 'bounded rationality', they introduce the concept of *bounded emotionality*. Simon introduced the modifier 'bounded' to suggest that rationality – typically defined as intentional, reasoned, goal-directed behaviour aimed at maximizing gain – is limited and restricted by various organizational constraints, such as institutional practices and rules. Because individuals make choices based on incomplete information, explore only a limited range of alternatives and attach only appropriate values to anticipated outcomes, members of an organization rarely make optimum, 'purely' rational choices, Simon argues. Hence, organizational rationality is best understood as bounded. Taking this as their starting point, Mumby and Putnam's concept of 'bounded emotionality' refers to

> an alternative mode of organizing in which nurturance, caring, community, supportiveness, and interrelatedness are fused with individual responsibility to shape organizational experiences. Individualizing is joined with relatedness. The term *bounded* shifts in meaning to incorporate the *inter-subjective limitations* or the constraints that individuals must exercise in a community. (1992: 474 *original emphasis*)

They argue that this concept of 'bounded emotionality' as a basis for alternative modes of organizing reflects the desire to nurture relational development, marginalized within dominant modes of organizing, that are based largely on 'bounded rationality'. Goals are arranged in a heterarchy, which Marshall defines as an organization that:

> has no one person or principle in command. Rather, temporary pyramids of authority form as and when appropriate in a system of mutual constraints and influences. The childhood game of paper, stone, and scissors provides a simple illustration: paper wraps stone, stone blunts scissors, scissors cut paper. There is no fixed hierarchy, but each is effective, and recognized in its own realm. (1989: 289)

Thus, heterarchical goals and values are flexible. Two examples of heterarchical organizations which are founded on 'bounded emotionality' which Mumby and Putnam identify are the female weaver's guild examined by Wyatt (1988) and the feminist organization Redwood Records

(Lont, 1988). Following Lont (1988), they argue that Redwood Records illustrates the ways in which egalitarianism, supportiveness and diversity of interests can intertwine to form a profitable organizational community based on a work environment of informality, supportiveness and consensual decision-making through which Redwood Records 'preserved its philosophy and found unity through diversity of interests' (Mumby and Putnam, 1992: 477). Acknowledging that the organization of Redwood Records may be perceived as somewhat utopian, Mumby and Putnam go on to argue that bounded emotionality, as a principle of organization, can function equally well to frame interaction in traditional, commercial organizations as a more effective and efficient mechanism for decision-making. In short, Mumby and Putnam argue that

> having employees develop skills in listening, negotiating and understanding feelings is more liberating that turning them into emotional robots. . . . Thus, through an emphasis on bounded emotionality, *the marginal aspects of organizational experience can be recaptured* (namely, the private, the informal, the physical, and the emotional). (1992: 478–9 *emphasis added*)

They make it clear, therefore, that this approach does not involve an abandonment of instrumental goals of productivity and profit. Rather, 'recapturing' bounded emotionality does not even call for a radical restructuring of current organizational forms but implies simply a re-inclusion of what is currently marginalized or ignored. Thus, in proposing bounded emotionality as an alternative heuristic, Mumby and Putnam attempt to activate a 'play' between oppositional pairs, namely rationality and emotionality, that, they argue, is obscured by current organizational theory and research. However, it seems that they do so ultimately in the service of instrumental, organizational ends. In this sense, the broadly poststructuralist approach to organization theory that they adopt provides us with what seems to be, essentially, a reification device for performance imperatives already embraced within mainstream managerialism. As Martin, Knopoff and Beckman have put it recently, '"bounded emotionality" . . . encourages the constrained expression of emotions at work in order to encourage . . . a deeper and more intimate form of controlling employees' (1998: 429).

For those who have developed a more critical, non-performative perspective on this 'recapturing' of emotion, the incorporation of emotion into work organizations means that some types of work require employees to undertake unacceptable levels of emotional management and display, with potentially detrimental effects on their sense of self. From this perspective, then, 'bounded emotionality' simply means emotional exploitation, in a form that has come to be understood critically, therefore, as a profoundly alienating and fragmenting aspect of contemporary work organizations. It is to this more critical understanding of emotion in organizations that we now turn.

Critical approaches to emotion in organizations

Critical perspectives on emotion have drawn attention to the ways in which the socio-cultural milieu shapes organization within society and, in particular, its commodification and management in the contemporary workplace. Much of the critical analysis of the 'production' of emotion in work organizations has emerged largely from the Marxist-inspired critique of capitalism and, particularly since the 1970s, out of attempts to synthesize elements of Labour Process Theory, feminism and organization theory. Within this tradition, emotion is understood as shaped by social relations, biology and human labour, so that a dialectical relationship is seen to exist between a person's sensuous relations with the material world and the meanings brought to bear on those relations. Consequently, critical perspectives tend to share with postmodernism the view that emotions are not essential qualities, but are dependent on interaction with others for their emergence. We do not become subjects – emotional, intersubjective beings – except in relation to others. Some of those who adopt a critical perspective on emotion in organizations also share with postmodernism a rejection of the central tenets of positivistic social science that are seen to have added considerably to the marginalization of emotion in organizational theory (see, for instance, Hosking and Fineman, 1990).

From this perspective, emotions are understood not as the unfortunate aberrations or by-products of insufficiently rational systems, or as 'intruders' into the bastion of male rationality. Rather, it is seen as necessary to fundamentally 'rethink the relation between knowledge and emotion and construct conceptual models that demonstrate the mutually constitutive rather than oppositional relation' (Jaggar, 1989: 157) between them. Both critical and postmodernist approaches emphasize, then, that emotions 'contra centuries of dominant Western dualistic thinking, are central to reason, even when ideologically denounced as its antithesis' (S. Williams, 1998: 757). Critical accounts emphasize, however that the distortion of emotion is intensifying with its increasing commodification, engendered by more flexible and service-orientated organizations such as in the airline industry (Hochschild, 1983), tourism (Adkins, 1995), burger chains and financial services (Leidner, 1993, 1999), for instance. It is with regard to this latter point that postmodern and critical approaches are at their most divergent. Whereas postmodernism tends to celebrate the liberation of emotion from modernist rigidity, more critical approaches are concerned with the way in which emotion is distorted by the exploitative and alienating forces of capitalism in its various guises including, and especially, in so-called postmodern organizations.

Emotional arenas

The incorporation of emotion into organizational life has perhaps been explored most thoroughly by Fineman (1993, 1994), who, broadly speaking, adopts a critical approach to emotion in organizations. For Fineman, organizations constitute *emotional arenas*, that is, 'emotions are within the fabric of . . . work life' (1994: 79) and are reflected, for instance, in the evocation of work organizations as families, communities or as social groups, ideas perpetuated by social calendars and extensive 'training' that conflate formal and informal aspects of organizational culture. For instance, stage-managed meetings and reward ceremonies, 'graduation' ceremonies and 'away days' all have a distinct evangelical tone that is intended 'to keep spirits high' (1993: 20) he argues. Significantly, many of these 'emotional' events occur outside normal working hours and so blur the boundaries between work and non work, between who and what 'belongs' to the organization and who and what does not, functioning in important ways to breath life into a managerially-inspired vision of organizations as emotionally-bound collectivities. Obligations on organizational members to participate in social events, outside the organization's 'normal' space and time, are seen as opportunities to share 'real' (dis-organized, un-managed) feelings safely within a receptive audience of peers (Van Maanen, 1986; Van Maanen and Kunda, 1989). In this sense, such emotional 'safety valves' are seen to provide a useful outlet through which 'bad' feelings can be safely expelled in a controlled environment and their potentially anti-organizational effects nullified. Thus, 'apart from being individually cathartic, the social sharing of normally hidden feelings creates a subculture through which organizational members can emotionally bond, feel at one' (Fineman, 1993: 21). In this sense, potentially anti-organizational emotions become subject to 'strategic renegotiations' (1993: 22) so that the possibility for emotional leakage, *within* the organization's time and space, is minimized.

For Fineman (1994), then, by effectively organizing out 'bad' (unprofitable) feelings, by implication, the productive energy associated with 'good' feelings can (and should, the prophets of EQ have argued) be channelled into the labour process. Hence, organizations increasingly seek to develop a social reality in which emotions become commodities for achieving instrumental goals of perfomativity through recruitment, selection, socialization and the evaluation of employees as 'emotive subjects' (Hearn, 1993). In a similar vein, Hatcher (1999) has argued, with particular reference to the training and education of managers, how the specific concept of 'passion' has been increasingly mobilized, particularly in writing by management consultants and gurus. She notes how 'new forms of management training set out specifically to train managers in what passion feels like, and when and how it should be felt and displayed in relation to their work practices' (Hatcher, 1999: 5–6). Her critical account identifies what she terms 'practices of the heart', that is, a range of discursive techniques through which emotional commitment is instrumentalized and 'transformed into ordered passion', susceptible to control and functional engagement (1999: 19). Critical approaches to organizations such as these emphasize, then, that managers and employees alike are increasingly required to personify the desired emotional ethos of their employing organization. Other accounts have emphasized that emotional engagement at work, particularly for those who are employed specifically as service providers, demands the performance of what has come to be understood as 'emotional labour'.

Emotional labour

A wide range of organizational contexts clearly exists in which employees are required to manage their own emotions and those of others in the service of their employing organization, some of which require an emotional ethos characterized by solemnity (as in the case of undertakers), by intimidation (debt collectors, for instance), or hostility (in the emotional disposition associated with police interrogators, for example). However, most empirical consideration in organizational analysis has been given to the more common contexts where employees' emotional dispositions are designed to induce or reinforce positive feelings of organizational identification within a commercial exchange, that is, to those occupations that are concerned primarily with providing 'service with a smile'.

The literature on emotions in a variety of customer service occupations documents abundantly organizations' formal and informal efforts through recruitment, training and socialization to try to ensure that employees display the desired organizational emotions. The fixed grin of jovial employees at Disneyland (Van Maanen and Kunda, 1989), the aggressive disposition of debt collectors (Sutton, 1991) and the routinized 'have a nice day' sentiments of fast-food servers (Leidner, 1993) all reflect a display of emotions which, it could be argued, have effectively become the property of the employing organization. Such rationalized and commodified emotions have come to be understood in the critical analysis of contemporary work organizations as the outcome of *emotional labour*. This term and its recent popularity in organization theory can be attributed largely to the work of Hochschild (1979, 1983, 1993, 1998). For Hochschild, 'emotional labour' involves the management of human feeling within the labour process, as shaped by the basic requirements of capital accumulation, 'to create a publicly observable facial and bodily display' (1983: 7). According to Hochschild, emotional labour consists of two components: controlling the emotions of others ('emotional management') and controlling one's own emotions ('emotional labour'). These two aspects are linked dramaturgically (in their performance), for such work 'requires one to induce or suppress feeling in order to sustain the outward countenance that produces the proper state of mind in others' (1983: 7).

In an organizational environment of apparently intensified competition and de-humanization (Bauman, 1993), how a service is delivered has come to be perceived as central to overall organizational success. As a result, those employees who operate as 'front-line' service providers, be they providing nursing care or selling hamburgers, and who are thus perceived as key representatives of their organization, have become the focus of considerable managerial intervention into almost every aspect of their presentation of self. As Noon and Blyton have noted, 'customer-facing staff are situated in crucial "boundary-spanning" positions which link the organization to external individuals or groups' (1997: 128). Jan Carlzon (1987), as Chief Executive of a major airline, sums up the nature of such service interactions and their organizational significance as 'key moments of truth' on which those who come into contact with an organization form lasting judgements of the organization as a whole. When emotions become commodities they are clearly liable to become standardized and inauthentic (Hochschild, 1983), however As Leidner (1993) has noted, emotional labour cannot be standardized in the same way as other forms of labour, because to do so requires stable and predictable working conditions that cannot be guaranteed when people are the raw materials. Similarly, uniformity of output, a major goal of Fordist techniques of organization, constitutes a poor strategy for maintaining quality control in the commodification of emotions, since customers often perceive uniformity in emotional display as incompatible with quality. That said, just as we realize the person behind the counter in a McDonald's fast-food restaurant does not really care whether we have a nice day or not (Leidner, 1993; Ritzer, 1996), so we recognize the insincerity in the smile of the flight attendant (Hochschild, 1983). In other words our experiences of service encounters suggest that a certain level of instrumental reflexivity is not uncommon. This involves what Fineman (1994: 83) has referred to as an 'emotional conspiracy', in which neither party in a commercial exchange quite believes the 'genuineness' of feeling that the other is portraying, 'but each is willing to applaud a good act – and good acts are the stuff of effective commercial transactions'. The successful performance of emotional labour – pulling off a good act – typically requires 'a complex combination of facial expression, body language, spoken words and tone of voice' (Rafaeli and Sutton, 1987: 33). This combination seems to be secured and maintained primarily through processes of selection, training, supervision and monitoring of employee presentation and performance (Leidner, 1993; Tyler, 1997; Tyler and Abbott, 1998). Leidner has argued that emotional labour is therefore managed

> by taking care in the selection of employees; through initial training and ongoing efforts at indoctrination; through the design of systems, routines, and technology that guide workers on the job; and by instituting mechanisms of monitoring or surveillance. (1999: 85)

In most service occupations that involve 'front-line' interaction with the public, the way in which employees deliver a service has thus come to represent an increasingly important aspect of that service and, in some cases, actually constitutes the service itself. In this sense, the 'service and its mode of delivery are inextricably combined' (Filby, 1992: 37) to the extent that, in many respects, the distinction between the service and the service provider is conflated. In recent years, the range of organizational activities demanding the performance of emotional labour – and the ontological conflation on which it depends – has expanded and intensified such that a basic assumption of a critical analysis is that a gap inevitably arises between what Snyder refers to as 'the public appearances and private realities of the self' (1987: 1). Drawing on a combination of Goffman's dramaturgical approach to the performance of identity roles, as well as a Marxist perspective on alienation, Hochschild in particular has argued that the commercialization of human feeling forces people to 'accept as normal the tension they feel between their "real" and their "on-stage" selves' (1983: 185).

Many of the studies of emotional labour also highlight particular supervisory practices (Van Maanen and Kunda, 1989), often involving self and peer surveillance (Tyler, 1997), which, when combined with the various demands of the work involved, can result in the performance of emotional labour becoming especially problematic for the individual. Such demands can involve, for instance, the requirement that a particular emotional display – such as smiling for the entire duration of a long flight – be maintained over long periods of time often in working environments that are entirely unconducive to maintaining such displays (Bain and Boyd, 1998). Similarly, emotional labourers tend to be required to maintain an appropriate emotional display to customers who are being rude or offensive (Adkins, 1995; Filby, 1992; Hochschild, 1983), resulting in many of them experiencing difficulties in performing this aspect of their work and, as such, devising various coping strategies. At their simplest, these strategies may involve employees retreating to spaces constituting 'back stage' areas (where customers and possibly co-workers are not present) to let off steam or simply to 'switch off' (Van Maanen and Kunda, 1989: 67). Leidner suggests that workers resort to their scripts as a way of emotional separation, arguing that 'routines may actually offer interactive service workers some protection from assaults on their selves' (1993: 14).

Another strategy identified involves a more empathetic form of deflection. For instance, in dealing with situations involving emotional conflict, Hochschild (1983: 105–8) reports that flight attendants are trained to perceive difficult or offensive passengers as people who are experiencing problems in their personal lives or who are afraid of flying, and to manage their emotions accordingly. Underlying this aspect of their training is the requirement for attendants to respond positively to emotional conflicts and to manage them in such a way as to always 'think sales' and so, essentially, to rationalize an otherwise 'irrational' organizational interaction.

Consequently, as Hochschild has argued, 'just as we may become alienated from our physical labour in a goods-producing society, so we may become alienated from our emotional labour in a service-producing society' (1979: 571). This sense of alienation – from the products of their labour and from the labour process itself, from their co-workers and from their own human nature – may cause emotional labourers to feel false and estranged from their own 'real' feelings, an experience which Hochschild (1983: 90) terms 'emotive dissonance'. Similarly, emotional labourers are understood to 'suffer from a sense of being false, mechanical, no longer a whole integrated self' (Ferguson, 1984: 54), and of not being able to switch themselves 'back on' and re-engage their sense of self outside of their work. Critical analyses emphasize, therefore, the ways in which the performance of emotional labour fragments and alienates individuals, who 'often estrange themselves from their work as a defence against being swallowed by it' (Ferguson, 1984: 54). In sum, then, critical perspectives on the incorporation of emotion into work organizations have highlighted, as Leidner has put it, that

> management techniques for directing and monitoring interactive service workers extend managerial control to aspects of workers' selves usually considered outside of the scope of employer intervention. Bureaucratic controls are also extended beyond the boundaries of the organization through the management of customer behaviour. (1999: 81)

What such approaches have emphasized, then, is that employees, managers and customers in various ways have all become increasingly subject to attempts to rationalize their emotions, that is, to efforts to subject emotionality to various management techniques and discourses. While critical approaches have also drawn attention to the ways in which both workers and consumers may derive some benefits from the routinization of service encounters based on attempts to rationalize emotion (Leidner, 1993, 1999), what they also tend to highlight is the extent to which an instrumental approach to human emotion and social interaction raises some troubling ethical issues, not least in terms of its effects on the sense of self of those involved.

Towards the postemotional organization?

Throughout this chapter, we have examined a number of ways of thinking about emotions within contemporary work organizations. While distinct in many respects, what they share in common is a recognition of the need to re-centre the emotional dimension of organizational life as both a theoretical and practical concern for those involved in both the study and management of work organizations. As such, it may perhaps seem somewhat premature to refer to the idea of a post-emotional organization. Yet, this is an idea that has already been developed by Meštrović (1997) in his critical account of what he terms the *postemotional society*. For Meštrović, post-emotionalism does not refer to the simple absence of emotion from society, but rather to what he views as its mechanization, rationalization and commodification. Thus, extending Ritzer's (1996) McDonaldization thesis and the work of the Frankfurt School (which he argues neglected the importance of emotions and focused overly on cognition and rationality), he argues that contemporary western societies are entering a new phase of development, a phase in which synthetic, quasi-emotions have become the basis for the widespread manipulation by what he terms the authenticity industry (consisting of a combination of the culture and service industries) (Meštrović, 1997: xi), resulting in a 'McDonaldization' of emotions. Much like Willmott's (1992) analysis of cultural 'excellence', Meštrović also extends Orwell's focus on manipulation in *1984*, arguing that the culture industry, in its manifestation as the authenticity industry, also manipulates the emotions, and not just cognition, noting that: 'in addition to Orwell's original depiction of the almost exclusive manipulation of ideas, rational content, and habits of the mind, emotions and habits of the heart are also manipulated' (Meštrović,. 1997: 2).

Now while Meštrović's thesis is directed at the broader socio-cultural condition, much of what he has to say has deep affinities with the more critical literature on the subject of emotion within organizations. For example, he suggests that 'postemotionalism can account for the emergence of a distinctly new and mechanized emotion-speak' (Meštrović, 1997: 62) and uses the organizational example of Disney and what he sees as its efforts to create an artificial community premised on emotional attachment to the corporation and its values. He argues, then, that 'the McDonaldization of emotions has been an attempt to . . . create Disneyesque, artificial realms of the authentic' (1997: 98). Drawing also on Durkheim, he points out in this regard that 'the main difference between traditional rituals and postemotional rituals seems to be that traditional ones serve as tools to bring out spontaneous emotions as part of collective effervescence while postemotional rituals are mechanical, routinized attempts to simulate authentic collective effervescence' (1997: 111).

Imitative rites such as affixing totemic symbols to everyday objects – one of our colleagues never goes anywhere without her much prized cigarette lighter emblazoned with the corporate logo, for instance – to foster a sense of collective belonging (as recognized in many critical and not so critical accounts of corporate culturalism) bespeak the emotional hunger of post-emotional societies, Meštrović argues. For him, post-emotional societies are those in which 'mechanization has extended its imperialistic realm from technology and industry to colonize the last bastion of nature: the emotions' (1997: 146). Thus, the concept of post-emotionalism emphasizes that what appears to be postmodern disorder, creative chaos or a genuine attempt to embrace the apparently irrational and thus potentially disorganizing dimensions of emotional life, to celebrate the Otherness of feelings, desires and intuitions, 'turns out to have a hidden order of its own, and to be highly automatized, rehearsed, and planned' (1997: 2).

Post-emotionalism, then, can be seen to encapsulate quite succinctly the critical conception of organized emotions considered in the latter part of this chapter, exemplifying as it does a vision of an organizational world full of emotions, yet devoid of any 'real' emotional content. However, this is not to dismiss the potential of a postmodern-inspired re-cognition of the emotional Other of systemic rationality as a potentially resistant or critical force in the face of contemporary practices of control and regulation. Genuine passion, rage and love all continue to simmer within organizational life, threatening to spill over as disruptive forces, negating the logic of order and the control that continues to characterize the structuring of organizational relations of power and domination (see Burrell, 1997). What a more critical reading of such developments suggests, however, is that what cannot be ignored is the fact that this space can also be a highly circumscribed one that is equally amenable to mechanized processes of order and regulation or, in Meštrović's terms, post-emotionalization. For as Marcuse (1986 [1964]) noted, the de-sublimation of the non-rationalized dimensions of human life can, if approached in a 'rationalized' manner, produce perhaps the most effective mechanism of control and repression, a process which an uncritical celebration of the emotional in organizational life may itself, albeit unwittingly, serve to perpetuate.

Conclusion

In discussing emotion in organizations we have endeavoured to identify not only the various factors underpinning its emergence as an increasingly significant concern within organization theory, but also another pertinent example of the impact of postmodernism both on the management and study of organizations. From a broadly modernist perspective considered at the beginning of this chapter, emotion is perceived as a relatively undesirable appendage to reason, as irrational, or rather as non-rational. From this vantage point, emotion should either be excluded from organized life or, as has been proclaimed more recently, rationalized and managed as yet another quantifiable resource. Emerging largely as a critique of this approach, what appears to be a postmodernist orientation towards the conceptualization and analysis of organizational emotionality emphasizes that emotion and its expression should be both valorized and celebrated as a previously silenced Other of modern organizational rationality. Broadly, then, postmodernized modes of organization, from this perspective at least, would recognize emotion as one of its intrinsic elements, inaugurating a climate in which passion and pain, tears and laughter would be understood as central to organizational life.

Yet, as we argued is the case with regard to the broader theme of culture within organizations, the boundary between these two perspectives appears to be somewhat blurred. For even where emotions are valorized, in Cooper's (1998) conception of 'EQ' or in Mumby and Putman's (1992) 'bounded emotionality' for instance, an important caveat remains; namely, that organizational emotion, whether merely tolerated or openly celebrated, is required to be both expressed and managed 'properly'. So while the apparent shift towards a postmodernist mode of organization, marked by an embracing of affectivity, is certainly suggestive of a concomitant displacement of strategic rationality, it seems to achieve this only in favour of a new kind of instrumentality, an instrumentality that, as Fineman has noted, 'aims to harness positive emotion as a "success" ingredient' (1994: 86).

In the latter part of the chapter, however, we also outlined the insights of a range of more critical approaches to understanding organizations as emotional arenas that demand the performance of emotional labour and management from the heart, so to speak. Here, we drew largely on the work of those who have sought to understand emotional organization as the commodification of that which was previously excluded from the realms of work organizations, or as the colonization of the organizational Other for primarily instrumental ends. This approach has emphasized, concomitantly, the extent to which the emotions of employees are considered fair game for employer intervention when self-presentation and interactive service style are integral parts of the labour process, as increasingly seems to be the case in contemporary western economies. This latter approach has also highlighted, in line with a more critical reading of postmodernism, the ways in which organization theory has been weakened by its failure to acknowledge its own presupposition of a hierarchical dualism that places emotions outside of the realm of rational organizations and their analysis.[2] Hence, the (re)discovery of the emotional has also provided an important critical lever, one that has helped to expose certain mechanisms that are utilized within systemic modes of organizing that have depended on the erection of crude dualistic frameworks, suppressing certain voices while valorizing others. By incorporating some of the conceptual insights of postmodernism into a more critical theorization of emotion in organizational life, such approaches have tended to emphasize emotion as a constitutive organizational Other, as the irrational on which the rationality of organizations depends and which recent developments in organization theory have 're-cognized' as central to the process of organization and its managerial mediation. Thus, at the level of epistemology, rationality can be seen to need emotionality as its Other, to be able to assert the superiority of rationality in order to sustain its privileged position within the management of work organizations. This more critical incorporation of postmodernist ideas into the study of work organizations emphasizes, therefore, that once we strip away layers of reified 'rationality' from our understanding of organizational life, a veritable cornucopia of emotion is revealed. Seen in this light, emotions can be understood as fundamentally 'within the texture of organizing' (Fineman, 1993: 1). In this sense, then, it seems that a postmodernist critique of the logocentric character of modernist organizational rationality could potentially provide a powerful resource in any critical assault on the instrumentality that continues to pervade contemporary organizational life and its study.

In this respect, the material considered throughout the latter part of this chapter has also emphasized that the rationalization of emotion, as indicated, for instance, by the routinization of human interactions by large corporations and other bureaucracies, is a trend that seems to epitomize the levels of de-personalization, de-humanization, manipulation and superficiality that characterize many work organizations in their current form. In this sense, attention, emotion and simply recognition have become the scarcest of resources in our so-called 'postemotional society' (Meštrović, 1997). A critical understanding of emotion in organizations therefore needs to be grounded in a critique of the promotion of organized emotional exchange as both a cause and reflection of the extent to which such interaction occurs within an increasingly competitive organizational environment. In such an environment, one in which the actual goods and services being offered for sale (be they airline seats, hamburgers, widgets or whatever) are relatively indistinguishable, considerable significance is attached not only to the physical or material nature of the service offered, but also to its psychological, aesthetic and emotional nature – to the 'experience' of the service. But does this imply that an increasingly instrumantal attitude towards the 'self' is gaining acceptance? Since many service organizations call on workers to turn relatives and friends into customers, and to attempt at least to turn customers into friends, will the boundary between work organizations and personal relationships[3] be eroded further? As Leidner (1999) has noted, the defining qualities of interactive service work require that organization theory recasts some of the questions that have traditionally framed the study of work organizations. Reflecting on the organization of emotions in the workplace links broad questions concerning subjectivity, the ethical underpinnings of social interaction and the scope of organizational power to shape social life. In the following chapter, we consider these questions more specifically in relation to sexuality, postmodernism and work organizations.

Notes

1   As Albrow (1992: 318) notes, the German translated here as 'impersonal' is 'sachlich' in Weber's *Economy and Society* (1978), which means both 'attending to the matter in hand' and 'businesslike'.

2   Of particular note here is the way in which Alvesson and Deetz's (1996) attempt to outline a postmodernism of resistance is characterized by a largely Derridean critique of a 'philosophy of presence'.

3   It could be argued that, in a capitalist society at least, this is a boundary that provides some degree of protection against exploitative abuses of power and invasions of privacy (to which Weber alluded in his use of the term 'Gerhaus' as a description of bureaucratic organizations, see Kanter [1977]).

6

Organization, Postmodernism and Sexuality

Anything that suggests erotic excess always implies disorder. (Bataille, 1962: 170)

This society turns everything it touches into a potential source of progress *and* of exploitation, of drudgery *and* satisfaction, of freedom *and* of oppression. Sexuality is no exception. (Marcuse, 1986 [1964]: 78 *original emphasis*)

In the final chapter of this part, we consider what remains perhaps one of the most taboo topics within contemporary organization theory, namely sex and sexuality. Certainly, the separation of sexuality and organization, based on the juxtaposition which Bataille alludes to above, means that sexuality as a 'frontier' of control and resistance within organizational life (Burrell, 1984: 102) – itself both organized and organizing – seems to have been somewhat neglected. However, even where this has begun to change, recent accounts of the role of sexuality in the workplace have tended to focus particularly on sexuality and organizational power relations, highlighting most notably the organizational control of women through sexual discrimination and harassment. While such accounts are clearly important to understanding the lived experience of work organizations, it could be argued that what has been omitted from any sustained empirical or theoretical attention has been the idea of 'organization sexuality' (Hearn and Parkin, 1987) more generally, that is, the mutually constitutive relationship between sexuality and organization. Indeed, it seems fair to argue that what Judith Butler (1990a) has termed the 'heterosexual matrix' – the normative relationship that is deemed to exist in contemporary western societies between sex, gender and sexuality – and the ways in which this matrix is organized in and through work, has been something of a neglected aspect of organizational analysis. Thus, despite an increasing number of references to the significance of sexuality to work organizations and vice-versa (see, for a notable example, Brewis and Linstead, 2000a), and to attempts to manage and rationalize sexuality, the relationship between organization and sexuality continues to be marginalized from the discourses that are seen to constitute the discipline. Hence, the analysis of work and its organization has continued to proceed relatively separately from a much more flourishing concern with sexuality in social theory more generally. In this sense, Eagleton's (1996: 69) suggestion that in the 1960s 'everyone shifted over from production to perversion' seems something of an over-statement when applied to the study of organizations. Indeed, organization theorists appear to remain resolutely unaffected by his corollary that 'there's nothing more sexy than sex' (Eagleton, 1996: 69). Hence the 'paradox' of organization sexuality: 'enter most organizations and you enter a world of sexuality', but read what has been written about them (with perhaps, the notable exception of the Whitehouse) and 'you would imagine these organizations, so finely analyzed, are inhabited by a breed of strange, asexual eunuch figures' (Hearn and Parkin, 1987: 3–4).

In what follows, we consider the relationship between organization, sexuality and postmodernism. In so doing, we attempt to reflect, in particular, on the possible implications of a proliferation of 'postmodern sexualities' (Simon, 1996) for contemporary work organizations. In our first section, we review the location of sexuality in the 'organization of production' paradigm that Burrell and Hearn (1989) identify as being shaped by a triangle of modernism, 'big science' (Lyotard, 1984) and productivity. We begin with a consideration of the central tenets of 'modernist sexuality' (Hawkes, 1996), characterized by the association of sexuality with 'nature', the 'scientific' classification of sexual subjectivities and the primacy of heterosexuality. We then examine the emergence and influence of sexology, the 'science' of sexuality, and its relationship to what Gramsci (1971) termed a 'Fordist sexuality'. We then consider processes of (i) 'de-sexualization' (the exclusion of sexuality from organizations) and (ii) over-inclusion (the incorporation of sexuality into organizational imperatives) (Burrell, 1984).

In the second section, we go on to explore the impact of postmodernism on the relationship between sexuality and organization. In particular, we consider the potential contribution of queer theory, based on a performative sexual ontology (Butler, 1988, 1990a, 1990b), to a critical analysis of 'sexualization' – the commodification of sexuality – in work organizations. Finally, we reflect critically on the extent to which the 'over-inclusion' (Burrell and Hearn, 1989) of sexuality in work organizations since the 1960s at an empirical level signifies a potential shift towards a de-stabilizing postmodern mode of organization characterized by a 'liberalization' of sex, or conversely, a post (neo)-Fordist flexible organization of sexuality in line with an intensification of the accumulative imperatives of modernity (Hawkes, 1996).

The modernist organization of sexuality

In her historical-sociological account of the development of modern conceptions of sex and sexuality, Hawkes (1996) argues that in addition to the parameters of modernity more usually addressed – technological progress, the spatial and social organization of populations, the triumph of reason and so on – there was an additional element of the process of modernization that is seldom the focus of commentary or analysis, namely, the ordering, and indeed organization, of sexuality. As she puts it, 'the suppression of the irrational which was the corollary of modernity led to a renewed focus on the disruptive potential of sensual pleasure' (1996: 31) and so to the organization of sexuality on an unprecedented scale. Hawkes argues that given the central dynamic of asceticism and the spirit of modernity, sexuality was a prime candidate for rationalization throughout the modern era. This was reflected not simply in the outright prohibition of sex, but through the reordering of ways of knowing, thinking and speaking about sexuality, of what is prioritized and marginalized in modernist sexual orthodoxy; in other words, in the organization of sexuality. Weeks (1989) notes that such cultural discourses – both cognitive and normative in their organizing capacities – probably originated in early Christianity, becoming enshrined in statute during the sixteenth century. In his *History of Sexuality*, Foucault (1979, 1985, 1986) emphasizes how they have received scientific legitimation in the modernist conception of sexuality since the eighteenth century.

Hawkes (1996) emphasizes that, at the heart of this *modernist sexuality*, are three basic organizing principles. Perhaps the most fundamental and enduring is a scientific association of sexuality with 'nature'. Conceived as a biological essence, sexuality is understood as a natural, pre-social ontology, classified as the property of individual subjects and residing in the biological constitution of the body. Consequently, certain parts of the body and how we use them came to be designated for sexuality, while others were forbidden as physically and morally dangerous, or as inefficient. Secondly, and related to this, was the emergence of sexual 'types' – homosexual, heterosexual and so on – and an enduring convergence of behaviour and identity, according to which sexuality came to be understood as an aspect of the inner self. Though posited as the source of the capacity for reason and moral judgement, this core or inner self also came to be seen, in Freudian psychoanalysis, for instance as the locus of sensuality. Finally, modernist sexuality was constrained by the primacy of (re)productive (hetero)sexuality, so that a persistent presence in the construction of healthy, moral and rational 'modern' sexuality was (and remains, we could argue) the privileging of heterosexuality.

As Hawkes emphasizes, the self-appointed guardian of this modernist attempt to organize and ultimately contain sexuality was the emergent patriarchal bourgeoisie. As Mort (1987) argues, appropriate sexual behaviour became a yardstick against which this class sought to distinguish

itself not only from its socio-economic inferiors, but also from what it collectively viewed as the debauched excesses of the decadent and waning
aristocracy.[1] 'Modernist sexuality' was driven, then, largely by a concern to
preserve male dominance (M. Jackson, 1987) and to secure social status for
the bourgeoisie during a period of rapid social change and, therefore, came
to assume a deeply gendered and class-based character. As a consequence
of this modernization of sexuality, and the imperatives underpinning it,

... those manifestations of desire which were deemed to have negative consequences for the maintenance of the patriarchal bourgeois hegemony – women's
sexual autonomy, same-sex desire, expressions of youthful sexuality and auto-
eroticism – were marginalized and even outlawed. (Hawkes, 1996: 3)

Through a process of modernization, sexuality therefore became increasingly subject to systematic organization. Furthermore, in a period in which
scientific approaches to the management and investigation of human
behaviour were dominant (see Chapter 1), it is perhaps no surprise that
scientific analyses of sex also emerged in western societies during the late
nineteenth and early twentieth centuries. Characteristically janus-faced –
that is, both radical and 'modernizing' and at the same time instrumental
in remoulding a conservative (pre-modern) sexual orthodoxy – 'the emergence of sex as an object of study was one of the major features of the social
sciences of the period and stands as a central moment in the constitution of
modern sexuality' (Weeks, 1989: 141).

Underpinned by the pursuit of science in the search for the 'truth' about
an 'essential' and biologically-determined sexuality, sexologists such as
Ellis (1913), Kinsey, Pomeroy and Martin (1948, 1953), and Masters and
Johnson (1966), each of whom played a key role in establishing sexology as
a 'science', espoused an implied, if not conscious, denial of subjectivity and
moral judgement in a body of work which reflected this scientific approach
to human behaviour. For instance, in his presidential address to the 1929
Congress of the World League for Sexual Reform, Hirschfeld declared that
'a sexual ethics based on science is the only sound system of ethics' (cited
in Weeks, 1986: 111). In this sense, it has been argued (Brecher, 1970;
Robinson, 1976) that sexologists advocated an Enlightenment-based sexo-
logical revolution in which prejudice, religious moralism and authoritarian
sexual codes would dissolve in the light of scientific reason. Hence, as
Weeks has observed, 'sexual knowledge and sexual politics marched hand
in hand as the sexologists ... became the patrons of sex reform' (Weeks,
1986: 112). However, despite such apparently progressive ideals, related, in
the work of Ellis particularly, to a broader radical political agenda (see
Nottingham, 1998), sexology evolved throughout the modern era as a body
of specialized knowledge kept and maintained by expert 'sexologists' who
proclaimed themselves to be devoted to differentiating 'normal' from
'abnormal' sexual behaviour (a development that had important legal consequences). This meant that in the increasingly secularized world of
modern capitalism, as Hawkes has noted, 'the objectivity of science was to

assume the role of moral arbitration . . . and the servants of science inherited . . . the mantle of moral arbiter' (1996: 50). The central position of heterosexuality was, therefore, both retained and strengthened as 'what was once ordained by God was affirmed by the men of science' (Hawkes, 1996: 72).

Underpinning sexology in the pursuit of the 'truth' of sexuality, therefore, was (and remains) an ontological conflation of 'natural' and what is 'normal'. Despite the stronger emphasis on the social construction of sexuality (Evans, 1993; Gagnon and Simon, 1973; Weeks, 1985, 1986) from the 1960s onwards, and a strong shift away from the positivist influences of biology, medicine and sexology in the social-scientific analysis of sexuality, this essentialist ontology continued to exert a powerful influence on popular conceptions of the nature of human sexuality. As Carabine notes, this has left us with 'a legacy of sex as unavoidable, as given, an uncontrollable urge needing to be expressed. The belief is that we need to have sex regularly, especially in the case of men, otherwise there will be a dangerous build up of desire' (1992: 25). This is a view that legitimated the conviction that male sexuality is active and aggressive, and is fundamental to male identity and masculinity. Indeed, as M. Jackson (1987, *emphasis added*) has observed, the scientific model of sexuality constructed by sexologists 'is one which both reflects male supremacist values and promotes the interests of men by defining sex in male terms, . . . *thus facilitating* . . . *the increasing sexualization of western women* which has taken place since the nineteenth century'.

Thus, the 'scientific' pursuit of 'accurate knowledge of the fundamental instincts upon which life is built' (Ellis, 1913: 103) should be seen, we would argue, as fundamental to the progressive subjection of human sensual experience to modernist organizational imperatives. Hawkes in particular has argued that through the process of sexual 'modernization' and the subjection of sexuality to scientific discourse, modernity came to be characterized by a 'sexual mode of production' (Hawkes, 1996) according to which issues of efficiency and outcome in relation to (hetero)sex came to the fore. For Hawkes, modernist regimes of sexual efficiency came to replace pre-modernist discourses of physical and moral danger, as the science of sex offered a blueprint for the effective and efficient rationalization of the erotic, presenting us with both a desired end and an efficient means to that end – a Taylorization of sex. (This is a theme to which we return in due course.) The fear of sexual danger came to be replaced by a fear of sexual dysfunction, manifest in anxieties about performance and in the efficient deployment of resources, most obviously apparent in the promotion of 'family planning'.

What all this suggests, then, is the emergence of a sexual economy in which the expression of sexual desires and pleasures, deemed superfluous to the (re)production of modern organizations, was considered wasteful in both the physiological and moral sense. An important feature of the spirit of modern capitalism was thus an asceticism, one mediated through rationality. Within this context, modernist sexual asceticism can be understood as a re-ordering or prioritizing of aspects of human behaviour rather than as an outright sexual prohibition, according to which ascetic discipline entailed the elimination of irrational spontaneity and, consequently, the formal exclusion of sexuality from the life of the work organization (Sayer, 1991), a process that Burrell (1984) referred to in his seminal paper on organization and sexuality as 'de-sexualization'.

Organizational de-sexualization

The idea that sexuality and rational efficiency are somehow incompatible and that, as such, sexuality should be excluded from workplace activities is illustrated well, it has been argued, in Weber's work on the development of the ideal rational bureaucracy. Bologh (1990: 291) in particular has observed that for Weber, 'love and greatness were incompatible'; the former was deemed by him to be responsible for extinguishing the vital spark of drive and ambition in man (sic) whereas the latter was understood to be based on 'discontented activity'. As Burrell observes, from the perspective of Weber's bias towards discontented action, it is almost as if he 'wishes us to celebrate the celibate' (1992: 71). Hence, Weber argued that modern organizations required that erotic impulses be contained within purposive frameworks of reproductive marital alliance.

While largely developed in a somewhat theoretical and abstract environment, these general principles were also not lost on the managers of real (rather than ideal type) work organizations. Among factory owners, and the emerging breed of professional managers, sexual activity increasingly became associated with a lack of production and thus a decrease in efficiency. Accounts by Walby (1989) and Hearn (1992) have emphasized the extent to which the modern workplace was organized largely according to management attempts to segregate, marginalize and suppress sexuality. As Burrell notes, since the late eighteenth century a range of 'management control systems were formulated in which the spending of time and the spending of the body became the key focuses of attention' (1997: 219). Where tactics of gender segregation did not work, workers in a wide range of industries were routinely fined for engaging in any form of sexualized interaction during working hours (De Grazia, 1962; Rodgers, 1978) or, as in the case of Wedgwood's head clerk and cashier, faced outright dismissal (cited in Burrell, 1997: 217), as sensual asceticism came to be widely associated not only with efficient organization, but more generally with the civilizing process (Elias, 1978, 1982).

Thus, in terms of the dominance of certain forms of sexuality – monogamous, reproductive, heterosexual – the expansion of competitive capitalism was closely related to the emergence of the bourgeois political economy of sexuality outlined above, an economy in which the quest for productivity implied the idealization of economy and self-restraint in sexuality and a revulsion towards all forms of pleasure-seeking sexualities, including spending one's semen on 'unproductive' purposes. According to Lofstrom (1997), this bourgeois sexual economy presented itself as the paragon of morality, characterized by a sexual ethos of thrift and discipline. It was not, however, merely towards the regulation of heterosexual activity that such logic was directed. In particular, Greenberg (1988) has also suggested that as the capitalist economy developed, from the nineteenth century onwards, into a more merciless struggle, the legitimacy of bureaucratic organizations required impersonality and an even more rigorous exclusion of any emotional or sexual relations that might appear to erode rationality.

Consequently, the rivalry between men inherent in capitalism became exacerbated such that a heteronormative culture of organizational life became almost unquestionable. As Adam has noted, as 'affectionate male bonds became irreconcilable with the fastidious austerity of the businessman and sober practicality of the male workers' (Adam, 1985: 663), they became increasingly condemned. Hence, the pronounced taboo on sexuality, particularly between men, was as much a manifestation of a bourgeois political economy of sexuality, as it was of the (initially) religious or moral conception of 'natural' or 'normal' behaviour outlined above.

For some, the rationalization of sexuality, of which the condemnation of homosexuality is but one notable example, can best be understood in terms of a framework of (Fordist) relations of production (Hawkes, 1996; Jackson and Scott, 1997). For Jackson and Scott (1997), the trends outlined above towards a rational construction of the (hetero)sexual, coupled with a 'scientific' approach to the management of sexual activity, contributed significantly to the *Taylorisation of sex*. Borrowing from Taylor's principles of scientific management, they argue that the execution of this philosophy in a Fordist mode of organization – associated with de-skilling or with limiting skills to those needed for specific, repetitive task performance – constitutes an important framework within which to understand sexuality in the modern era. They also note that

> sexual skills are defined and delimited in specific ways. The social construction of sexual aptitude assumes that these are not craft skills passed down through generations, but require specialist training founded on expert knowledge. In this regard, sexuality has become caught up in the rationalizing motor of modernity. (Jackson and Scott, 1997: 558)

In equating modernist sexuality with scientific management, Hawkes (1996) and Jackson and Scott (1997) adopt a similar approach to those critical social theorists who have argued that this modernist organization of sexuality was indeed conducive to, and should not be separated from, Fordist accumulation imperatives. Critical theorists, such as Gramsci (1971), Reich (1962) and Marcuse (1972 [1955]) have observed how Fordist modes of regulation extended well beyond the immediate site of production, as sexuality in the modern era became excessively sublimated to the interests of calculative rationality. Emphasizing that the objectifying effects of the capitalist labour process must be fought, at least in part, on the terrain of sexuality, Reich (1962) argued that sexual liberation was a fundamental key to social freedom, a disruptive energy that could fragment the established order blocked only by the power of capitalism and its 'civilizing' effects. Marcuse (1972 [1955]: 42, 102) argued similarly that the 'performance principle' governing capitalist civilization was fundamentally dependent upon the 'repressive organization of sexuality' – the irreconcilable conflict between alienating labour and Eros. Marcuse linked alienation with the repression of sexuality, as a component of Eros or the 'life instinct', arguing that sexual relations are controlled by and for the harnessing of human energy into production (and reproduction). For him, only a post-capitalist society would allow for an eroticization of labour based on the organization of work according to genuinely inter-subjective rather than alienated social relations:

> The transformation of sexuality into Eros and its extension to lasting libidinal work relations, here presuppose the rational re-organization of a huge industrial apparatus, a highly specialized societal division of labour, the use of fantastically destructive energies, and the cooperation of vast masses. (Marcuse, 1972[1955]: 153)

In a much earlier analysis, published in the 1920s, Gramsci had also observed how the regulation of sexuality and of sexual behaviour occurred through what he referred to as 'a process of psycho-physical adaptation to specific conditions of work . . . not something "natural" or innate, but [which] has to be acquired' (1971: 296). He argued that the formation of this sexual habitus was a necessary element in sustaining the mass production techniques of Fordism, which required that sexuality be mechanized and excluded from the sphere of work organizations. Just as the activities of workers in the work process must be shaped carefully towards a given end, so their appetites outside the workplace must reflect the prevailing ideology of ordered rational action. For Gramsci, 'the truth is that the new type of man demanded by the rationalization of production and work cannot be developed until the sexual instinct has been suitably regulated and until it too has been rationalized' (1971: 297). Gramsci suggested, therefore, that a distinctly *Fordist sexuality* was a necessary correlate of mass production and consumption, one that was characterized by 'a new sexual ethic' (1971: 296) of regulation and rationalization, of sexual asceticism, suited to Fordist modes of production and work organization. For Gramsci (1971: 300), then, modern work organizations demanded a Fordist sexuality, characterized by regulation, rationalization and discipline, 'assimilated . . . in the form of more or less permanent habits'.

Burrell (1984, 1992) conceptualizes this organization of sexuality as a gradual process of *de-sexualization*, shaped by a combination of

> (i) the civilizing process and the development of religious morality, combined with (ii) the evolution of a calculative rationality according to which sexuality is

perceived as a nonrational, uncontrollable factor, to be suppressed in the interests of efficiency and order and, finally, (iii) the development of control over time and the body. (1984: 113)

As he puts it, 'with modernity came surveillance, bureaucratization and desexualization' (Burrell, 1992: 72). De-sexualization implies 'a managerial effort to repress sexual relations and expel them from the organization into the "home"' (1992: 70). The rationale for de-sexualization, he argues, has sometimes taken the form of medical advice to employers, based on a theory of equilibrium of bodily fluids; it has sometimes been based on religious beliefs, sometimes on the social norms associated with the civilizing process (Elias, 1978, 1982) and sometimes on the need for discipline (Foucault, 1979). As Burrell notes, 'whatever the rationale, the expulsion and repression of sexuality have been key management goals' (1992: 71). Burrell's de-sexualization thesis is thus predicated on the assumption that modernist work organizations suppressed sexuality through dual strategies of *eradication* (of sexuality from work organizations) and *containment* (of sexuality within the non-work sphere). The 'suppression of sexuality, therefore, involved both eradication and containment, inside and outside work respectively' (Burrell, 1984: 99), and the process of organizational de-sexualization both a means of subordinating and/or rationalizing out certain forms of sexuality.[2]

However, simply to conceptualize the relationship between modern organizational activity and sexuality as one shaped solely by the exclusion of the latter would be mistaken, as Burrell himself emphasizes. For, as Burrell argues, the modernist de-sexualization of work organizations was also characterized by a related process involving the 'over-inclusion' of sexuality in organizational life. It is to this 'silent inclusion' (Burrell and Hearn, 1989: 13), one that simultaneously valorized yet denied the existence of sexuality within modern organizations, that we now turn our attention.

Over-inclusion and 'organization sexuality'

Focusing on the *over-inclusion* of sexuality into organizations, Hearn and Parkin (1987) argue that sexuality and contemporary work organizations exist in a dialectical relationship whereby workplaces construct and are constructed through sexuality. That is to say, despite formal proclamations on the exclusion of sexuality from the workplace, sexual relations remain pervasive throughout organizations, particularly through the power of men (over sexuality and women); the power of the public sphere (over sexuality and the private); the power of production (over sexuality and reproduction) and the power of reproduction (over sexuality). Thus, for Hearn and Parkin (1987), the 'paradox' of organization sexuality is that, far from being excluded from the workplace, sexuality is an integral part of the workplace. It is present in the organization of work time and space

(Hearn et al., 1989), in organizational cultures (Gherardi, 1995; Mills, 1994), in the sexualization of bodies (Brewis, 1998; Martin, 1990; Trethewey, 1999) and in gendered rules and organizational control (Witz and Savage, 1992). This can be seen particularly at the level of organizational symbolism, with powerful organizations frequently seeking to assert their market supremacy through, for example, phallic skyscrapers, fast cars and, more overtly, representations of successful and powerful men. As Hearn and Parkin also note, sexuality pervades the language of work organizations: markets are 'penetrated' and the outcome of competitive struggles means that some are inevitably 'fucked' or 'screwed' (1987: 147–8).

Adopting a similar approach to conceptualizing the relationship between organization and sexuality, Brewis and Linstead (2000a) have recently addressed the extent to which 'sex' and 'work' continue – mistakenly in their view – to be perceived as antithetical, arguing that not only does sexuality pervade work organizations, but that sexuality in everyday life is itself highly organized. Drawing on a range of theorists associated with post-structuralism, including Bataille (1962), Foucault (1979, 1985, 1986), Deleuze and Guattari (1984), as well as a variety of empirical sources, they explore some of the ways in which organizational behaviour is shaped by sexuality. Much like Hearn and Parkin's (1987) earlier work, their analysis emphasizes the mutually constitutive and highly complex relationship that can be said to exist between sex and work.

Perhaps nowhere is the intimacy – and, indeed, complexity – of this relationship more obvious than in what has been termed *sexualization*, through which sexuality becomes integral to the labour process (Adkins, 1995; Tyler, 1997). In much the same way as emotion (see Chapter 5), many work organizations seem to utilize women's sexuality as a means of pursuing strategic organizational goals. Recent empirical research has highlighted sexualization in the tourist industry (Adkins, 1995), in waitressing (E.J. Hall, 1993), in the betting and gaming industry (Filby, 1992), in secretarial work (Pringle, 1989a), in the work of flight attendants (Hochschild, 1983; Tyler, 1997) and, perhaps most obviously, in prostitution or 'sex work' (Brewis and Linstead, 2000b; McKeganey and Barnard, 1996; O'Connell-Davidson, 1995; Scambler and Scambler, 1997). Filby in particular has argued that in the performance of sexual labour, the distinction between service work and sexuality is conflated so that 'gender constructions are part of the total package which constitutes the product' (1992: 37). Filby's account emphasizes that in selling their sexuality, sexual labourers are dependent upon their tacit skills and assumed capacities as sexual subjects who are expected to initiate sexual exchanges themselves. What this research has highlighted is the extent to which 'doing sexuality' at work is increasingly conflated with 'giving good service' (E.J. Hall, 1993), so that primarily women, in a number of disparate roles and in a wide variety of occupational and organizational settings, are classified and utilized for their sexual characteristics. Such accounts emphasize the harnessing of female sexuality and the extent to which, as Filby has put it, 'the figures, the personality and the bums'(1992: 23) are all increasingly important commercially.

Within this context sexual discrimination (DiTomaso, 1989), male domination (Collinson and Collinson, 1989; Sheppard, 1989) and unwanted sexual attention in the form of harassment (Cockburn, 1990; Gutek, 1985; Gutek et al., 1990; York, 1989) can all be understood as fundamental aspects of organization sexuality, and its 'over-inclusion' into organizational power relations. As Folgero and Fjeldstad (1995) have argued, due to their inherent characteristics, service organizations in particular are a prime breeding ground for sexual harassment, although the extent to which this is the case is rarely in focus because of the gendered, cultural norms governing occupations which are based largely on the incorporation of sexuality into service work, notably the expectation of 'sexual exchange' (Adkins, 1995). As Sims, Fineman and Gabriel have put it, 'women's sexuality is far from peripheral in most of these jobs' (1993: 151).

Building on Pateman's (1988) work on the sexual contract, Silvia Gherardi (1995) argues that in many work organizations a sexual exchange underpins the employment contract in that the organization purchases the right to command, within certain limits, differently sexed bodies and to structure the ways in which they express their sexuality, exploiting this sexuality when it has value (for the organization) and repressing it when it proves useless to the organization or impedes production (Gherardi, 1995). She emphasizes that not only gender differences are co-opted by organizations, but that employees' sexual skills are also incorporated so that, within certain limits, the organization acquires control over the sexuality of its employees as well as, in doing so, its customers or clients. In this respect, she emphasizes the extent to which sexualization can function as a mode of socialization, as 'organizations deploy the sexual skills of their employees to flatter, to smooth, to satisfy and to ensnare the customer' (Gherardi, 1995: 43). As Tancred-Sheriff (1989) has also emphasized, the sexualization of commercial relationships is particularly evident in 'boundary roles' – those where the employee encounters people or environments external to the organization. Following Tancred-Sheriff, Gherardi argues that in such settings sexuality can act as an instrument of control through which women are used simultaneously to socialize and to seduce those who come into contact with the organization.

Developing this focus on the socializing effects of sexualization but turning her attention to the employment relationship, Gherardi also notes how, for those employed in what Tancred-Sheriff terms 'adjunct control jobs', 'participating in the authority of others, representing it, exercising it vicariously, is seductive to the extent that the position of subordination is legitimate and psychologically acceptable' (Gherardi, 1995: 44 emphasis added). For Gherardi, the seductiveness of authority over others can compensate those who occupy otherwise subordinate roles psychologically, thus serving to reproduce existing power inequalities within organizations and the employment relations upon which they rest. All of those who come into contact with the organization (employees, customers, suppliers and so on) are understood to be seduced by the organization itself, so that potential resistance to the organization is neutralized. In Gherardi's account, sexuality is of great interest to organizations, then, not simply in terms of its commodification, but in its more subtle manifestation as seduction: 'it eroticizes the workplace and weds control with pleasure' (1995: 45).

This aspect of her approach – a focus on the seductive nature of organizational power – is at the heart of what could be conceived of as an S/M (sado/masochistic) analysis of organizational life. Gherardi emphasizes that the sexual context of the employment contract, the pleasures of organizational eroticism and the seduction of organizational power, mean that organization sexuality can be understood as 'a relationship with sadistic and masochistic characteristics', one which, of course, presupposes the participation of consenting adults (1995: 61). What is significant about her approach, in this respect, is that sexuality is not only the object of her analysis – as a commodity, for instance – but also provides the analytical framework within which organizational power relations are conceptualized. In this sense, her approach is reminiscent of that developed by Hollway (1991) who, in a similar vein to Knights and Willmott's earlier work (1989), focuses on the centrality of 'productive desire' to organizational governance.[3] Hollway argues that, given the extent to which anxiety and psychological 'lack' are predominant features of the subjective experience of contemporary western societies, the seductive nature of power is fundamental to the reproduction of organizations. In this respect, she argues, productive desire is engendered through individuals being seduced by organizations into pursuing organizationally desirable modes of identity, securing strategies of control and, therefore, a sense of self through oppressive organizational discourses and practices. Although Hollway does not make the connection herself, a similar S/M analysis can be applied to her understanding of organizational power relations in so far as, for Hollway, it is precisely the seduction of organizational identification, and the 'authority' accorded to those who occupy 'adjunct control' jobs for instance, that facilitates the seemingly pleasurable reproduction of asymmetrical organizational power.

It is not only where women operate as front-line service providers, or in adjunct control functions, that their sexuality is subject to a process of over-inclusion, however. Trethewey (1999), in her study of women working in a professional and, as such, usually managerial capacity, has exposed the ways in which such women are constantly aware of, and respond to, their prescribed status as sexual beings. Her research findings suggested, above all, that such women are frequently occupied by what they considered to be the need to monitor and control manifestations of their sexuality, particularly in terms of the potential for their female bodies

to display 'spillage, slips, leaks and excess' (Trethewey, 1999: 438). As she
goes on to note,

> women's bodies may overflow via pregnancy, menstrual bleeding, emotional
> displays and unruly clothing. The excessively sexual or undisciplined body
> draws attention to the otherness of the female, private body in the masculine
> sphere of work. (1999: 438)

In particular, Trethewey's female respondents identified clothing as an
important tool for occluding corporeal manifestations of their sexuality.
Tight clothing, 'plunging necklines' and 'short skirts' were all identified as
potentially detrimental to a woman's occupational credibility; functioning
as signifiers of excessive sexuality or of a lack of professionalism within the
workplace. In Trethewey's account, female sexuality was thus acknowledged, by the women in particular, as something men found uncontrolled
or uncontrollable, constituting a present and continuous threat to organizational order and male domination.

Yet, even where exclusion appeared to be the dominant strategy pursued
by these women, they continued to find themselves subject to competing
discourses on sexual appropriateness. Where the priority was to disguise
or disrupt the embodied expression of their sexualities, this could only be
pursued within certain acceptable limits. For example, the women interviewed generally observed the fact that to dress in such a way as to
excessively disguise their sexual identities was to run the risk of being
perceived as too masculine, or even worse (sic), a lesbian. Trethewey's
(1999: 443) interviewees thus point out how, when seeking to dress 'appropriately' for work, they had to be careful to wear clothes that were 'not too
sexy and not too prudish', 'pretty but not too feminine', 'interesting but not
too suggestive', 'tailored but not too tight'.

Certainly, one important consequence of such studies is a realization
that any analysis of organization sexuality, and in particular the process of
sexualization, therefore needs to highlight the extent to which 'we . . .
cannot think about sexuality without taking into account gender' (Weeks,
1986: 45). The commodification of gendered sexuality and the management of sexual orientation in the workplace bring into focus that, as Mills
has argued (1989: 31), 'in a world in which women are viewed as subordinate to men, in which heterosexuality is the norm and in which
organizations expect behaviour to conform to a view of "normal" gender
relations, sexuality becomes an embodiment of power relations'.

Sex and the modern(ist) sensibility

Sexuality, within the broadly modernist parameters we have encountered,
remains deeply enmeshed within the language and practices of exclusion
and appropriation. Like emotion, it has been historically perceived as one of
the 'Others' of rationality and order. Base and natural, inimical to a vision of

efficient organization, sexuality has been apparently, at one level at least, organized out. Even beyond the immediate work environment, where sex and sexual activity may have had their place, excessive or indeed non-reproductive sexual activity was deemed by some as wasteful. This was especially the case when it threatened the ability of workers to commit the required amounts of dedication and energy to the organizational tasks, when it became not only wasteful but, above all, inefficient. More often than not, of course, it was the discourses of morality and civility that were mobilized in the assault on such wanton behaviour, yet underlying organizational de-sexualization was, or so it would seem, a paradigm of performance that was central to the maintenance of the machinery of industrial production.

Yet, as we have observed, this tells only half the story. While the rationalizing forces of modernity denounced the realm of sexual pleasure, the structures of male privilege and power remained intact. Where sexuality could not be eradicated, therefore, it became appropriated particularly in the form of female sexuality, as yet another commodity – serving both the capitalist market and the essentialized male sexual appetite. As Burrell (1997: 220) notes in his discussion of satyriasis – excessive sexual desire in males – despite the rationalizing logic of modernity, men of power and influence were careful to separate the need for a process of organizational de-sexualization from their own interests and desires. Yet, however one conceptualizes the varying relationships between organization, sexualization and gender, one thing that has remained relatively constant in the above discussion is the omnipresence of power and control. Be it the exclusion of sexuality on the grounds of rational efficiency, or its over-inclusion as a commodity subject to instrumental rationality, its relationship to enduring structures of economic and patriarchal power parallels the modern attitude to nature, of which sexuality has come to be so closely associated, for sexuality, particularly female sexuality, is conceptualized as the harbinger of chaos and disorder to organizational life. One may seek to control it, even package and sell it, but as the women interviewed in Trethewey's study so acutely observed, allowed free range, it presents a threat; a threat to the rational order of modernity.

In the following section, we explore a postmodernist critique of the modernist tendency to present sexuality as the necessary object of control and regulation. As such, we explore the idea that sexuality and its analysis provides something of an antithesis to the view that automatically equates sex in organizations with oppression and exploitation, and consider the ways in which postmodernism has drawn attention to the pleasures of sexuality in the workplace and, in particular, to its disruptive potential.

Postmodern sexualities

As we have noted throughout the book, the broad thrust of postmodern thought has been to vilify the perceived marginalization or domination of nature by the technologies of a technocratic and instrumental rationality so closely associated with the modernization of socio-cultural and economic life. This conceptual bifurcation between nature and culture, passion and reason has in turn placed sexuality firmly in the category of the tempestuous, erratic and thoroughly non-rational dimension of life, ripe for the attention of the technocrats, engineers and organizers of a rational world vision. As such, a postmodern defence, if not celebration, of the sexual is perhaps an inevitable outcome of such an oppositional stance. Certainly, this is true, but it is not the first and only attempt to develop such a critique. As we noted earlier in this chapter, those who have shared a critical position on the worst excesses of modernity's instrumental logic (Marcuse, 1972 [1955]; Reich, 1962) have also voiced their concerns over the excessive technologies of repression that sexuality has encountered as a direct outcome of the modernization process.

Central to this critique was the proposition that prior to capitalism there had been relative sexual freedom, but that as capitalist modernity required an efficiently exploitable, reproductive and malleable labour force, non-procreative 'wasteful' sexuality became repressed. While the idea that human sexuality has, under modernity, come to be the object of strategies of power and control is one not lost on those who would adopt a postmodern perspective, a number of important theoretical divergences exist between a postmodern critique of modernist sexuality and the broadly critical modernist approach adopted by Gramsci, Marcuse and Reich. First, postmodernism is characterized by a firm rejection of what is viewed as the underlying essentialism of such critical accounts. For Marcuse it would seem that 'polymorphous' human sexuality is an essential quality, one that is acted upon by various regimes of power and domination, repressing its authentic, or 'true' experience and expression. While a post-structuralist approach to sexuality shares in common with critical theory the conviction that a hegemonic sexuality is the outcome of regimes of power, at the heart of the former is a Foucauldian rejection of the idea that sexuality is the source of 'truth', or the essence of human nature, an idea that tends to be attributed to the latter. Rather, sexuality is conceived as destabilized, decentred and de-naturalized.

Secondly, contemporary approaches to sexuality that have been influenced by postmodernism tend to view the current reconfiguration of contemporary industrial societies facilitative of the opportunity to explore a myriad of sexual possibilities. Postmodernists argue, therefore, that the dissolution of traditional social structures, the ascendance of secularism over religion, and the relatively recent separation of sexuality from procreation all suggest a slow yet consistent process of what Simon (1996) has termed *sexual post-modernization*.

As we outlined in Chapter 1, postmodernism is perceived as the 'time of the sign', as an era when media images and 'regimes of signification', such as 'sexy' adverts for otherwise unsexy products and services or the organizations that provide them, have become the primary feature of human experience. In a similar vein, postmodern sexuality can be understood as characterized by a progressive disengagement of the modernist association of sexuality with reproduction (Hawkes, 1996), and a proliferation of available sexual identities as 'lifestyle' choices which are no longer perceived as essential expressions of a sexual 'nature', and by a rejection of the science of sex in favour of a performative ontology based on process, paradox and play. In his account of the postmodernization of sexuality, Simon thus emphasizes the power of symbolism, the significance of language and metaphor, pluralism and change as constitutive of human sexualities in what he terms the 'postparadigmatic age' of postmodernism (Simon, 1996: 9), an age characterized by an intense pluralization, individuation and a multiplicity of choices, emerging from rapid social change as our normal condition. Simon argues that, under these circumstances, the postmodern serves as a challenge to the tired habituation of old metaphors, particularly those derived from biology. His postmodern approach to sexuality supplants biologically-grounded metaphors with socially-derived ones, most notably those associated with the 'script'. He suggests that human sexualities are best understood as dramas, and that heterosexuality constitutes a sexual 'genre', a fixed formula which makes life and sexuality easier to market in much the same way as any other dramatic performance. His perception of sexuality is of an aspect of social life that is increasingly multiple, fragmented, diffuse and contested, forged out of the contingent circumstances of choice, pluralism and complexity that ultimately link together in the creation of a sexual self. The reflexive, social construction of a sexual self is highlighted through contexts of complexity, choice and plurality. To put it simply, a postmodern sexual ontology is understood in terms of 'a postparadigmatic phase where consensual meanings have dissolved into pluralism, authority has weakened, "choices" have proliferated, time and space have become reordered and the natural has been deconstructed and denaturalized' (Plummer, 1996: xiii).

Where postmodernists differ from a more critical understanding of this dissolution into sexual pluralism that focuses on the increasing scope for commercialization and commodification (Weeks, 1985) is that, in the potential chaos of perpetual change, postmodernists claim to identify enormous potentiality. In the separation of sexuality from religion, from traditional family structures, communities, politics and restricted forms of communication, a space is seen to emerge for new kinds of sexuality and, thus, of subjectivities. Postmodern sexualities are understood to be characterized by 'a de-naturalization of sex' (Simon, 1996: 30), by the proliferation of a plurality of meanings, acts and recursive identities (Plummer, 1995), and by pastiche and an indeterminate blurring of boundaries (Gergen, 1991). From a postmodernist perspective, as Plummer has put it, 'a supermarket of sexual possibilities pervades' (1996: xv).

In this respect, one particular signifier of a possible shift towards a postmodern sexual ontology which is often cited is that heterosexuality has 'ceased to be a fixed terrain' (Hawkes, 1996: 106). While careful not to overstate the significance of this development, Creith (1996) sees the de-centring of heterosexuality as indicative of a significant shift in the social organization of sexuality. While she sees this shift as connected with com-mercialization and commodification, she argues that a shift away from political definitions of lesbianism towards those focused much more on sexual relations and identity has opened up new ways of destabilizing the modernist primacy of heterosexuality. Thus, for Creith, the contemporary focus on lesbian chic marks not so much the end of sexual politics but the formation of a new (stylized, postmodern) form of sexuality.

More critically, perhaps, than what appears to be (in our view at least) simply a convergence of the reflexive project of the sexual self with an intensification of the (highly modernist) imperatives of the 'sexual sell' (Friedan, 1963) is the emphasis that postmodernism places on rejecting the normative underpinnings of modernist sexuality. As Weeks has put it, postmodernism emphasizes that the 'political and moral implications of sexual enlightenment were at best ambiguous and at worst dangerous as they contributed a scientific justification for essentially traditional or authoritarian positions' (Weeks, 1986: 112). A postmodern sexuality is thus characterized, crucially, by 'a de-essentializing and a de-naturalizing thrust' (Plummer, 1996: xi). Yet if, as Foucault has suggested (1979: 149), 'sex is without any norm or intrinsic rule that might be formulated from its own nature', how can we determine appropriate or inappropriate sexual behaviour without recourse to scientific knowledge and the 'truth' of nature? In other words, how can we 'know' sex and its organization in a postmodern era? How can we know, for instance, what is and is not appro-priate in terms of sexuality and its incorporation into contemporary workplaces?

Foucault's (1985, 1986) own attempt to grapple with questions of sexual ethics in the second and third volumes of his *History of Sexuality* published at the end of his life, focuses on the pre-modern 'aesthetic existence' of Greek and Roman civilizations. Asking us to reflect on the ways of life that could be valid for us today, Foucault argues that what we lack is not a tran-scendent truth but a way of coping with the multiplicity of truths that postmodernism proffers. He proposes a 'radical pluralism' that points away from an absolutist morality, one grounded on a fundamental human nature and truth, to a radical ethical pluralism that is based on an assump-tion of the existence of diversity and a positive endorsement of variety as a necessary accompaniment of our increasingly complex world. His argu-ment is founded on an acceptance of diversity as the norm and the necessity to evolve the appropriate means of thinking and 'knowing' about sexual multiplicity. This radical, aesthetic conception of sexuality suggests that what is ethical in terms of sexual relations is whatever is consensual and 'feels right'.

What this emphasis on a postmodern sexual ethics seems to suggest, then, is that the fixed points that organized and regulated our sexual beliefs and activities during the modern era – religious, scientific, familial, heterosexual, monogamous – have been radically challenged since the latter half of the twentieth century. With the increasing promotion of sexual desire, the tolerance of sexual pleasure as a means to an end seems to have been replaced by the positive promotion of such pleasures as an end in themselves. In this sense, sexuality has shifted, it has been argued, from a (modernist) ascetic to a (postmodernist) aesthetic ethic. In this shift, the old bourgeois values of thrift and self-restraint, of 'saving' oneself rather than 'spending', have given way to an emphasis on sexuality as an aesthetic experience (Simon, 1996).

Postmodernism, sexuality and the work organization

What, if anything, can this postmodernized conception of sexuality contribute to the study of organizational relations? First and foremost, it suggests, at the very least, an understanding of sexuality within organizations that is neither exclusionary nor repressive but one that recognizes the liberating and playful nature of sexuality as a potential release from the rationalizing imperatives embedded within contemporary organizational forms. As Sims, Fineman and Gabriel have noted,

> sexual fantasies are an escape from the ordinariness of work [as] sex talk breaks the monotony, introduces a playful element in a highly controlled environment. Sex talk also reminds people that their bodies are not just labouring instruments hiding inside uniforms and suits, but are also sources and objects of pleasure and desire. (1993: 148)

Focusing on sexuality as 'an escape from the ordinariness of work', Pringle emphasizes that sexuality might move organizations towards what she refers to as 'erotic bureaucracies' (1989a: 89) in which, among other things, 'sexual pleasures might be used to disrupt male rationality and to empower women' (1989b: 166). Influenced by post-structuralist perspectives including, most notably, the work of Foucault, Pringle's account of secretaries conceptualizes sexuality as something of a contested terrain on which power struggles are fought out. In characteristically Foucauldian fashion, she argues that in work organizations both power and sexuality are 'everywhere' (1989a: 90), and are subject to a constant process of re-negotiation characterized by power and resistance such that sexuality in the wokplace is not simply repressed, sublimated or subjected to controlled expression (Marcuse, 1972 [1955]), but is 'actively produced in a multiplicity of discourses and interactions' (Pringle, 1989a: 91). For Pringle, then, making sexuality visible in the pursuit of 'erotic bureaucracies' will involve 'an exploration of what it means to be sexual *subjects* rather than objects' (1989a: 101 *original emphasis*). In this sense, she argues that post-structuralism provides a potentially critical approach to deconstructing existing configurations of sexuality and organization.

A similar approach to Pringle's, advocating the *re-eroticization* of the work organization, has also been developed by Burrell (1992), who suggests that workplaces should be organized on the basis of 'a more joyous, playful attitude to life and to fellow humans, where sensuality and feeling are enhanced and where the erotic plays a more central role in our day-to-day lives' (Burrell, 1992: 78). For Burrell, re-eroticization is antithetical to both organizational de-sexualization and over-inclusion in its attempt to encourage erotic encounters in work organizations as a means of undermining oppressive power bases. Re-eroticization, then, involves an alternative to the 'managerialist appropriation of sex and sexuality by recognizing, allowing and playing with the pluralistic erotics of organizations outside of the instrumental control of management' (Brewis and Grey, 1994: 71). In some respects, this potentially signals a shift towards a postmodern organization, in so far as, as Brewis and Grey have argued, 'the bureaucratic mode of organization does not sit well with re-eroticization, which is fundamentally about potential, playfulness, unpredictability and danger' (1994: 73), so that re-eroticization has stronger affinities with an anti-organization theory (Burrell and Morgan, 1979) than it does with bureaucratic, quintessentially modernist ways of doing and understanding organization. Even at his most celebratory, Burrell is clearly aware, however, of the extent to which a re-eroticization of the workplace potentially opens up the way for increased sexual harassment and commodification. As such, he makes it clear that he is not implying a re-sexualization of organizations where this merely involves an increase in sexual relations embedded within established patriarchal and capitalist structures. Instead, he proposes a radical process of re-eroticization in line with Bakhtin's 'carnivalesque', one in which 'the hierarchy of the official order is overturned and the lowly are able to mock the high' (Burrell, 1992: 80). On this basis, Burrell argues that

> re-eroticization is the attempt to reintroduce serious polymorphic emotions into human organization at any level. It involves spontaneous involvement of the masses and their willingness to experiment with many forms of social organization – collectives and co-operatives, communes and communal acts. (1992: 78–9)

While this may appear a highly attractive proposition, even this more measured conception of re-eroticization is not without its problems. Most notable is its apparent lack of any clear vision of just how such a re-eroticization could be approached without a far broader re-organization of hegemonic gender relations and the role that sexuality is deemed to play in the structuring of regimes of identity. As Brewis and Grey also note, 'little detail is given . . . as to what the erotic workplace would actually look like' (1994: 73). In their own critique, however, Brewis and Grey give more attention to the theoretical difficulties of re-eroticization than to its practical implications, arguing that as a thesis it is based on an appropriation of a somewhat artificial version of the feminine and also on the endorsement of potentially violent forms of sexuality, concluding that 're-eroticization theorists are therefore mistaken in their evocation of a sexual Utopia free from the workings of power' (Brewis and Grey, 1994: 80). Burrell himself has since questioned the very basis of such a vision, indicating its utopianism and reflexively acknowledging the fact that it may be as much the outcome of a phallocentric worldview as that which it seeks to challenge (Burrell, 1997: 236), a point we return to shortly.

If we are to be suspicious, then, of any call to re-centre the erotic or sexual dimension of organizational life, what else can a postmodern emphasis on the indeterminacy and, indeed, celebration of sexuality and sexual identity offer the critical study of organizations? One relatively recent addition to the lexicon of organization theory has been that of *queer theory* (Parker, 1999; Tyler, 2000). Queer theory derives from the interplay between lesbian and gay studies and postmodernism and has been articulated most fully in the work of Judith Butler (1988, 1990a, 1990b, 1993). For Butler, sexual desire and sexual orientation, far from constituting innate dispositions, are created and lived through the specific constructs of linguistic categorization and re-iterative performance. Following Foucault, she argues that what underlies the performance of gender and sexuality are not dispositions of the body, but discourses governing such performances which create the illusion of underlying dispositions centred on a stable and coherent gendered, sexual identity, so that 'such acts, gestures, enactments, generally construed, are *performative* in the sense that the essence or identity that they otherwise purport to express are *fabrications* manufactured and sustained through corporeal signs and other discursive means' (Butler, 1990a: 136 *original emphasis*).

For Butler, then, the radical programme that could derive from such a realization is one of creating what she terms 'gender trouble'. To create gender trouble means to destabilize these fabrications by 'playing' with them to demonstrate their performative nature and, in doing so, to parody the idea that they refer to innate essences, as in the performative ontology of 'queer' (Butler, 1990a). Queer theory therefore emphasizes the discursive constitution of gendered and sexual categories based on a performance ontology, and seeks to bring the binary classification on which they are based into question. Queer theory promotes the idea of sexual plurality and explores the destabilizing potential of sexual transgressions. It thus constitutes a radical challenge to the enduring modernist concept of a stable, sexual identity, emphasizing instead 'a concept of self which is performative, improvisational, discontinuous, and processual, constituted by repetitive and stylized acts' (Meyer, 1994: 2–3).

As such, two main challenges to both the social organization of sexuality and sexuality within work organizations are posed by queer theory. First, mechanisms of the social construction of heterosexuality are exposed and challenged. Queer theory reveals that, in order to construct a 'seamless heterosexual identity', heterosexuality demands a continuous performance. The ubiquity and potency of the scripts of gender are seen as testimony to the inherent instability of the connections between sex, gender and sexuality: 'if heterosexuality is compelled to repeat itself in order to establish the illusion of its own uniformity and identity, then this is an identity permanently at risk' (Butler, 1990a: 29). Secondly, as Sontag puts it, 'the whole point of camp is to dethrone the serious' (1966: 288).

This later point perhaps represents the most intriguing threat to the gatekeepers of work organizations, in that, in the camp version of 'play', the pleasures of sexuality threaten to undermine the seriousness of organizational life and, indeed, the very process of organizing. In this respect, it might be suggested therefore that parodic sexual performance provides a potential means of resisting organizational identification, particularly for those lesbian and gay employees who are heterosexualized by 'organization sexuality' (Hearn and Parkin, 1987), while also being able to 'play' with sexuality and gender as a subversive strategy, that is, to make 'gender trouble' in organizations by drawing on sexuality as a resource to be mobilized in the service of individual or collective, rather than organizational, ends. This element of organizational performance *potentially* constitutes a valuable resource in the development of strategies of resistance to organizational identification and heterosexualization as the regulative norm of organizational, sexual subjectivity.

Extrapolating out from this argument, Parker (1999) has suggested that what queer theory may be able to contribute to our understanding of organizational relations is a focus on the ways in which organizational employees, specifically managers, can be understood to be performing a role. This observation leads him to posit the idea that, by adopting a 'queer' perspective, organization theorists can contribute to the development of a radical theory of organizations, as well as suggesting a subversive strategy of resistance among such managers. The former revolves around the aforementioned observation of the performative dimension of managerial activity, that is, the conceptualization of management as a series of provisional, localized enactments and, at one and the same time, a collection of structured and power-ridden activities. The latter derives from the realization that, as Parker puts it, 'what might be called "camp" management would be a form of practice which would dramatically enact its provisionality, its fragility, without constructing a fictional outside to the discourses of management within organizations' (1999: 16).

Perhaps more important than this, however, is that it could lead to a radicalized mode of reflexivity among those who seek to study organizational life, a mode of reflexivity that forces those who ask the questions to realize their own investment in the maintenance of certain performances, which are both self and other determined, while at the same time de-stabilizing simple dualistic categories such as I/we and us/them that contain such modes of understanding within static relations and categorical positionings. As such, while moving beyond the particular concerns of queer theory with the performative dimensions of sexuality and gender *per se*, Parker offers a radicalized proposition based on a more general 'queering' of organization theory, a proposition that would seek to combine the deconstructive impetus of postmodern thought with a politics of 'subversion and transgression as a habit in itself' (1999: 17). Attempts such as these to develop a postmodern-inspired theory of organization focus on sexuality as both a means of organizational liberation and a potential tool of subversive disruption. In the penultimate section of this chapter, we therefore attempt to reflect on the critical potential of a postmodern emphasis on the free-play of sexualities for understanding contemporary work organizations.

Repressive desublimation and the 'sexual promise'

While the language surrounding the postmodern celebration of sexuality appears to be clothed in a (post-) politics of radical subversion and a trans-gression of modernist imperatives of performance and efficiency, critics of the idea have argued that the promise of postmodern erotic plurality is tempered by a continuation and, in some cases, an intensification of certain modernist realities. Hawkes, in particular, argues that the apparent identi-fication of a postmodernization of sexuality has gone hand in hand with an increased commodification process, one that, in itself, does not 'indicate an unproblematic weakening of the heterosexual hegemony' (1996: 143). Rather, she observes that such challenges are simply part of what she terms 'flexible heterosexuality' (Hawkes, 1996). That is to say, the liberalization of heterosexuality reflects many of the features of 'flexible accumulation', most obviously an organization of the work process which is dependent on rapidly manufactured and short-lived consumption patterns for its vitality, and on a de-politicizing and intensifying evocation of sexuality in the pur-suit of profit. Thus, for example, she notes how 'the popularization of lesbian chic by mainstream sexual culture seeks to appropriate radical sex and make it "style", while simultaneously defusing its potential and rewriting it as commodity' (Hawkes, 1996: 142–3), so that style and image allude to the potential of a 'pick and mix' sexuality, but do not promote it. Sexuality has, in other words, become commodified and commercialized as a matter of 'choice', as part of a new regime of regulation and accumu-lation in the guise of postmodernism.

Tyler (1999) associates this process with the continued expansion of the rationalization and performative principle of modernity through the increasing prevalence of managerial-inspired discourses within 'everyday life'. Taking as her analytical focus the content of a range of 'lifestyle' mag-azines, she charts the ways in which, while open and playful in their discussions of human sexuality and sexual relationships, such magazines continue to provide highly prescriptive narratives on how to 'manage' one's sex life, especially in the face of greater career and workplace demands. While the style may therefore be reminiscent of the idea of a postmodernization of sexuality, in which sexual activity is represented as an open and expressive activity, the underlying rationality remains starkly modernist and instrumentalist. Drawing on Bauman (1998), Tyler thus con-cludes that, despite the liberatory connotations of the celebration of sexual experimentation and freedom espoused in such magazines, the underlying reality is that of 'a burden of liberation according to which greater freedom of choice turns out to be yet another pressure to perform, requiring a "controlled de-control" not dissimilar to that which characterizes the tempo of the "informal" aspects of contemporary workplace participation' (1999: 24).

Other feminist-inspired writers such as Brewis (Brewis and Grey, 1994; Brewis et al., 1997) have also noted that the postmodernist-inspired celebration of the disruptive potential of sexuality, in the aforementioned re-eroticization thesis developed most notably in the work of Burrell, for instance, is likely to achieve little more than a 're-affirmation of the degraded feminine, a "welcoming back" of the feminine and the values and behaviours customarily associated with it – sensuality, caring, openness, play, emotionality, etc. – into the public sphere' (Brewis et al., 1997: 1295). As such, it is charged with merely serving to re-enforce repressive dualisms as well as overlooking the existence of structural constants, constants which act as 'important constraints' (Brewis et al., 1997: 1297) on the ways in which people can behave. These include, for instance, women's continued familial dependence, their increasing exploitation as sexualized, low-paid workers, and intensifying regimes of bodily appropriation. However, this does not mean that, in this instance, a more postmodernized approach to the question of organizational sexuality is dismissed altogether. Rather, Brewis, Hampton and Linstead appeal to the need for the kind of playful strategy, reminiscent of queer theory, in which individuals are free to 'recognize and creatively exploit their own ambivalence, their masculinity/femininity, rationality/emotionality, in ways which enable them to meet, and if necessary, reconstruct their performative goals' (1997: 1300).

Are, then, the insights and resistive strategies associated with re-eroticization and queer theory, for instance, representative of a genuinely subversive, postmodernized approach to the structuring of sexuality within organizations? Well, while broadly sympathetic to the ideals that such an approach professes, we remain sceptical that they represent a sufficiently effective tactic in the face of structurally enduring technologies of control and appropriation. As Burkitt has noted (1998: 489), 'parodying dominant norms is not enough to displace them' and, as such, parodic sexual performance may simply result in a very superficial challenge to the discursive categories of gender, sexuality and organization without addressing, simultaneously, the structural context of such discourses. In this respect, Burkitt argues (1998: 491) that Butler's approach, in common with the post-structuralism on which she draws ultimately collapses into language and discourse, both the subject and the networks of power relations in which subjectivity is located, involving a linguistic reductionism which provides an inadequate basis for a critical understanding of sexuality and its organization. Indeed, this is one of the main criticisms made of those post-structuralist approaches to language and subjectivity that we discussed in Chapter 1. As Stein and Plummer (1996) have also suggested, there is a dangerous tendency in queer theory to ignore the materialities of lived 'queer' experience and of how that experience is organized. Holliday (1998), through her analysis of the film *Philadelphia*, for example, highlights the resilience of heteronormative organizations to counter-hegemonic sexualities in the deployment, for example, of AIDS as a powerful legitimating force in homophobic discourse and practice. In this example, it transpires that material exclusions are legitimated with reference to powerful cultural discourses – in this case the archetype of homosexuality as deprivation and disease.

We would argue, therefore, that the disruptive or dis-organizing potential of sexuality remains highly vulnerable to the performance imperatives of contemporary work organizations, both in terms of commodification and the re-appropriation of elements of its 'style' into the mainstream. We acknowledge that queer does represent a potentially destabilizing and, in the context of work organizations, dis-organizing force, by citing an opposing reality – identifying an alternative to the heterosexual matrix as the dominant mode of organizing the relationship between sex, gender and sexuality (see Butler, 1990a). Yet, as M. Hall notes (1989: 138), queer sexualities face what Laing (1970: 76) referred to as 'the danger of being engulfed within a framework that one had hoped to break out of'. As Hall notes: 'The rare lesbian who reveals her orientation, and who survives the consequences of violating the gendered expectations which structure the organization succumbs, then, to the organization in another way' (1989: 138).

Queer sexualities are thus vulnerable to re-appropriation or 'over-inclusion' as Burrell (1984) might put it. This is highlighted in Humphrey's (1999) account of the organizational experiences of lesbian women and gay men who are employed in a variety of public sector occupations in the UK, which concentrates on career trajectories 'beyond the closet'. Humphrey argues that 'those who dare to come out . . . will tread a precarious tightrope between being *out and pursued* for their specialist knowledges and *out and persecuted* for their presumed perversities' (1999: 134 *emphasis added*). With regard to the latter, Humphrey's respondents emphasize that coming out at work involves a never-ending process of constant renegotiation *vis-à-vis* each new audience if the ever-present presumption of heterosexuality is to be refuted. With regard to being 'out and pursued', her account also emphasizes the extent to which, because sexuality continues to be excluded from the self-consciousness of work organizations, lesbian and gay employees tend to become the carriers of sexual consciousness on behalf of their organizations, in virtue of what are often perceived as their unique positions and insights. What this means is that it is 'in virtue of their unique position as victims and survivors of heterosexism that lesbian and gay employees have been ideally placed to recognize and in some cases remedy the sexual inequalities ingrained within their workplaces' (Humphrey, 1999: 142).

While this designation of lesbian and gay employees as consciousness-raising 'experts' clearly has some significant democratic potential that should not be overlooked (Humphrey, for instance, emphasizes the ways in which several of her respondents depicted a dialectical consciousness-raising process whereby the more out and proud they became, the more their colleagues noticed sexual ignorance and injustice and requested assistance), there are clearly important dangers that also need to be recognized. In this celebration of organizational Otherness – be it for personal, professional or political ends (Humphrey, 1999: 138) – what Hall (1989) refers to as the 'private mutinies' of gay and lesbian sexualities expose themselves to being forfeited or 'stylized' into the mainstream while the privileged and critical potential of queer, and its perverse viewpoint, is incorporated into the fold of the organization. The potential for sustained dissent (which Humphrey acknowledges is problematic for lesbians and gay men at work) is thus re-organized, included. While it is predicated on and offers the potential for a 'dis-organization sexuality', the appearance of queer sexual politics does not necessarily indicate, therefore, an unproblematic weakening of heterosexual hegemony within work organizations and the rationalizing logic that underpins its political economy.

In contrast, we would tend to agree with Jackson and Scott (1997) when they argue that the proclaimed diversity and choice of post-Fordist or post-modernist sexuality represents, rather, an intensification of the rationalization of modernist sexuality according to largely Taylorist principles of organization. As such, in the post-Fordist sexual era of adaptability, versatility and re-skilling, the continued proliferation of expert knowledges makes it difficult for us to be the authors of our own sexual scripts, either within, or increasingly outwith, the environment of the work organization. Thus, just as 'disorganized capitalism' (Lash and Urry, 1987) is not a departure from the capitalist imperatives of modernity, 'for all its emphasis on flexibility, post-Fordist sexuality . . . is more an extension of some of the underlying principles of Taylorisation than a challenge to it' (Jackson and Scott, 1997: 566). Post-Fordist sexuality is still, it seems to us, geared towards the maximization of profit. Whether in the form of production, consumption or reproduction, it remains inextricably tied to the capitalist imperatives of modernity.[4] As Marcuse argued nearly fifty years ago, the ability to simultaneously desublimate and repress the sexual drive provides one of the most powerful resources for the motivation of humanity in the service of goals directed not towards human emancipation, but towards increased servitude and responsiveness to the very forces that require the suppression of sexuality in the first instance.

Conclusion

Having considered, over the length of this chapter, sexuality both as a component of organizational life and as something that is itself organized, we wish to make just a few brief points by way of conclusion. The effect of a postmodernist perception of sexuality seems to have been an endorsement of the idea that the incorporation of sexuality into the everyday life of work organizations is the outcome of a radical 'postmodernization' of sexuality (Simon, 1996), that is, the product of contestation, struggle and resistance in which radical strategies have brought about a reconstruction of its organizational expression. However, we would argue that this is too simplistic a proposition. For if we look more carefully we can see that it is the perpetual evolution of organizational life and the commensurate shift towards an intensification of the incorporation of those most personal and intimate traits that have their most startling expression in the (re)production of 'organization sexuality' (Hearn and Parkin, 1987). The aggregate effect of this has been that the changes taking place in contemporary 'organization sexuality' have all been entirely commensurate with the atomization of the inter-subjectivity that underpins eroticism (Bataille, 1962), signifying not a break with, but rather a continuation of, the instrumental dimension of the logic of modernity.

This is not to say that we do not ascribe a significant degree of value to the questions postmodernism, as a body of ideas, has raised with regard to the issue of organizational sexuality. As Bauman (1990), who, if not a champion of postmodernism, is someone who is deeply sympathetic to its potential as a tool of critique, has noted, central to the project of modernity has been the mastery over unruly nature, within which a distinction between rationality and irrationality has featured as a recurring motif. It is this insight that, while not necessarily strikingly original, has also led to a critical understanding of how sexuality became designated as

> . . . something not to be trusted and not to be left to its own devices, something to be mastered, subordinated, remade so as to be readjusted to human needs. Something to be held in check, retrained and contained, transferred from the state of shapelessness into form – by effort and by application of force. (Bauman, 1990: 165)

Yet, for us at least, it is this insight that leads us to embrace not the promise of a playful and celebratory postmodernism, but rather the realization that perhaps the most striking aspect of modern sexuality is the co-existence of, on the one hand, a promotion of pleasures and, on the other, the progressive strengthening of the organizing parameters of what constitutes sexuality. It is these themes that reinforce our view that the promotion of organizational sexuality, be it through organizational re-eroticization or the queering of organizations, signifies not a radical disjuncture in the history of modernity, but rather threads of historical continuity that are not, in themselves, indicative of anything but an adaptation of the instrumental logic pervading organizational life to the destabilizing character of postmodern culture.

Notes

1   As depicted so graphically in the novels of De Sade, for instance.
2   See Mills (1994) for an example of the application of this distinction to the analysis of a particular organization, in this case British Airways.
3   A similar approach to organizational power is adopted by Jackson and Carter (1986) who, drawing on Deleuze and Guattari's (1984) distinction between Desire and Interest, argue that corporate imagery consists of various seductive devices, designed to entice manufactured lack into a desire willing to be controlled (see also Jackson and Carter, 1985).
4   As in, say, Microsoft's alleged encouragement of romantic liaisons within the company so as to promote greater levels of organizational synergy (see Sampson, 1996). This is a theme that has also been articulated recently by Shere Hite in her book *Sex & Business* (2000), in which she emphasizes the importance to corporations of harnessing the sexual energy created by gender differences at work.

Overview

In the second part of this book, we shifted our attention away from providing what was a relatively straightforward account of the various intersections between postmodernism and organization theory, towards a critical exploration of the increased emphasis that, in recent years, seems to have been placed on the management and theorization of the cultural, emotional and sexual dimensions of organizational life. Although these aspects of organizational life have traditionally been suppressed in both the management and theorization of organizations, they have also, as some of the more reflexive contributors to the discipline such as Burrell (1997) have emphasized, constituted an enduring sub-text within organizational life, often underpinning the very processes of organizing that sought to exclude them. It is our view that what unites much of the work we have considered thus far, in relation to both the management and theorization of organizations, is the desire for 'getting a bit of the Other' (Moore, 1988; see also Brewis and Grey, 1994: 77). In other words, for reclaiming that which has previously been excluded.

As well as attempting to provide a relatively concise introduction to the ways in which organizational Others, such as culture, emotion and sexuality, have increasingly penetrated organization theory, however, we have also sought to explore just what they may suggest to us about the possible development of the relationship between work, postmodernism and organization. As such we took these developments as, in part, indicative of a series of shifts within both organization theory and management practice that can be seen to reflect many of the postmodern themes we encountered in the first half of the book. In particular these include an evident concern with the study and management of previously marginalized dimensions of human experience that, under the rubric of modernist science, have been deemed at best peripheral, at worst dangerous, to the orderly and rational practice of organization.

In Chapter 4, we considered the impact of the cultural turn on organization theory, noting how, since the late 1970s, culture has become somewhat paradigmatic in both the management and study of work organizations and has certainly been a major influence on shaping the increasingly complex nature of the relationship between these two concerns. Considering various perspectives on culture within organizations, ranging from what we termed the corporate-functionalist, symbolic-interpretive, postmodern-fragmentary and critical-emancipatory, we identified a range of postmodern themes and ideas in the relatively recent concern with culture in organizations, notably, for instance, the conception of organizations as cultural phenomena. While an attempt to apply the cultural values and practices of Japanese organizations to western corporate life, an endeavour that implies an emphasis on flexibility, diversity, community and so on (Ouchi, 1981), constitutes one notable example of the relationship between contemporary modes of organizing work and a possible process of postmodernization (Clegg, 1990), we also argued in Chapter 4 that the relationship between the cultural turn and postmodernism can be seen to run even deeper, in the expansion of so-called new styles of cultural management (Peters, 1989; Peters and Waterman, 1982). In this respect, we drew on the work of Willmott (1992) in particular, who has emphasized that the appeal by many of the champions of corporate culture to managers to promote a closer integration between an employee's sense of self and the priorities of the organization suggests something of a postmodern process of cultural de-differentiation in the conception and management of work organizations and, particularly, of the subjective dimension of organizational life. Hence, we tended to identify a distinction, throughout the chapter, between approaches that tend to celebrate the creative potential of culture as an untapped resource and more critical, analytical attempts to understand the role of culture and its management in contemporary organizations.

We then, in Chapter 5, went on to explore the role of emotion in contemporary work organizations, paying attention to both the rationalization and analysis of the affective dimension of organizational life. Rather than the range of perspectives that we identified in the continually burgeoning literature on culture in work organizations, we worked here with a broad distinction between, what seemed to us at least, to be a fundamentally modernist perspective on the exclusion of emotion from work organizations and a concern, of a more postmodernist tenor, with harnessing the creative energies of emotional commitment and, particularly, emotional intelligence. However, we also argued here that in terms of their basic commitment to a largely functionalist focus on managing emotion, that is, with rationalizing the irrational, a modernist perspective on emotion and a more celebratory postmodernism share much in common – primarily a concern with harnessing emotion in the pursuit of a performance imperative. In this sense, we distinguished such approaches from more critical accounts of organizations as 'emotional arenas' (Fineman, 1993), the performance of 'emotional labour' (Hochschild, 1983) and the commodification of the 'irrational' dimension of human existence. The latter tend to focus more on developing a critique of the detrimental effects emotional management has on employee subjectivity than is the case in relation to a more celebratory postmodernist-inspired emphasis on emotion as the key to organizational success that we considered in the first part of the chapter.

Similar themes emerged from our analysis in Chapter 6, which focused on the role of sexuality in organizations. Here we began by considering the modernist designation of sexuality as the irrational, disorderly, anti-organizational Other, exploring the dual strategies of eradication and containment that Burrell argues constituted organizational 'de-sexualization' (Burrell, 1984). We then went on to consider more critical perspectives on the repressive aspects of modernist sexuality (Hawkes, 1996), drawing largely on the work of critical theorists such as Gramsci (1971), Marcuse (1972 [1955]) and Reich (1962), going on to focus on the corollary of de-sexualization, namely the 'over-inclusion' of sexuality in organizations. Such modernist conceptions of sexuality were then distinguished from post-modernist-inspired approaches, which tend to celebrate the playful, disruptive potential of sexual energy and its dis-organizing impetus. In this context, we also explored the work of those who advocate a 're-eroticization' of organizations and the development of what Pringle has termed 'erotic bureaucracies' (Burrell, 1992; Pringle, 1989a, 1989b). We finally evaluated some aspects of the potential contribution of queer theory to the development of a postmodern organization theory, one that is both deconstructive and critical in its approach to understanding the role played by sexuality in shaping (and potentially resisting) repressive aspects of the subjective experience of contemporary work organizations.

Although there are certainly many differences between each of the three themes that we considered here, in terms of their relationship both to work organizations and to postmodernism, what culture, emotion and sexuality share in common, it seems to us at least, is a designation as the irrational, anti-bureaucratic 'Other' of work organizations. In our view, it is this designation that postmodernism has, in various ways, sought both to celebrate and to challenge. On the one hand, it seems to be the case that a range of discursive resources that have contributed to the popularization of a functionalist and, we would argue, instrumental project of recapturing the Otherness of organizations can be characterized as broadly postmodern in their celebratory, yet also ultimately reactionary, tenor. These appear to involve, as Rose (1990) has noted, the identification of supposedly new ways of relating the 'irrational' attributes of employee subjectivity to organizational objectives. Particularly evident in the various proposals and prescriptions to be found in the literature on organizational excellence, corporate culture, emotional intelligence and so on, these approaches tend to combine the postmodern principles of plurality and play with an overriding emphasis on the pursuit of employee perfomativity. In this literature, many of the thematic concerns of postmodernism can be identified in those management styles that have come to be associated with the harnessing of culture, emotion and sexuality as under-exploited resources.

This ultimately instrumental incorporation of the ideas of postmodernism into much of the 'how to' literature can be seen to produce reified conceptions both of the organizational form and of individual employees. With regard to the former, much of this literature conceives of the organization simply as a vessel into which the creative energies of irrationality, disorder and dis-organization, extolled as newly-discovered renewable resources, can (and should) be poured, and also of the individual employee. In terms of the latter, employee subjectivity tends to be thought of in terms of 'entrepreneurial' rather than 'bureaucratic' styles of management; as a creative energy that can be released into the organization through the 'liberating' effects of contemporary managerial techniques and practices – those that 'thrive on chaos' (Peters, 1989) and ensure that employees fall in love (Harris, 1996) with their organizations, and so on.

In apparent contrast to this colonization of the language and, some would argue, of the radical agenda of postmodernism, a number of alternative, and seemingly more critical, approaches have sought to embrace the theoretical openness of postmodern meta-theory, not to enhance organizational performativity but, primarily, to enrich our understanding of organizations. First and foremost, such approaches tend to reject any attempt to impose an ordered or functionalist 'model' on to the organizational lifeworld. Rather, organization is conceptualized as diverse and heterogeneous, inaccessible to positivistic research strategies bequeathed to organization theory by the legacy of the natural sciences. These more critical attempts to incorporate the ideas of postmodernism into organization theory can, we would argue, be credited with enhancing the field in several ways. In particular, this latter approach has broadened our understanding of the ways in which organizational life is 'enacted', focusing on those themes or Others that organization theory has traditionally marginalized yet which, as we have argued throughout the second part of this book, appear to be far from marginal to the contemporary management, and lived experience, of organizations. This is emphasized, particularly, by recent analyses that have sought to demonstrate the presence of culture, emotion and sexuality as 'anti-organizational' permeations of modernist organizations that were constituted, at least in part, on the negation of such subjective phenomena and their organizational presence.

Reflecting on the issues raised in these chapters it seems to us, then, that postmodernism has had a significant influence on the ways in which the lived experience of contemporary organizational life has come to be understood. From this perspective, those changes that have occurred in modes of organizing, primarily since the 1960s, that we discussed in the first half of the book, have been understood variously as an attempt to recapture the Otherness of organizations, that is, to colonize the previously excluded, marginalized or simply overlooked aspects of work organizations. In transforming the ways in which we think of organizations, attempts to infuse organization theory with postmodernism have also, it could be argued, encouraged those who write (about) organizations to be more reflexive, novel, deconstructive and so on in their approach. Consequently, recent debates within the field have been shaped, particularly, by several recurring themes such as power, subjectivity, knowledge and textuality and by an injection of concepts and ideas from the arts and humanities. In this sense, it seems that postmodernism has demanded that organization theory begin to address questions, of reflexivity for instance, that it has been avoiding for too long, and also to explore approaches to understanding organizations that have been otherwise overlooked.

What does it all mean, and does it really matter?

If nothing else, then, postmodernism seems to raise important questions for organization theory and, in doing so, draws our attention to some of the more marginalized aspects of power, exclusion, subjugation and so on. Yet, in relation to the concerns of a postmodern meta-theory that we outlined in Chapter 1, it seems that postmodernism remains somewhat problematic in terms of its own analytical potential and explanatory power to respond to the questions it raises. How can inequalities in power be 'real', for instance, if organizations exist only in a society characterized by 'hyper-reality', or in which everything that exists is merely a 'text'? It seems to us that the emergence of what Willmott (1998) has suggested is a 'new sensibility' in organization theory, one that is concerned with 're-cognizing the Other', needs to re-think its understanding of the Otherness of organizational life in such a way as to subject some of the conceptual insights of postmodernism, and the many questions that a postmodernist approach to organization theory raises, to a re-invigorated critical account of work organizations. The latter, we would suggest, needs to be able to convey a sense of the dialectical nature of recent developments within the management and study of organizations.

As we indicated in our introduction, one of the primary concerns of this book is to chart the impact that postmodernism has had on both the analysis and structuring of organizational life, how the kinds of tensions we have identified thus far manifest themselves in both theory and practice, and how these various tensions are apparently mediated within organizations. In this context, we believe that while the particular examples of the 're-cognition of the Other' (Willmott, 1998: 234) that we have considered in this part of the book resonate with a number of postmodern ideas, they also reflect recurring themes that have continued to characterize more critical approaches to understanding organizational life. Without doubt, we have a richer conceptual understanding of sexuality, emotion and culture as constitutive elements of the process of organization because of the various insights of postmodernism that we have examined thus far. Yet the need is, we believe, to move beyond its parameters and to re-focus our attention on some of the concerns and insights of critical modernism. Such an approach needs to emphasize, in particular, that postmodernism, rather than implying newly-emergent organizational forms or novel ways of organizing, reveals instead the extent to which 'rationality' requires, as a condition of its very existence, the simultaneous creation of a realm of the Other, be it personal, emotional, sexual or 'irrational' (Pringle, 1989a: 89). More than this, we would argue that contemporary organizations require the rationalization of the irrational – the colonization of organizational Otherness – and it is to this colonization process that we turn our attention in our final chapter.

The chapters that have contributed to the second part of the book suggest to us, then, that we need to think more critically about the many questions that postmodernism raises for work organizations and their study than postmodernism itself allows us to; to think about the ways in which all aspects of contemporary work organizations, particularly the business partners of rationality and irrationality, (re)produce modernist organizations in a purportedly postmodern form. With this in mind, we consider, in our final chapter, one particular theme that has recurred throughout our analysis thus far, namely, the role played by subjectivity in shaping the relationship between work, postmodernism and organization.

PART 3

7

Organization, Postmodernism
and Inter-subjectivity

[Ethical Life is] is a seeing into (*An-schauen*) which does not dominate or suppress but recognizes the difference and sameness of the other . . . when the other is seen as different and as the same as oneself, as spirit not as a person, as a living totality not as a formal unity, then empirical consciousness will coincide with absolute consciousness, freedom with necessity. This can only be achieved in a just society. (Rose, 1981: 69)

To build connections and to gain the full commitment of employees, we must come out from behind our desks and embrace an 'in-your-face' passion for employee interaction. . . . Do not just ask for two-way inter-action – demand it! Aggressively go after it. (Harris, 1996: 43/44)

Within the social sciences the term 'unintended consequences' is often used to describe the results of human actions that were neither foreseen, nor, as the term suggests, intended by the actors in question. An example of this may be, say, the collapse of a company as the result of several indi-viduals selling their shares in its stock, merely in an attempt to release some of their personal capital. While the collapse in the value of the com-pany, due to the resultant panic on the stock market can be in part attributed to their actions, it is unlikely that this was ever their intent. In authoring a book on postmodernism we have had to face some of the unintended consequences of this particular action ourselves. Most notable has been the labelling of our work and, indeed, our more general theoretical orientation as 'postmodern' by a number of our colleagues and peers. While we were aware that, by writing a book on postmodernism that will (hopefully) be read by students of organization, we would in some way contribute to the discourse we were seeking to chart, it was never our intention to court the label 'postmodernist'.

We do not concur, for example, with the view that modernity necessarily represents a failed or essentially flawed project. Nor are we convinced that postmodern meta-theory, in itself, offers a substantially more radical, anti-systemic or emancipatory approach to the theorization of organizational relations than certain aspects of its so-called modernist predecessors. Rather, what we have tried to suggest is that not only do many of the themes and issues raised by postmodernism reflect concerns within previously existing traditions within social theory, but that the insights presented under the label of the postmodern have often contributed to the emergence of strategies of managerial control that have, in effect, undermined a movement away from repressive social relations based on instrumentality and heteronomy.

Of course, such protestations are unlikely to absolve us completely from the critical attentions of those who are particularly hostile to the meta-theoretical claims of postmodernism and/or its incorporation into this particular field of study. Most likely, for them, this book will be viewed as yet another hapless attempt to promote a perspective on organizations that represents little more than the misappropriation of what is, at best, a fanciful creation of disenchanted European intellectuals, or, at worst, a deliberate attempt to obscure the introduction of a reactionary agenda within the social sciences.

Alternatively, our attempt to maintain a critical perspective on much of the material we have considered here will, undoubtedly, produce equal dismay among those who have defended the radical claims of postmodernism to promote the deconstruction of oppressive power relations and offer new and significant insights into the complexity and disorder of organization(s). From this quarter, we may well be decried as little more than unreconstructed modernists, dabbling in ideas beyond our grasp and, in turn, perpetuating the follies of modernist social science that would best have been discarded.

In response to accusations such as these, we are certainly prepared to make two admissions. First, in writing this book we admit to having taken postmodernism seriously. However, as we have previously indicated, this does not mean that we support unreservedly the claim that work has become a postmodernized and, as such, less rationalized or systemically organized activity. As we noted in Chapter 2, the empirical evidence that would be required to support such an assertion appears notably thin on the ground. Nor do we accept that postmodern meta-theory represents an entirely novel or appropriate means of subjecting organizations to radical critique. However, we are unable to deny the fact that postmodernism, as a cultural and intellectual discourse, does appear to have been increasingly implicated in the emergence of a range of analytically distinct organizational practices, and that it has informed a series of challenges to the intellectual principles of western rationalism that both underpin and legitimize the concerns of mainstream organization theory. As such, while particularly critical of the relativistic and ahistorical tendencies of postmodernism, we would suggest that a range of critical questions that have emerged within organization theory over the last decade or so would have been far less likely to have seen the light of day had it not been for the challenge that postmodernism has presented to more orthodox ways of framing the nature of work and its organization. In making this claim, then, we agree with several of the more reserved critics of postmodernism such as Tsoukas (1992) and Carr (1999) when they argue that the

> postmodernist desire to take up the already accepted answers and problematize them; to turn many inherited structures of thought on their head; and to focus on what is unproblematically assumed, is a valuable contribution to . . . reflexive rationalism in so far as we are able to appreciate things which we ignored before. (Tsoukas, 1992: 647)

Our second admission elaborates on one of the reservations intimated above. While we broadly welcome the ways in which postmodernism has illuminated previously marginalized aspects of organizational life, we are less than convinced by its ability to theorize adequately the consequences of these insights. Our feeling is that this is particularly apparent in relation to the possibility of developing a substantively critical account of organizations, maintaining our concern that an emancipatory project is not well served by abandoning a commitment to notions of 'truth' and 'progress' that would appear to be anathema to those who hold to a postmodern worldview. However, this is not a view based purely on our own reservations about the potentially debilitating consequences that may derive from a commitment to the epistemological and ethical relativism that has become such a trademark of postmodernism. It is also grounded in our conviction that the theoretical tools required to address critically many of the issues that postmodernism has raised already exist within what has been described, drawing on Cooper and Burrell (1988), as critical modernism, particularly that tradition of thought that has come to be termed Critical Theory.[1] This is not to say that we believe Critical Theory is not without its own problems and limitations. However, in terms of many of the issues that postmodernism has set out to address, we would assert that Critical Theory, in many ways, not only pre-empted postmodern metatheory in terms of its concerns and general diagnosis of the modern condition, but provided a framework within which critique is able to resist many of the totalizing and essentially repressive tendencies that derive from the modern valorization of a narrow conception of rationality while, at the same time, seeking to avoid the postmodern descent into nihilistic relativism so damaging to critical political discourse.

Admissions and hand-wringing aside, then, our primary aim in this chapter is to try to develop our own account of the relationship between work, postmodernism and organization, and to consider just what Critical Theory can offer to such a project. In doing so, we do of course acknowledge a number of complementary attempts to integrate Critical Theory into organization theory. However, in addition to this, we also endeavour to make our own efforts relevant to several of the concerns we have raised throughout this book. Most notably, we argue that in valorizing the Otherness of organizational life, postmodernism has, in turn, provided a conceptual, and indeed practical, space within which the Other has been subject to a range of intensified strategies of instrumental rationalization, most evident in an increasing concern with employee subjectivity. In attempting to understand this process, we stress the need to re-examine what, for us, is the foundation for a critical theorization of subjectivity as one possible approach to theorizing the nature and impact of postmodernism on organization theory.

Postmodernism and subjectivity

While, as we have noted throughout the previous chapters, the increased popularization of postmodernism within organization theory is not short of its critics, one area of particular concern has been the ways in which many of its meta-theoretical insights have been incorporated into the analysis of employee subjectivity within workplace relations of control and resistance. This not only exemplifies the significance of postmodernism in relation to this particular issue, but also, in our view, cuts to the quick of many of the issues we explored in the second half of the book. As Newton (1999: 413–14) has pointed out in this respect, the current interest in questions of subjectivity can be attributed to three main propositions. First, the rise of corporate culturalism has signalled what is seen by many as a concerted attempt to 'manage' employees' subjective aspirations. Secondly, workplace discourses surrounding emotion and other supposedly non-rational modes of cognition reflect an understanding of the need to take into account the affective, non-rational dimension of employees' motivation and how this can be directed. Finally, a concern with subjectivity is seen to reflect the postmodern problematization of the relationship between structure and agency, particularly in relation to the post-structuralist critique of the realist proposition that social structures exist independently of subjective understanding and that, in turn, actors' subjectivity can be understood as an essentially pre-social quality. Furthermore, as Newton goes on to note, this is an issue complicated further by the primacy afforded to reflexivity within postmodern meta-theory, a primacy suggesting that 'the *subjectivity of organizational writers* is central to the study of, and prescriptions for, the management of organizations' (Newton, 1999: 414 *original emphasis*).

It is perhaps not too unreasonable to claim that the *current* interest in subjectivity within organization theory can largely be traced back to Braverman's (1974) study of the organization of the labour process under capitalism, and his self-professed attempt to try to exclude any consideration of the subjective dimension of labour. As Knights and Willmott (1989: 537) have noted, this was largely a political gesture in so far as Braverman's principal aim was to identify employee alienation as an outcome of the objective nature of capitalist relations of production, rather than as the subjective outcome of an individual orientation to working conditions. As such, Braverman rejected the idea that workers can somehow be liberated from alienating economic and social relations simply through programmes of job enrichment and work humanization. However, this exclusion of the subjective dimension of alienated labour subsequently inspired a number of critical interventions (for example, Burawoy, 1979; Cressey and McInnes, 1980; Storey, 1983) which, in various ways, sought to address Braverman's neglect of the role of subjectivity in the workplace.

It was in the context of a search for a theory of the 'missing subject' of Labour Process Theory (LPT), as P. Thompson (1990: 114) has put it, that a number of writers subsequently turned to Foucauldian post-structuralism, and particularly to the idea that subjectivity should be understood as the outcome of discursive practices (Knights, 1990, 1995, 1997; Knights and Willmott, 1989; Willmott, 1990b). Knights and Willmott, especially, were critical of the traditionally Marxist foundations of LPT that served to posit the subject as an apparently pre-given category, one that is subsequently colonized through, or alienated by, organizational or managerial ideologies. In contrast to this they argue that managerial activities, particularly those increasingly associated with so-called post-bureaucratic management styles, attempt to generate a condition of identification between managerially-directed imperatives and subjectively-held aspirations and, as such, are designed to generate the illusion of an individualized, pre-social subjectivity. Such activities, they argue, end up effectively promoting individual endeavour and, as such, strengthen the grip of organizational technologies of power. As Knights and Morgan put it in relation to 'corporate strategy':

> The discourses and practices surrounding strategy have to be seen as social constructs, which have the effect of constituting managerial, and labour subjectivities that enhance the productive power of organizations through subjectively 'locking' individuals and groups into their tasks and commitments. (1991: 270)

This particular approach, while specifically concerned with the relationship between power and subjectivity within organizations, is also underpinned by a broader philosophical assault on the modernist duality of object and subject and the superior status it ascribes to either the agency of the subject in the face of structural constraints or, alternatively, to the efficacy of reified social structures to generate subjective compliance to external priorities and imperatives. For Knights (1997), this dualistic mode of understanding the world merely reproduces the very logic of hierarchy and oppression operating, as it does, within a representationalist episte- mology that is itself premised upon an ontology of the world that posits both the subject and its objective environment as 'scientifically' accessible object domains, distinct from the discursive resources utilized to describe and explain them.

Willmott (1990b, 1994, 1995b), while also adhering to a largely post- structuralist conception of the subject as the outcome of discursively generated categories of meaning, has sought to refine this approach through an attempted reconciliation of the Foucauldian stress on micro- relations of power with a more Marxian-orientated form of meta-critique. In doing so, he argues that the efficaciousness of discourses of power/knowledge and their subjectivizing outcomes can be understood largely in terms of the individualizing logic of capitalist modernity. Willmott suggests that the social and cultural differentiation process cen- tral to modernity has resulted in a plethora of possible avenues of subjective self-constitution which, on the one hand, offer a range of oppor- tunities for 'self-invention' and, at the same time, result in a subjective state of angst and a 'heightened sense of indeterminacy, freedom and responsibility' (Willmott, 1994: 109).

This, for Willmott, is a condition that in turn produces a state of frag- mentation that leaves the modern self vulnerable to the 'diverse disciplinary powers' (1994: 108) of corporate governmentality. Willmott argues that such indeterminacy results in subjects who are 'seemingly capable of autonomous action, yet who are also acutely vulnerable because [they] are held individually responsible for [their] actions' (1990b: 369). Thus, the subject, in an attempt to mitigate against this sense of ontological fragility, is frequently drawn into self-confirming discursive relations of 'identity fetishism' (1990b: 369) that reinforce their subjection to regimes of disciplinary control and subjectification. Such behaviour is understood then to reinforce and legitimate a dualistic mode of under- standing that establishes the idea of the subject as an autonomous entity somehow distinct from those discursive resources and material practices upon which identity is dependent. Wilmott's response to this is to call for a non-dualistic mode of understanding that transcends the modernist belief in the sovereignty of the autonomous subject and the existence of objective categories of social structure and that, instead, seeks to 'decon- struct the idea of self identity as a sovereign seat of consciousness to reveal the subject as a tissue of contradictions that is precariously held together – or, better, bonded – by the ideological glue of identity' (1995b: 21).

This line of theorizing has, however, also inspired a range of critical responses, the majority of which have been directed as much at what is seen as the postmodern influence in this kind of theorizing, as the more substantive theorization of subjectivity *per se*. Reed (1997), as we noted in Chapter 3, has raised a number of concerns about what he considers to be largely postmodern-inspired attempts to challenge dualistic theorizations of subjectivity, and their tendency to conflate the ontological categories of subjective agency and social structure and, in the process, to diminish the explanatory potential of both. This critique is gauged in relation to Reed's view of postmodernism's proclivity, in an effort to deconstruct dualistic modes of understanding, to reject all forms of 'representationalist method-ologies' (1997: 23) that posit the existence of an external world, distinct from that constituted by the subject of such knowledge. This results, for Reed, in a situation in which

> [s]tructure is denied any kind of ontological status or explanatory power as a rel-ative enduring entity that takes on stable institutional and organizational forms generating scarce resources that actors, both individual and collective, have to draw on in a selective and constrained manner before they can 'move on' and 'make a difference'. (1997: 26)

Reed's view is that this is sufficient to raise serious difficulties for any endeavour to develop a postmodern-infused critical account of organi-zational power relations. His conviction is that postmodernism obscures any insight into the ways in which enduring relations of power and con-trol can be understood to direct and regulate patterns of behaviour and limit the range of possibilities and choices open to individuals. However, this is also compounded, in his view, by the propensity of such anti-dualistic modes of analysis to reduce concomitantly the agential power of social actors to influence and regulate structural processes. Thus, reduced to the product of externalized discursive formations, not only is structure denied any causal capacity, but its corollary, subjective agency, also seems to be erased from the equation of organizational power and control.

It is this latter point that has also fuelled the work of a number of more vehement critics of the impact of postmodern thought on organization theory and, in particular, its stress upon a non-dualistic account of organi-zational life (Ackroyd and Thompson, 1999; Austrin, 1994; P. Thompson, 1993; Thompson and Ackroyd, 1995; Thompson and Findlay, 1996). For Thompson, rather than reinstating the missing subject into LPT in partic-ular, and organization theory more generally, all postmodernism has achieved is to deprive the subject of any causal and, as such, agential capacity through its reduction of the subject to little more than a discur-sively generated fiction. Denied any ontological status, the subject is debarred from undertaking an active and purposeful role in opposing the relations of power and motivation that LPT views as inherent to capitalist modes of organization. This is a problem that is compounded, for Thompson, by Willmott's proposition that even where individuals and collectivities may be seen to act in a way that affirms their autonomy and individuality, this serves merely to reinforce the subjectification process that underpins the repressive logic of capitalist modernity. As Thompson notes, in conjunction with Ackroyd,

Even when employees are not entirely subjugated, seduced or self-disciplined, they are prisoners of their own identity projects. For not only is the search for particular secure identities constantly undermined, the search for security *per se* is a self-defeating trap. (Ackroyd and Thompson, 1999: 160 *original emphasis*)

In this respect, then, critics of postmodern organization theory, such as Thompson, have tended to emphasize the extent to which employees, as active and self-interested subjects, reappropriate regimes of power (see, for example, Thompson and Findlay, 1996). As such, they reject both the onto-logical assumptions of postmodernism, as well as what they consider to be the epistemological inadequacy of a mode of looking at the world that views resistant practices as merely reinforcing the disciplinary structures of organizational governance, resulting in what they consider to be an unac-ceptable level of apoliticism. In contrast, they call for a way of 'doing' organizational research that recognizes the agency of employees and their ability to challenge and attempt to undermine managerially-directed strategies of control (Thompson and Ackroyd, 1995).

A similar, if somewhat more sympathetic, critique can be found in the work of Newton (1998, 1999). Here, the main focus of attention continues to be a critical analysis of the apparent lack of any concrete theory of the role of the active subject within postmodern and, particularly, Foucauldian-inspired studies of workplace activity and, concomitantly, of the role of materially stabilized and asymmetrical power relations in the structuring of organizational life. The latter concern is illustrated by Newton with particular reference to Grey's (1994) study of the career development of aspiring accountants, and Du Gay's (1996) more extensive consideration of the relationship between identity, labour and consump-tion. In the case of Grey's study of careers in accountancy, for example, Newton argues that it almost completely disregards the idea that individ-uals may seek to pursue career advancement for its associated material rewards favouring, instead, an analysis based on a Foucauldian assump-tion of the interrelationship between the discourse of career advancement and the pursuit of an enduring sense of self (Newton, 1998: 424). In much the same way as Thompson, Newton is also concerned by what he con-siders to be the Catch-22 implications of an approach that views any resistant practices by employees as themselves potentially indicative of their salience. As such, he clearly remains uneasy with a conception of the subject that is apparently devoid of any purposeful agency, observing that 'it is hard to gain a sense of how active agential selves "make a difference" through "playing" with discursive practices' (Newton, 1998: 426).

Of equal importance for Newton, however, is what he considers to be the failure of post-structuralism to address adequately the duality of subject and object that it professes to overcome. Rather, he sees, particularly in the work of Knights and Willmott, something of an ontological sleight of hand occurring. In other words, for Newton, the dualistic nature of more tradi-tional forms of analysis is seemingly side-stepped rather than resolved, through the repression of subjectivity as an analytical variable (Newton, 1998). However, while his own attempt (Newton, 1999) to invoke the socio-historical work of Elias (1978, 1982, 1991) in the critical analysis of workplace subjectivity is certainly informative, particularly in its theorization of subjectivity within the framework of 'changing social and political structures of particular epochs' (Newton, 1999: 417), its relative neglect of an adequate theory of the relationship between inter-subjectivity and the objective domain results in a model that remains, to the likely disdain of most postmodernists, subject centred. In other words, it maintains the primacy of the subject as an individualized, rational agent isolated in the pursuit of its own sense of self and, as such, it seems to fall at the final hurdle of developing a viable alternative to the subject/object dualism that Newton seeks to address in his appropriation of Elias's social theory.

Critical Theory and inter-subjectivity

Considering not only the ideas encountered above, but also many of the themes that have re-emerged constantly throughout this book, it would seem to us, then, that perhaps the most striking problem that has arisen from the impact of postmodernism on organization theory is that of how we can understand the relationship between employee subjectivity and the apparently shifting nature of contemporary organizational life. This is not to suggest, however, that this is the sole issue at stake within such debates. Nevertheless, we do believe that it provides one possible avenue along which a fruitful re-evaluation of the relationship between work, postmodernism and organization might be pursued. In particular, what is at stake, or so it would seem to us at least, is the need to develop a theoretical approach to organizational subjectivity that is both sensitive to the capacity of the subject to engage actively and purposefully within his/her environment, yet that does not slip into a crude and essentialist subject centrism. Naturally, this is something of a tall order and, as such, we do not claim to offer a definitive or uncontestable response to this challenge. However, we do believe that it might at least be possible, by revisiting what could be understood as the critical precursor of the postmodern sensibility, to provide an alternative means of conceptualizing not only how the subjective and objective dimensions of human beings exist in a state of interdependence but also, in doing so, to bring critical insight to the impact of postmodernism as an historical and culturally-located phenomenon on our understanding of this state of existence.

The reflexive critique of modernity

As we have suggested, both in the early stages of this chapter, and at different junctures throughout the book, despite the protestations of some of the more fundamentalist defenders of postmodernism, modernism as an intellectual and cultural tradition has never been lacking in terms of those willing to mount a reflexive critique of its own limitations. A notable example of this is the work associated with the Frankfurt School of Critical Theory, a group of German intellectuals whose writing has, thus far, spanned a period of around seventy years. While both extensive and complex, central to Critical Theory has been a concern to develop a critical understanding of what its various adherents have viewed as the contemporary crisis of modernity – a crisis underpinned by the distortion of the emancipatory potential of human reason and an accompanying closure of opportunities for the development of autonomy and responsibility that has come to dominate the post-Enlightenment period. Drawing on a range of intellectual resources ranging from the philosophies of Hegel and Nietzsche, through the political economy of Marx, to the sociology and cultural criticism of Weber and the psychoanalytic theory of Freud, Critical Theory has come to represent what can perhaps be described as the critical conscience of modernity.

The Frankfurt School

It is common today to distinguish between two generations of thinkers associated with the Frankfurt School and its particular brand of Critical Theory. The earlier, or first generation's work is exemplified most notably in the published works of Theodor Adorno (1973 [1966], 1974 [1951]), Max Horkheimer (1994 [1974]; Adorno and Horkheimer, 1973 [1947]) and Herbert Marcuse (1972 [1955], 1983 [1941], 1986 [1964]), whose writings spanned a period of some forty years, culminating in the mid to late 1960s. The later, or second generation's work is associated largely, though not exclusively, with the contemporary contribution of Jürgen Habermas (1972, 1987a [1985], 1987b [1969], 1993 [1981]). While differing in many respects, what unites the two generations is a commitment to developing a critical appraisal of contemporary western culture and, in doing so, to render transparent the maintenance of what they consider to be social relations of domination and repression.

Taking the earlier generation as our starting point, what is of particular interest to us here is the way in which Critical Theory has addressed the nature of subjectivity and its uneasy relationship with the historical development of the capacity for critical reason. Critical Theorists such as Adorno, Horkheimer and Marcuse were fundamentally committed to the idea that the human faculty of reason was the key to an emancipated human condition. That is to say, only through grasping the critical and self-reflexive potential of reason would humanity achieve the status of autonomous subjectivity. As Alvesson and Willmott note in this regard, autonomy for Critical Theorists refers broadly to 'the capability of human beings to make informed judgements that are not impeded and distorted by socially unnecessary dependencies associated with subordination to inequalities of wealth, power and knowledge' (1996: 13). This is a formulation that draws heavily on Critical Theory's roots in Hegel's philosophy of history and a belief in the dialectical evolution of reason as the march of freedom through history. While we develop this theme more thoroughly later in the chapter, for Hegel, human freedom could be attained only if, and when, humanity came to realize its constitutive role in the world through the meaning we give to it. As such, critical reason is seen as the means by which humanity would reconcile itself with the social world that it had created, one now freed from reification and, thus, domination. As Marcuse put it, for Hegel, the subject must '*set out to organize reality according to the demands of his free rational thinking instead of simply accommodating his thoughts to the existing order and the prevailing values*' (1983 [1941]: 6 *emphasis added*).

The faculty of critical reason is not something that is given for Critical Theorists, however, but an attainment that must be struggled for through a dialectical process of affirmation and negation. For while human beings ascribe meaning to, and thus construct, the world they inhabit, the subsequent objectification of that world opposes and diminishes the constitutive role of subjectivity in the generation of that social reality. Thus, particularly in the guise of positivist philosophy, under the conditions of modernity reason is reduced to the role of detached observation, the 'function' of which is merely to record and categorize reality. Reason is divested of its critical apprehension of the interdependence of subject and object. In contrast, the role of a genuinely critical reason is to question and negate the world as objective reality and, in doing so, to expose the reified relationship between subject and object and the inadequate realization of subjectivity within existing social relations and the modes of its organization.

For Critical Theorists, then, what has come to characterize modernity is the reduction of critical reason to a technocratic or *instrumental rationality* – one that prioritizes means over ends or efficiency over value in the Weberian sense. While deeply embedded within capitalist relations of production and exchange, instrumental rationality is not, however, simply reducible to capitalism as perhaps would be judged to be the case in a more orthodox Marxian reading of the determination of the consciousness of an age by the requirements of the economic base. Rather, from the perspective of Critical Theory the crisis of modernity is understood as the particular outcome of a dialectical interrelationship between the material and the ideational domains or between economy and culture. It is within this context that Critical Theory seeks to expose the ways in which instrumental modes of reasoning, combined with the accumulative logic of industrial capitalism, have produced rationalized modes of social and cultural domination that exclude alternative ways of thinking or being in the world. As Marcuse lamented in this respect:

We live and die rationally and productively. We know that destruction is the price of progress as death is the price of life, that renunciation and toil are prerequisites for gratification and joy, that business must go on, and that the alternatives are Utopian. (1986 [1964]: 145)

At the heart of this diagnosis of modernity is a belief that the outcome of such a restructuring of the faculty of critical thought, and its subjugation under a technical rationality that merely posits the 'real' as rational, is an arresting of the dialectical process that might otherwise lead to the realization of human subjectivity. In his writing on those institutions of modern capitalism that provide entertainment and information to the populous, and in a vein that is not dissimilar to Willmott's analysis, Adorno (Adorno, 1991; Adorno and Horkheimer, 1973 [1947]) emphasized that what he termed the *culture industry* functions primarily as a technology for the 'fettering of consciousness'. For Adorno, the culture industry 'impedes the development of autonomous independent individuals who judge and decide consciously for themselves' (1991: 92) through the provision of a set of values that secure for them a sense of well-being, and a (mis)conception of their own subjective identity. This resulted in what he termed a 'subjectless subject' (cited in Dews, 1987: 227); a product of the rationalizing tendencies that result in an understanding of the subject as a socialized object, one both knowable through, and ultimately reducible to, instrumental reasoning and its concomitant logic of exclusion and/or domination.

In questioning the status of the subject under the conditions bequeathed by capitalist modernity, the analysis professed by Adorno and his colleagues certainly seems to resonate closely with the post-structuralist motif of the 'death of the subject' and its reduction to the product of socio-historically located forms of discourse. However, this would be a misleading assertion to make in so far as, in the terms of engagement posited by Critical Theorists, the possibility that an autonomous mode of subjectivity might arise within history remains a cornerstone of their emancipatory philosophy. What Critical Theory does reject nevertheless, is the assertion of the existence of an essential pre-social subject, a proposition that is deemed to ignore the dialectical quality of subjectivity as an outcome of the perpetual interdependence of Self and Other. In Adorno's view in particular, to signify a state of existence as a 'subject' in isolation from its relationship to the totality of inter-subjective experience would be to engage in a form of identity thinking (Adorno, 1973 [1966]) in which the subjective 'I' is posited as that which is identical with itself. As Best and Kellner observe in this regard, the idea of an essential or socio-culturally isolated subject is, for Adorno therefore, misleading because in Critical Theory '[a]ll experience and thought is mediated – by language, society, and a set of social relations and objects. There is no pure subjectivity which confronts pure objects: the subject is mediated by objects and vice versa' (Best and Kellner, 1991: 230).

Taking this conception of subjectivity as fairly paradigmatic of the earlier generation of Critical Theorists, it can be argued that what underpins their critique of the modern condition of subjectivity is not so much a concern with the colonization of an essential, pre-social self, as exemplified in more orthodox versions of Marxism, but rather, with the ways in which the *process* of subjectivity is arrested as a consequence of the instrumentalization of the sites through which it is mediated inter-subjectively. As such, while the emergence of a critical subjectivity is something that the Frankfurt School clearly viewed as 'a goal to strive for' (Best and Kellner, 1991: 233), this was not a goal premised on some essentialist notion of a pure, *a priori* conception of subjectivity. Critical Theory is also markedly different in its approach to the ontological status of subjectivity from the postmodernist critique of essentialism and the concomitant positing, particularly by those postmodern meta-theorists whose work we discussed in Chapter 1, of a dualistic relationship between Self and Other, subject and object. Rather, the self-realization of the subject is premised, for Critical Theorists, upon the possibility of an interdependent relationship between Self and Other, albeit one that is increasingly rendered impossible by the reifying effects of the logic underpinning capitalist modernity.

Habermas and communicative action

The early work of the Frankfurt School, and particularly its conception of subjectivity, has been both inherited and challenged by one of the most prominent contemporary Critical Theorists, Jürgen Habermas. For Habermas (1987a [1985]), despite their conception of rational subjectivity as a processual quality, his Frankfurt School predecessors' approach is undermined by what he considers to be their continued faith in the emergence of critical reason and a philosophy of subjectivity that remains essentially 'subject-centred' (1987a: 294). By this he means that, Habermas, the first generation of the Frankfurt School remained committed to a conception of reason as both the driving force behind, and the final realization of, subjectivity that was seen to reside in the process by which the individual comes to attain a bounded sense of his/her own individual self-consciousness. While Habermas shares the concern of the earlier Critical Theorists with the repressive consequences of the undue valorization of instrumental reason, or what he has termed 'purposive-rational action' (Habermas, 1987b [1969]: 91), over and above a more substantive conception of rationality, his own critical project is based on what he considers to be the emancipatory potential of a *communicative rationality*, one grounded in a philosophy of inter-subjectivity (Habermas, 1984), rather than a subject-centred rationality grounded in a philosophy of consciousness. Thus, underpinning Habermas's brand of Critical Theory is a more pragmatic concern with the desire to reconstruct the possibilities of an undistorted inter-subjectivity, one grounded in communication and language.

In developing what he considers to be a potentially emancipatory approach to the social sciences, Habermas (1972) proceeds from a typology of what he terms cognitive or *knowledge-constitutive interests* that, in his view, underpin the generation and legitimization of all knowledge claims. These comprise:

- *empirical-analytical* knowledge that has an interest in control and classification, and so should be judged only according to its correctness in applying rational-purposive criteria;
- *hermeneutic-historical* knowledge that has an interest in understanding, and so should be judged according to its adequacy of meaning and interpretation;
- *critical-emancipatory* knowledge that asks not only 'what is?', but also 'what ought to be?', and as such directs its activities at questioning social relations that result in unnecessary levels of repression or domination. Critical-emancipatory knowledge should be judged according to its emancipatory potential.[2]

While not dismissive of the important role empirical-analytical and hermeneutic-historical interests have to play in the accumulation of knowledge, what Habermas stresses is the need for these to be informed by a critical-emancipatory interest if they are to contribute to the pursuit of the Enlightenment goal of human emancipation and progress. In many ways, it is this proposition that leads Habermas to a condemnation both of positivist/functionalist accounts of science, and of postmodernism. For, in both instances, Habermas perceives a renunciation of the critical-emancipatory interest involving an evasion of any sense of a normative foundation for science and the necessary pursuit of what Benhabib terms 'the minimal criteria of validity' (1990: 125). His defence of 'the project of modernity' (Habermas, 1993: 103) is thus based on an acknowledgement of the increasing predominance of an instrumental or technocratic rationality within society, yet is combined with a belief in both the need for, and the possibility of, an alternative rationality underpinned by the pursuit of a critical-emancipatory interest.

However, it is not only the apparent lack of any room for normative commitment that troubles Habermas in relation to postmodernism. He is also concerned by the process of subjective dissolution that haunted his mentor Adorno and which, he argues, is celebrated within much of the postmodern genre that we considered particularly in Chapter 1. As Habermas notes in this regard:

> They [the postmodernists] claim as their own the revelations of decentred subjectivity, emancipated from the imperatives of work and usefulness, and with this experience they step outside the modern world. . . . They remove into the sphere of the far-away and the archaic the spontaneous powers of imagination, self-experience and emotion. The instrumental reason they juxtapose in Manichean fashion is a principle only accessible through evocation, be it in the will to power or sovereignty, Being or the Dionysiac force of the poetical. (1993: 107)

In contrast, then, Habermas seeks to develop what he considers to be a normative account of social relations, one that rejects a non-social conception of reason and subjectivity as well as the postmodern and thus, in his view, nihilistic assault on the categories of truth and value. To achieve this he calls for what he terms an ethical-epistemic shift towards a 'paradigm of mutual understanding' (Habermas, 1987a [1985]: 310). As such, Habermas's social philosophy is premised upon a direct critique of what he considers to be the undue emphasis placed on the potential of the individual to reach a state of self-contained, authentic subjectivity which he views as an inevitable, if unintended, outcome of the 'paradigm of consciousness' that underpinned the work of his predecessors within the Frankfurt School. In its place, he seeks to offer a genuinely radical *social* philosophy of the subject that avoids the monadic implications of traditional philosophy by emphasizing the role of language, the communicative nature of inter-subjectivity and the processes through which individuals are 'socialized through communication and reciprocally recognize one another' (Habermas, 1987a [1985]: 310). In other words, as Benhabib (1992: 71) puts it, for Habermas 'the "I" becomes an "I" only among a "we", in a community of speech and action'. In Habermas's view, then, Critical Theory must be based less on a conception of 'transcendental reason' accessible merely through isolated reflection or contemplation, and more a Hegelian philosophy of inter-subjectivity.

Challenging postmodern meta-theory, then, Habermas endeavours to identify the necessary conditions for an adequate critique of modernity within the modern tradition itself, distinguishing between reason as such and a subject-centred, instrumental reason. On this basis, he develops what he terms 'a theory of the pathology of modernity from the viewpoint of . . . the deformed realization of reason in history' (1984: 7), emerging as a defender of the emancipatory potential of a more substantive and inter-subjective concept of rationality, while sharing with early Critical Theorists, and indeed certain postmodern meta-theorists, a critical disposition towards its oppressive and destructive appropriation. It is through this appropriation that instrumental reason, based on outcome and performance, is understood by Habermas to invade the everyday sphere of inter-subjective understanding, a process that he terms the 'colonization of the lifeworld' (Habermas, 1984). Re-emphasizing Hegel's understanding of reason as inter-subjective, Habermas identifies 'a different model for the mediation of the universal and the individual . . . provided by the *higher-level inter-subjectivity of an uncoerced formation of will* within a communication community existing under constraints toward co-operation' (1987a [1985]: 40 *original emphasis*). On this basis, Habermas claims to 'put modernity back on the road – both philosophical and practical – to *democratic self-organization* achieved through communicative action' (Frank, 1992: 153 *emphasis added*).

Structuring Habermas's conception of inter-subjectivity and the will to co-operate therefore, is a distinction between instrumental and communicative action. The former reflects the common concern, within Critical Theory, with a mode of rationality that prioritizes means over ends, techniques over goals, and operates without reflection on the rationality or 'justness' of the goals themselves. In contrast, the latter, Habermas argues, is orientated towards understanding and agreement, and an emancipation of the potential of inter-subjectivity. Underpinned by a focus on the pragmatics of the speech act, Habermas's inter-subjective theory of communicative action is thus grounded in a commitment to social solidarity and the utopian potential of the medium of language to facilitate mutual recognition or what he terms 'communicative rationality'. Habermas (1984) terms the standard by which such rationality can be evaluated the *ideal speech situation*, characterized by an absence of coercion, and the recognition of the authority of rational argumentation.[3] For Habermas, then, communicative action is not an end in itself, but rather an element in the pursuit of communicative rationality as a universal emancipatory force. As he puts it:

> To the extent to which it suggests a concrete form of life, even the expression 'the ideal speech situation' is misleading. What can be outlined normatively are the necessary but general conditions for the communicative practice of everyday life and for procedure of discursive will-formation that would put participants *themselves* in a position to realize concrete possibilities for a better and less threatened life, on *their own* initiative and in accordance with *their own* needs and insights. (1984: 69 *original emphasis*)

Habermasian critical theory therefore proceeds from a recognition of the need to maintain a rigorous critique of the tendency of instrumental rationality to colonize the emancipatory potential of inter-subjectivity and the conditions upon which it depends. It also maintains, however, a confidence in reason as imperative to discursive will-formation[4] and so is premised on the conviction that, in order to sustain the emancipatory potential of modernity, we must also be both critical and reflexive in our approach to it.

For those committed to the development of an organization theory that is both critical of systemic modernism, yet also wary of the anti-foundationalist claims of postmodernism, it is perhaps unsurprising therefore that the relatively contemporary work of Habermas has proven to be something of an inspiration. The appeal of Habermas's work in this regard rests largely upon its critical approach to the subjection of rationality to the imperatives of technical cognitive interests outlined above. Its portrayal of the 'superiority of interests based on emancipation' (Burrell, 1994: 13) and the possibility of non-coercive, communicative rationality as the foundation for 'democratic self-organization', as Frank (1992: 153) puts it, has proven to be particularly appealing. In terms of understanding contemporary work organizations and the various themes that we have explored throughout previous chapters, Habermas draws attention to the ways in which the non-instrumentalized aspects of the social world, and with them the potential for communicative action, are colonized by the instrumental rationality underpinning systemic modernism. For Habermas this results in an arresting of the processual nature of inter-subjectivity and the subjugation of the critical and emancipatory potential of communicative action to the systemic imperatives of technical rationality – a process that we have argued can be identified in relation to contemporary (and so-called postmodern) management practices discussed in previous chapters. In this sense, Critical Theory, and Habermas's work in particular, appears pertinent to many of the questions of power, subjectivity and organizational identification that postmodernism raises for organization theory, and which have shaped recent debates on postmodernism and work organizations considered in previous chapters.

Habermas, Critical Theory and organization theory

Regarding more traditional approaches to the study and management of organizations as oppressive and objectifying, a growing recognition has emerged, over the last ten years or so, of Critical Theory's capacity to reinvigorate the emancipatory potential of the discipline. As Deetz has noted in this regard, 'central to such a project is an understanding of the relations among power, discursive practices and conflict suppression as they relate to the production of individual identity and corporate knowledge' (1992: 22). Attempts to integrate Critical Theory and organization theory tend to emphasize the ideological use of science as an objective authority in mainstream organization and management theory and are defined, in large part, by a concern to be both emancipatory and self-reflexive. As Steffy and Grimes (1986: 325) have put it, any attempt to integrate Critical Theory into the analysis of organizations 'assumes that organization science is a social practice and as such, must give an account of itself'. One notable example of such an attempt is the work of Alvesson and Willmott (1992a, 1992b), who have emphasized the need for an emancipatory and reflexive understanding of organizations and their management. Inspired by Critical Theory, they advocate an approach that would resist technicist and 'objective' views on organizational processes and, instead, draw attention to asymmetrical power relations. Their work has stressed the need to explore the partiality of shared and conflicting interests, paying attention to the centrality of language and communication in much the same way as Habermas does.

While much of this work acknowledges the writing of the early theorists of the Frankfurt School, particularly Adorno and Marcuse, the vast majority has tended to focus on the more recent contribution of Habermas and his theory of communicative action discussed above[5] (Alvesson and Willmott, 1992a, 1992b, 1996; Burrell, 1994; Forester, 1992, 1993; Willmott, 1997b, 1998). Forester (1992, 1993), for example, in his attempt to develop a critical theory of public administration, planning and public policy, has applied Habermas's work to an analysis of communicative relations as they manifest themselves in the ways that policy and planning decisions are taken. For Forester, the aim of such an activity would be to make transparent 'how relations of class, power, ideology and policy-making may practically and systematically distort such institutionalized discourses' (1993: 159) and, in doing so, underpin and promote the need for 'the continual democratization of political discourse' (1993: 57) in all activities of public policy-making. In his account, Habermas's grand-theory is supplemented with a call for in-depth empirical research into the actuality of decision-making practices and their implementation, research that moves beyond the philosophical conception of the ideal speech situation and explores the 'actual social and political conditions' (Forester, 1993: 3) of communicative action.

Perhaps the most extensive example of an attempt to apply the insights of Critical Theory generally, and Habermas's work in particular, to the interrogation of contemporary organization theory, however, can be found in the work of Alvesson and Willmott (1992a, 1992b, 1996) referred to above. In *Making Sense of Management* (1996), Alvesson and Willmott's stated intent is to fashion what they see as a more pragmatic version of Habermas's theory of communicative action in an effort to promote a more ethically and politically defensible approach to management, one aimed at a broad audience of academic commentators and professional managers.[6] Developing their conceptualization of 'micro-emancipation' (Alvesson and Willmott, 1992a), the authors argue for a version of Critical Theory that is informed by both the post-structuralist (or postmodern) critique of meta-narratives and its valorization of local interventions into relations of power and domination, and by what they perceive to be the needs of management practitioners whose activities are themselves embedded within everyday communicative relations. Such an approach, they argue, should be adopted in an attempt to combine an exploration of processes of distorted communication with engagement in multiple and local projects of micro-emancipation. As such, they reject as overly utopian and abstract what they see as the 'grand project' (Alvesson and Willmott, 1996: 186) of Critical Theory, favouring instead a localized, yet globally contextualized, critique of particular practices and discursive forms. In an attempt to substantiate their position, Alvesson and Willmott provide several examples of possible strategies of micro-engagement, such as the adoption of forms of critical ethnographic practice, the development of more accessible and novel styles of writing by organization theorists, and the search for 'emancipatory elements in managerial texts' (1996: 183). In doing so, they develop what is clearly a dialectical sensibility in their acknowledgement of the simultaneous co-existence of both emancipatory and repressive elements within the practice and study of organizational life. They note, for example, how corporate culture can repress and yet, at one and the same time, provide opportunities for creative innovation among employees, potentially leading to a situation in which 'the ends and priorities of companies and working life' are questioned (1996: 185).

In our view, however, there is a danger in placing undue emphasis on localized or 'micro' practices of workplace emancipation, in that they potentially undermine the very project to which Alvesson and Willmott appear to be committed. Certainly, such an emphasis appears to suggest a weakening of the broader dialectical sensibility of Critical Theory that attempts to question 'the connection between the economic life of society, the psychological development of its individuals and the changes within specific areas of culture' (Horkheimer, 1989: 33). In seeking to make the project of emancipation 'more relevant and accessible to the more mundane world of management and organization' and by reducing the emancipatory concerns of Critical Theory to those that might make more amenable bedfellows for humanistic management theory and post-structuralism, they appear to lose sight of what, for us at least, is one of the definitive features of Critical Theory – the recognition that it is impossible to abstract out specific relational configurations from the totality of social ordering as a whole, or, indeed, to understand the subjective experience of organization in this way. As Sotirin and Tyrell have noted in this regard:

> in their determined (dialectic) effort to ferret out the emancipatory elements in contemporary management practices and in mainstream, progressive and alternative critical perspectives, they [Alvesson and Willmott] concede many of the criticisms of critical theory . . . and strike a tenuous balance between immediate relevance and broader socio-political transformation. (1998: 306)

This is not, however, simply a philosophical misjudgement in our view, but one that has potentially detrimental consequences for the political project of Critical Theory as a whole. For, to promote individual and localized strategies of emancipation and liberation that appear co-existent with (however transitionally) established structures of thought and organization may, in the end, serve more to reinforce the legitimacy of such structures than to provide emancipatory insights among those subject to them. Indeed, as Marcuse noted, the danger in such circumstances is that 'under the rule of a repressive whole, liberty can be made into a powerful instrument of domination' (1986 [1964]: 7). In many ways, the identification of such strategies of micro-emancipation with emancipation *per se* can itself be conceptualized as yet another form of identity thinking, one that is both true and false. While 'true' in so far as it represents the current condition of social possibility, such an approach is 'false', in our view, in that it ignores that these limitations are themselves historically contingent and, as such, can be exposed as non-identical with the concepts of autonomy and responsibility that Alvesson and Willmott (1996: 13) seek to promote. This is not to say that we oppose the idea that incremental gains in autonomy and responsibility within work organizations should be pursued. However, what concerns us in this respect is that such a re-formulation of Critical Theory can potentially lead to a valorization of mechanisms of repression that work in and through a series of reifications, replacing a concern with collective emancipation and autonomy with a focus on the individual benefits of slightly less obvious modes of control and domination, a shift in emphasis illustrated by Alvesson and Willmott's declaration that:

> Gains, however small, in terms of increased discretion and improved job satisfaction should be appreciated as such, and not be measured solely against Utopian visions of autonomy, creativity and democracy – visions that may have little meaning for the everyday experiences and struggles of many organizational participants. (1996: 186)

Our objection, then, is not so much directed at the idea that localized improvements in working conditions should not be pursued, but rather at the apparent claim that collective values such as autonomy, creativity and democracy should not provide the yardstick by which a Critical Theory of organizations should measure social change, because they have 'little meaning for the everyday experiences' of individuals. For, if Critical Theory is to provide anything of value to a critical organization theory, it is the realization that emancipation is about the realization of such values as social practices throughout every dimension of society, and that, in seeking to identify the practical application of such values, they must be understood as being fulfilled only when existing in a state of rational identity with the concepts of which they are the material expression. The fact that an apprehension of this ideal may not appear in the consciousness of those who are denied them should not, therefore, detract from one's desire to establish them as principles according to which we engage with organizational life in particular, and social relations in general.

Naturally, we are aware that such language may appear anathema to those who would seek to adhere more closely to a more postmodern mode of critical theorizing. Not only does it imply what they would see as a totalizing account of social relations; it also hinges on the positing of a privileged critical perspective. While we are sensitive to such criticisms, however, we are less than convinced by the alternatives as they have so far presented themselves. The apparent ease, as we discussed in the second half of the book, with which these aspects of postmodernism have been incorporated into a range of managerialist discourses and practices indicates to us the potential debilitating consequences of abandoning the ability of critical reason to understand the complex interplay of structured relations of domination and the concomitant emergence of instrumentalized modes of subjectivity. Equally, we would reject any attempt to uncouple Critical Theory's self-professed intent to combine dialectically the critique of macro-social relations from the everyday colonization of the inter-subjective processes of identity formation and critical reasoning. For, to do so has the potential merely to promote, perhaps albeit inadvertently, new representations of identity between practices which, while apparently fostering greater levels of individual autonomy in the workplace, intensify the very modes of instrumental reasoning that perpetuate the organization of society in such a way that closes off the possibility of critical reflection on the relationship between individual and collective subjectivity and the structuring of the social totality through which it comes into being.[7]

Our fear, then, is that giving too much ground to the postmodern assault on the aspirations of Critical Theory to provide a totalizing critique of contemporary social relations may serve more to reinforce the legitimacy of what are essentially repressive systems of human organization than to undermine them. That is not to say that, if Critical Theory is to contribute to a re-invigorated critical account of organizational life, it should simply ignore the issues that postmodernism has raised. Indeed, what we are particularly concerned with here is the development of a theory of organization that not only is grounded in Critical Theory, but that also attempts to address both the meta-theoretical issues raised by postmodernism and the impact that postmodern ideas have had on the structuring, and everyday life practices, of work organizations. One means by which this might be achieved, we would suggest, is to return to a theme that has recurred constantly throughout our account of the postmodern-inspired literature in this field, namely, the interrelationship that appears to exist between the constitution of subjectivity within the contemporary organizational domain and the cultural valorization of Otherness – the attribution of both ontological and epistemological value to previously excluded or marginalized aspects of subjective existence – the latter emerging largely as a consequence of the apparent decline of our faith in the universalism of Enlightenment rationality as the medium of social and political change.

Hegel and the dialectics of self-consciousness

The origins of the way in which Critical Theorists, particularly Habermas, have conceptualized the nature of rational subjectivity and its emergence through a dialectical overcoming of the duality of Self and Other is, as we have suggested, to be found in the phenomenological account of self-consciousness developed in the early work of the philosopher G.W. Hegel (1977 [1807]). As such, while now nearly two hundred years old, the ideas formulated by Hegel continue to address many of the questions and dilemmas faced by contemporary social theorists and their attempts to come to terms with the postmodern critique of the dualistic legacy of Enlightenment philosophy. Consequently, we would assert that, in revisiting the work of Hegel, we may be able to contribute to the development of a theoretical framework within which some of the more pressing issues raised above about the relationship between postmodernism and organizational life might be addressed.

As we noted earlier in the chapter, at the heart of Critical Theory is an Hegelian-inspired belief in the relationship between the evolution of the faculty of critical reason and the attainment of human freedom. For, in Hegelian philosophy, only when the subject comes to identify the nature of the world as organized in accordance with his/her rational will, does he/she come to be free from the domination of reified social relations and institutions. However, in contrast to what he understood to be the Enlightenment-grounded conception of the isolated consciousness achieving this realization through a process of individual self-reflection, Hegel believed that rational awareness and thus subjectivity, or in his own terms 'self-consciousness', could be attained only through a relational and historically-contingent process of inter-subjective recognition. At the core of this proposition is an understanding that human beings have a particular need that is unique to the species, the need both to desire and to be desired. All animals exist, of course, within this schema; they are all driven by desire. However, this desire can be seen as limited to an awareness of the need for the basic requirements of life such as food or the need to reproduce. What sets human beings apart is a particular type of desire, that is, the desire to be desired, and it is this quality that for Hegel is the key to self-consciousness or subjectivity.

What Hegel emphasizes, then, is the human need to be recognized as a self-conscious subject by other self-conscious subjects. In other words, we all desire to be recognized and valued as autonomous subjects by others who we ourselves deem to possess such qualities. Our sense of self is deemed to be deeply embedded in the recognition and approval of others; it is only through such recognition that self-consciousness, or subjectivity, is achievable. As such, we can only become fully aware of the Self through the recognition of the Other, for when we experience the Other we lose our sense of uniqueness and this can only be returned by their mutual recognition. Subjectivity, or self-consciousness in Hegelian philosophy, then, must be the outcome of a mutual and equal exchange of recognition between two equally valued subjects, who can only achieve such a state of being through partaking in this very process. As such, in Hegel's terms, 'Self-consciousness exists in and for itself when, and by the fact that, it so exists for another; that is, it exists only in being acknowledged' (1977 [1807]: 111 emphasis added).

Subjectivity, therefore, is not simply given in Hegelian philosophy, but exists, as we have stressed earlier, as a potential, in and through its basis in desire, a potential that can be achieved only through what is a phenomenological process of inter-subjective mutual recognition. This is not a freely given exchange of mutual recognition, however, but must be contested and fought for; an idea encapsulated in Hegel's (1977: 111) parable of the struggle between 'Lord and Bondsman'. Within this struggle, two consciousnesses, each determined to assert and maintain their own uniqueness in the face of something that is at one and the same time their 'Other' and their 'Self', come into conflict in a situation within which each is dependent on the recognizing gaze of the Other in order to affirm his/her own sense of Self.[8] This process is, therefore, one that requires the interrelationship between conscious beings who simultaneously view their 'Other' as both the same and different, as both subject and object. This results in a state of conflict whereby each consciousness seeks to negate the Other by reducing it to the status of object, thus asserting the uniqueness of his/her own subjectivity. Yet, the point is that this is a conflict doomed to failure as for each consciousness the truth of its own subjectivity lies only in the mutual self-recognition of Others, that is, in acknowledgement by equally self-conscious subjects. Thus a paradox arises in that, by seeking to negate the subjectivity of the Other, in an attempt to assert the uniqueness and status of its self-hood, each being negates the source through which a sense of self-identity or subjectivity can ultimately be achieved. For Hegel, then, it is a mutual 're-cognition of the Other' that sits at the heart of the processual nature of subjectivity, a state of existence that must be struggled for and fought over.

It is this ongoing struggle for mutual self-recognition, and the fears and conflicts that underpin it, which for Critical Theorists is the basis of the human condition. However, this conflict is not something that should be conceptualized only at the level of human inter-subjectivity. For the relationship between Self and Other is one that is mediated in and through social structures that themselves are a reflection of the level of self-consciousness of humanity in general. As Crossley notes in this regard:

> Self-consciousness is identified as being dependent upon the historical dynamic of social relationships. An analysis of consciousness is thus displaced by an analysis of concrete historical beings in concrete historical circumstances and intersubjective relations of recognition are conceived as social and political structures. (1996: 18)

While we would agree with Crossley's basic premise, we would not concur that Hegel 'displaces' his focus on consciousness by an historical analysis in any substantive sense. Rather, what Hegelian philosophy attempts to illustrate is the dialectical nature of the interdependence of the individual self-consciousness and the social totality, maintaining that self-consciousness can only be understood in relation to the socio-cultural and historical context within which it emerges and, in doing so, constitutes the world through its projection of meaning on to its external reality. For Hegel, therefore, self-consciousness, or subjectivity, is something that must be achieved at both the (ontogenetic) level of the individual and the (phylogenetic) level of social totality, for the conditions for both are mutually interdependent.

The struggle for recognition is understood, within Hegelian philosophy, to have become institutionalized through history in the form of social and political structures, as well as expressing itself in the phenomenology of everyday experiences. The fully self-conscious subject emerges as one that recognizes the necessary interdependence of Self and Other, subject and object and subject and subject, as the embodiment of the material, spiritual and psychological reconciliation of duality in all its forms. It is this potential condition that Hegel (1967 [1821]) refers to as 'ethical life' – a form of life embedded within an ideal set of social relations in which the conditions for mutual self-recognition have become a social and political reality. The subject of Hegelian philosophy and, we would argue, the subject of Critical Theory is not therefore the illusionary individualized subject of Enlightenment philosophy that postmodernism rejects. Rather, it is the self-conscious subject which, at one and the same time, neither desires nor needs to stand apart from the social totality nor seeks to dominate any aspect of it. As Gadamer has observed:

> When Hegel says that in reaching self-consciousness we have now entered the homeland of truth, he means that truth is no longer like the foreign country of otherness into which consciousness seeks to penetrate. It had only seemed to from the standpoint of consciousness. Now, in contrast, consciousness as self-consciousness is a native of the land of truth and is at home in it . . . it finds all truth in itself . . . it knows that it embraces the entire profusion of life within itself. (1971: 59)

Subjectivity, as self-consciousness, is understood to exist only as the potential outcome of the mutual and equal exchange of recognition, grounded in the desire for such an exchange, between equally self-conscious subjects. It does not pre-exist as a unified or 'essential' human state, nor is it something that can be achieved by the efforts of the heroic and isolated individual, but rather represents a potentiality that can be achieved only through a phenomenologically grounded journey of inter-subjective struggle for recognition, one mediated by the concrete historical and sociocultural environment within which it is embedded and of which, in turn, it is constitutive.

Hegel's assault on the dualistic traditions of western philosophy is fundamentally grounded, then, within a conception not only of the dialectical interdependence of Self and Other, but also of the need to locate this relationship within its concrete historical context. This is particularly important in that it provides, for us at least, a theoretical framework within which a critical theorization of the condition of the subject within modernity, developed most recently in Habermas's turn to language as the medium through which inter-subjectivity is realized, can be developed. It provides a framework within which the socio-economic demands of modernity can be understood to mitigate against the process of inter-subjective, mutual self-recognition through a basic denial of the ontological conditions under which such a process can evolve. This is based on the proposition that rationalization, by reducing subjects to the status of carriers of instrumentalized social relations, results in a process of 'mis-recognition', one that occurs not between evolving subjectivities, but between the objectified 'simulacra', to use Baudrillard's (1983a) terminology, of subjectivity. Such mis-recognition can be understood not as the result of a process by which an essential and self-contained subject is alienated from its true and stable nature, but rather as a result of the estrangement of the 'subject in becoming' from the inter-subjective processes upon which the potential for its realization depends.

Furthermore, this process of mis-recognition cannot be abstracted out from the historical context within which it is situated, for what the dialectic at the heart of Hegel's system in particular, and Critical Theory in general, enables us to recognize is that it is both constituted by, and constitutive of, that very context. As such, the stage at which self-consciousness or subjectivity is arrested is also experienced in concrete form through the concomitant arrestation of historical development, both in terms of the cultural values of society and the very material configurations of its dominant mode of organizing.

It is this dialectical philosophy of inter-subjectivity, grounded in the work of Hegel and its subsequent development in Critical Theory, that underpins our own critique of postmodernism and, in particular, its influence on the study of work and its organization.

Inter-subjectivity, work and postmodernism

The significance of the issue of employee subjectivity within work organizations has, as we have observed on numerous occasions now, been linked closely to a range of developments in their study and management. Critical accounts, in particular, have emphasized the ways in which managerial strategies associated with corporate culturalism and the like seek, in modernist terms, to *colonize* the subject or, in more postmodern accounts, to *constitute* human subjectivity, in the service of instrumental ends associated with industrial capitalism. Both approaches have been shown to have their limitations, however. While the former tends to rely on an essentialist conception of the pre-constituted subject, the latter seems to result in the apparent dissolution of the subject, as a meaningful ontological category, all together. While we would not seek to deny either the kernel of truth that exists within both of these perspectives, nor the pertinence of the critical work that has derived from them, the common problem for us is that both approaches continue to base their claims to 'truth' on what remains an essentially subject-centred philosophy. In other words, they conceive strategies of managerial control and exploitation as focusing on the isolated subject as the medium through which subjectivity itself can be either colonized or constituted discursively. It is the nomadic subject, shorn of its real socio-cultural locatedness, that becomes the object of analysis in both perspectives.

Drawing on the Hegelian-inspired tradition of Critical Theory discussed above, however, we would argue, in contrast, that what are often identified as managerial strategies of subjectification or subjugation are not so much a direct assault on the subjectivity of the individual, but rather, what we would term, *strategic mediations of process*. The latter operate through instrumental attempts to mediate the realm, or space, of the inter-subjective. Take, for example, the discourse of corporate culturalism that we discussed in Chapter 4, in which the values of community and mutuality are exalted

(Ouchi, 1981; Peters and Waterman, 1982). While much effort seems to be directed at mitigating against the worst excesses of subjective alienation, most notably in terms of low levels of motivation and thus productivity, this can be understood as being pursued through an arresting of the process upon which the *possibility* of a fully realized subjectivity is dependent. In other words, the inter-subjective process of 'becoming' is kept at a manageable and, therefore, productive level through attempts to mediate this process by technologies of rationalization and the corporate colonization of the space in which relations of mutual recognition might evolve.

This mediating process operates, we would suggest, in at least two ways. First, in seeking to establish the organization as the seat of meaning and value for the subject, the ontological interrelationship between subject and object becomes inverted. Rather than the subject (in becoming) existing as the source of meaning and action, such values are transposed on to the object realm of corporate culture and its concomitant symbolism in such a way as to attempt to bring about a form of transubstantiation through which the organization itself becomes personified,[9] and is then ascribed the status of a 'subject in being'. In other words, a process (of organization) occurs whereby rather than organizations existing as objective realities that serve to reflect the subjectivity of those who work in them, employees are required to identify subjectively with the organization as an external reality, as something Other than itself (the sum of its employees). This means that, on one level, the process of inter-subjective recognition manifests itself not as a subject/subject relationship, but as one between an objectified subject and a subjectified object, a relationship that is incapable of providing the mutual recognition that subjectivity, if it is to evolve and develop, requires. This is not, of course, a total closure of inter-subjectivity, for it is clearly not only in the workplace that opportunities for mutual self-recognition occur. As such, individuals are able to bring what may be viewed as surplus amounts of subjectivity into the workplace with them. It is at this point that a second strategy of mediation can be identified.

This relates to the concomitant, and at first sight contradictory, tenet of corporate culturalism, namely the promotion of shared commonalities among employees in the name of organizational community or clan membership. Engaging the philosophical framework developed above, such efforts can be understood as attempts to mediate the inter-subjective process of conflict and reconciliation that, as we noted earlier, is central to the ' becoming' nature of subjectivity. By reducing, or smoothing out, struggle within the workplace, both between individuals and between employees and management as collectivities, discourses associated with corporate culturalism that accord primacy to communitarianism, or more commonly 'teamworking', can be seen to be reliant on a contrived process of perpetual mis-recognition, seeking to ensure that the emergence of the subject is configured such that inter-subjective self-consciousness is pursued only through a managerially-mediated conception of identity. This means that the process of becoming a subject in contemporary work organizations can be understood to be one in which the process is more reflective of organizationally-prescribed and externally-imposed norms and values than self-reflexive. The result, therefore, could be understood less as an organizational community, characterized by mutual self-recognition, than as a reified form of 'ethical life', wherein subjectivity has come into being as a consequence of strategic planning on the part of those who exercise power and authority outside of the ethical sphere they themselves have sought to constitute.

This perspective is, at least in part, then, able to explain how the apparently contradictory discourses that feature so frequently within corporate culturalism, emotional labour and sexualization, namely loyalty to the corporation and its culture, as well as to colleagues, customers and clients, exist in a dialectical configuration, one shaped by unity and opposition. Furthermore, this analysis locates corporate culturalism and other forms of post-bureaucratic management within a critical understanding of the process of inter-subjectivity. This is one which, in our view, suggests how organizational subjectivity can be understood as the outcome not of mutual self-recognition, but of an imposed unity – a false reconciliation – of corporate and self-identity which, ultimately, denies the values of mutuality that may lead to the possibility of the kind of *genuinely* just and therefore ethical community alluded to at the beginning of the chapter (Rose, 1981).

Postmodernism and the re-cognition of the organizational Other

With this conception of so-called new management styles as *strategic mediations of process* in mind, we return, in the penultimate section of this chapter, to a theme that has recurred throughout the second half of the book, namely the relationship between postmodernism, organization and the 'rationalization of the irrational'. However, to do this we also need to address what has been noted as a significant absence in Critical Theory and in the work of the Frankfurt School in particular, namely, a concern with what can be understood as the affective, and thus irrational, dimension of the human condition. Somewhat scathing of what he considers to be Critical Theory's over-reliance on rationality as the antidote to the instrumentalization of society, Meštrović (1997) in particular has drawn attention to its neglect of the emotional component of life. For Meštrović, the members of the Frankfurt School, from Adorno to Habermas, focused in an exclusionary manner on the manipulation of consciousness (albeit through the medium of language in Habermas's case) and, in doing so, overlooked the ways in which the ideology of instrumental rationalization has colonized not only what and how we think, but also what and how we 'feel'.

While to suggest that, particularly in the work of the early Critical Theorists, no attention was given to the non-cognitive dimension of experience is somewhat erroneous (see in particular Marcuse, 1983 [1941]), Meštrović's observations do raise some important issues, particularly in relation to Habermas's communicative theory of inter-subjectivity. It seems evident within the theory of communicative action that, as Crossley (1996: 125) has observed, Habermas reduces inter-subjectivity to a 'narrowly cognitivist' outcome of linguistic communication. In doing so, he therefore excludes not only the emotional, but also the sensual and aesthetic dimensions of inter-subjective engagement that, more often than not, precede any linguistic interaction. This, we would argue, is debilitating to Critical Theory in at least two respects. First, it serves to blind us to the ways in which the non-cognitive dimensions of inter-subjectivity are subject to the strategic attentions of instrumental rationalization.[10] Secondly, emphasizing the inter-subjective as merely cognitive perpetuates a duality of thought, the critique of which sits at the heart of Critical Theory. For in raising reason and consciousness above the sensual and embodied dimensions of human experience, Habermas, in particular, neglects the integral Other of modernity (Burrell, 1984), perpetuating the identification of Self with a narrowly conceptualized account of what it is to be human. This is an outcome, perhaps, of his somewhat overly rationalist critique of postmodernism and his equation of its concern with the 'irrational' as representing a Nietzscheian-inspired assault on the equation of reason with progress (see Benhabib, 1990).

By returning to a dialectical understanding of the relationship between history and reason, however, this movement towards a 're-cognition of the Other' can be understood as a progressive development in that it suggests an historical overcoming of the false duality embedded within Enlightenment reasoning. That is, the increasing recognition of aspects of Self, such as emotion and sexuality, suggests a cultural shift in which a more holistic and, we would argue, dialectical understanding of the subject is starting to emerge. However, this should not in any sense be taken to suggest that we hold to a linear and essentially progressive conception of history. For as a genuinely dialectical understanding of history reveals, within any process of change, tensions and indeed struggles for dominance exist that may result in a number of indeterminate outcomes. This is the case especially, it could be argued, in relation to systemic modes of rationality which, while perhaps challenged by postmodernism, remain both intact and able to adapt effectively and efficiently as a result of the latter's materialization within the logic and practices of contemporary capitalism.

It is within this context, then, that our critique of what we have termed the rationalization of the irrational can be understood. While the recognition of the mutual interdependence of the cognitive and the sensual, the 'rational' and the 'irrational', represents, in part, a transcendence of the level of self-consciousness associated with modernity, the ever-present danger is that the cultural and material dominance of instrumental reason may arrest its realization. This, in turn, can be seen to result in a further mis-recognition of the relationship between the rational and the irrational, with the latter subsumed under the former, rather than existing in a mutual and constitutive relationship. Indeed, it is this latter state of affairs, it would seem, that characterizes the dominant relationship between the postmodern valorization of Otherness and its appropriation by the discourses and practices of the kinds of managerial strategy referred to in previous chapters.

Emotional labour, the sexualization of organizations, the promotion of organizational mythologies and even the pursuit of flexibility and teamwork within the organizational domain all reflect both the transcendence of modernist values and material practices based on the asymmetrical valorization of reason, order and calculability. At the same time, they represent a conflict between such values and a range of attempts to bring them back under the hegemony of instrumentalism that characterizes a modernism that, as Habermas originally put it, is 'dominant but dead' (1993 [1981]: 98). This, in turn, or so we would suggest, results in a situation whereby these valorized, yet largely colonized, discourses of the Other are brought predominantly into the service of mediating, and consequently arresting, the inter-subjective process of becoming within the workplace. By making knowable, and thus controllable, the sensual, affective dimension of subjectivity, subjectivity is turned back upon itself, reducing self-consciousness to an expression of the emotional and sexual values that are imposed as appropriate within the context of the work organization. Spontaneity and experimentation, and the conflict that may arise from the inter-subjective engagements of both individuals and collectivities, are thus denigrated and ultimately reified in favour of regimented, sanitized, and thus ontologically static, modes of subjectivity.

A final reflection

In drawing on our reflections on the relationship between work, postmodernism and organization to a close, we want to make a few final remarks. First and foremost, while the main aim of this book has been to draw together and introduce students of work and its organization to the literature and ideas that have been generated by the increasing interest in postmodernism within the discipline, we have, in this concluding chapter, attempted to develop our own re-appraisal of what we consider to be some of the pertinent issues arising from the book. At the heart of this is our belief that a critical reading of Hegel, and of the tradition of Critical Theory, may offer a possible starting point for understanding some of the restrictions that contemporary modes of organization seek to impose upon the dialectical, inter-subjective process of 'becoming' a subject. It has also sought to provide a critical, yet non-essentialist, response to contemporary debates in organization theory on the relationship between organization and subjectivity, and on the ways in which this relationship is shaped by various aspects of modernism and postmodernism, emphasizing, as it does, the importance of dialectical analysis. With regard to the analysis of contemporary work organizations, then, we would suggest that a dialectical theory of 'the mediations, or interconnections, that relate social phenomena to each other and the dominant mode of social organization' (Best and Kellner, 1991: 263) is a necessary prerequisite if we are to understand so-called 'postmodern organizations' as signifying, as we have suggested in earlier chapters, not a break from the imperatives of modernity, but a partial and incomplete transcendence of those imperatives.

With this in mind, and with particular regard to Chia's (1995, 1996) call for a postmodern organization theory that we considered in Chapter 3, we would argue that while his analysis is challenging, and represents an impressive demonstration of the depth of the postmodern critique of broadly modernist forms of analysis, Chia's dichotomous approach to postmodernism and modernism somewhat paradoxically suggests that escaping the problematic of dualistic thinking and theorizing requires a full substitution of 'postmodern' for 'modern' analysis. Hence, it could be argued that his schema exemplifies the systemic modernist proclivity for drawing boundaries, and for imposing an appearance of order and determinacy on an otherwise dynamic relationship, as well as exhibiting the postmodernist tendency towards embracing a somewhat paradoxically 'dehistoricized' periodization. Consequently, we would suggest that such an approach loses sight of the dialectical ontology at stake.

Attempting to respond to some of these problems, we would argue that, as a basis for the critical analysis of organizations, it is important politically and ethically to remain committed to an approach that strives to address how particular claims to truth come to achieve and maintain hegemonic status, emphasizing that it is exactly the overlooked supplement or 'Other' of formal organizations that is dis-covered (in the form of 'culture', 'emotion', 'sexuality' and so on), and that contemporary managerial discourses attempt to incorporate into organizations in order to transform the 'irrational' into a manageable, and therefore exploitable, resource. Keeping this point in mind, and attempting to respond to what we perceive as a notable weakness in analyses such as Chia's that contribute to what Reed (1993: 164) has termed the 'discontinuity thesis', we would thus advocate an approach to critical organizational analysis that is based on continuation rather than substitution. Here we share with Reed the conviction that organization theory needs to 'stress the underlying contradictions and tensions *inherent* within the modernist project and their continued relevance for assessing the future development of organization theory' (1993: 165 *original emphasis*). While the potentially critical and disruptive capacity of postmodernism to problematize and subvert aspects of organization in the name of emancipation should not be lost sight of, our preference is for a dialectical ontology of 'becoming' based on a philosophy of inter-subjectivity grounded in Hegelian critical theory. This is a philosophy that, in our view, allows one to subject the conceptual and theoretical insights of both modernist and postmodernist theory, as well as the concrete interrelationship between the subjective experience and structural evolution of contemporary work organizations, to critical analysis.

On this basis, then, we would argue that far from seeing the recent organizational emphasis on the 'irrational' as somehow postmodern, from its inception, modernity has always rested on, and wrestled with, its irrational foundations including, of course, 'the passionate sanctification of rationality itself' (S. Williams, 1998: 762). Instead of postmodernism, therefore, it could be argued that what we might be witnessing in the contemporary organizational era is modernity facing up to the limitations of its own disingenuous model of rationality and, in the case of contemporary work organizations in particular, an attempt to 'reclaim' that which has previously been excluded from the remit of rational organization. To call this postmodern, at this stage at least, would surely be misguided. What this situation indicates, it seems to us therefore, is that the rationalizing potential of modernity is clearly far from exhausted. As Williams concludes, 'it is simply undergoing a period of (uncomfortable) readjustment' (1998: 762–3).

Notes

1   Throughout this chapter we follow the convention, in contrast to say Morrow and Brown (1994), of using the capitalized term 'Critical Theory' to refer specifically to the work of those philosophers and social theorists associated with the work of the Institute of Social Research of the University of Frankfurt (more commonly referred to as the 'Frankfurt School'). See Wiggershaus (1994) for what is currently the most extensive history of the evolution of the ideas of this, sometimes disparate, group of thinkers.
2   See Willmott (1997b) for a discussion of Habermas's model of knowledge-constitutive interests in relation to the development of organization theory.
3   As Forester (1993: 3) notes, the concept of the ideal speech situation is one that is often misunderstood. Rather than a possible description of a utopian environment, or even a representation of actually existing practices, it refers to a 'counterfactual anticipation we make' that whenever we enter into meaningful discourse with one another, sound and reasonable argument will prevail as a prerequisite for entering into the exchange.
4   This can be seen to represent a liberal interpretation of Marx's conception of critical theory as 'the self-clarification of the struggles and wishes of the age' (cited in Fraser, 1989: 113).
5   Although an exception to this has been the recent work of Carr (1999) and Carr and Zanetti (1999) who have tended to be more concerned with the earlier work of the Frankfurt School and its dialectical foundations.
6   A move that suggests a marked evolution in Willmott's earlier, and more strikingly post-structuralist-orientated, work.

7   A pertinent, if admittedly extreme, example of the dangers inherent in such a reconciliatory approach can be found in Aktouf's (1992) attempt to steer management practice towards what he terms (misappropriately in our view) a radical humanism. Incorporating concepts traditionally associated with Critical Theory and its Marxian legacy, he seeks to appropriate the radical challenge to the instrumental conception of employees that is based on a perception of the individual as the passive cog in a machine, in the service of developing a more reconciliatory approach to management in which the employee becomes 'an active and willing accomplice' (Aktouf, 1992: 412).

8   This sense of fear and conflict that is a necessary aspect of any inter-subjective encounter is summed up in Sartre's (1990 [1944]: 223) renowned dictum that 'hell is . . . other people'.

9   This way of conceptualizing the distorted nature of the subject/object relationship owes a great debt to Marx's (1970 [1864]) formulation of 'commodity fetishism' as well as to its Hegelian origins.

10 In Hancock and Tyler (2000), partly in response to such observations, we explored, through a study of the work of female flight attendants, the ways in which the embodied and aesthetic qualities of such employees can be said to have undergone a process of 'aesthetic instrumentalization'.

References

Ackroyd, S. and Thompson, P. (1999) *Organizational Misbehaviour*. London: Sage.

Adam, B. (1985) 'Structural Foundations of the Gay World', *Comparative Studies in Society and History*, 27. 658–71.

Adkins, L. (1995) *Gendered Work: Sexuality, Family and the Labour Market*. Milton Keynes: Open University Press.

Adorno, T. (1973) *Negative Dialectics*. Trans. E.B. Ashton. London: Routledge and Kegan Paul (first published, 1966).

Adorno, T. (1974) *Minimu Moralia: Reflections from Damaged Life*. Trans. E.F.N. Jephcott. London: Verso (first published, 1951).

Adorno, T. (1991) *The Culture Industry: Selected Essays on Mass Culture*. Ed. J.M. Bernstein. London: Routledge.

Adorno, T. and Horkheimer, M. (1973) *Dialectic of Enlightenment*. Trans. J. Cumming. London: Verso (first published, 1947).

Adorno, T., Albert, H., Dahrendorf, R., Habermas, J., Pilot, H. and Popper, K.R. (1976) *The Positivist Dispute in German Sociology*. Trans. G. Adey and D. Frisby. Avebury: Ashgate (first published, 1969).

Aglietta, M. (1979) *A Theory of Capitalist Regulation: The US Experience*. London: Verso.

Agor, W.H. (1986) *The Logic of Intuitive Decision Making: A Research-based Approach for Top Management*. Westport, CT: Greenwood Press.

Agor, W.H. (1989) *Intuition in Organizations: Leading and Managing Productively*. Newbury Park, CA: Sage.

Aktouf, O. (1992) 'Management and Theories of Organizations in the 1990s: Toward a Critical Radical Humanism?', *Academy of Management Review*, 17 (3): 407–31.

Albrow, M. (1992) 'Sine Ira et Studio – or Do Organizations Have Feelings?', *Organization Studies*, 13 (3): 313–29.

Allen, J. and Du Gay, P. (1994) 'Industry and the Rest: The Economic Identity of Services', *Work, Employment and Society*, 8 (2): 255–71.

Althusser, L. (1969) *For Marx*. London: Allen Lane.

Alvesson, M. (1990) 'From Substance to Image', *Organization Studies*, 11 (3): 373–94.

Alvesson, M. (1991) 'Organizational Symbolism and Ideology', *Journal of Management Studies*, 28 (3): 207–25.

Alvesson, M. (1995) 'The Meaning and Meaninglessness of Postmodernism: Some Ironic Remarks', *Organization Studies*, 16 (6): 1047–57.

Alvesson, M. and Berg, P.O. (1992) *Corporate Culture and Organizational Symbolism*. Berlin: de Gruyter.

Alvesson, M. and Deetz, S. (1996) 'Critical Theory and Postmodernism Approaches to Organizational Studies', in S.R. Clegg, C. Hardy and W.R. Nord (eds), *Handbook of Organization Studies*. London: Sage. pp. 191–217.

Alvesson, M. and Willmott, H. (1992a) *Critical Management Studies*. London: Sage.

Alvesson, M. and Willmott, H. (1992b) 'On the Idea of Emancipation in Management and Organization Studies', *Academy of Management Review*, 17 (3): 432–64.

Alvesson, M. and Willmott, H. (1996) *Making Sense of Management: A Critical Introduction*. London: Sage.

Archer, M. (1995) *Realist Social Theory: The Morphogenetic Approach*. Cambridge: Cambridge University Press.

Ashforth, B.E. and Humphrey, R.H. (1993) 'Emotional Labour in Service Roles: The Influence of Identity', *Academy of Management Review*, 18 (1): 88–115.

Atkinson, J. (1985) 'The Changing Corporation', in D. Clutterbuck (ed.), *New Patterns of Work*. Aldershot: Gower. pp. 13–34.

Austrin, T. (1994) 'Positioning Resistance and Resisting Position: Human Resource Management and the Politics of Appraisal and Grievance Hearings', in J.M. Jermier, D. Knights and W.R. Nord (eds), *Resistance and Power in Organizations*. London: Routledge. pp. 199–218.

Bain, C. and Boyd, P. (1998) 'Flying So High with Some Girl in the Sky: Developments in the Airline Cabin Crew Labour Process', paper presented at the 16th annual International Labour Process Conference, Manchester, UK.

Barnard, C. (1938) *The Functions of the Executive*. Cambridge, MA: Harvard University Press.

Barns, I. (1991) 'Post-Fordist People?', *Futures*, November: 895–914.

Barthes, R. (1973) *Mythologies*. London: Paladin.

Bataille, G. (1962) *Eroticism*. Trans. M. Dalwood. London: Marion Boyars.

Baudrillard, J. (1981) *For a Critique of the Political Economy of the Sign*. St Louis, MO: Telos Press.

Baudrillard, J. (1983a) *Simulations*. New York: Semiotext(e).

Baudrillard, J. (1983b) *In the Shadow of the Silent Majorities*. New York: Semiotext(e).

Baudrillard J. (1988a) *Jean Baudrillard: Selected Writings*. Ed. M. Poster. Cambridge: Polity Press.

Baudrillard, J. (1988b) *America*. London: Verso.

Baudrillard, J. (1990) *Fatal Strategies*. London: Pluto.

Baudrillard J. (1993) *Baudrillard Live: Selected Interviews*. Ed. M. Gane. London: Routledge.

Bauman, Z. (1988) 'Is There a Postmodern Sociology?', *Theory, Culture & Society*, 5 (2/3): 217–37.

Bauman, Z. (1989) 'Sociological Responses to Postmodernity', *Thesis Eleven*, 23: 35–63.

Bauman, Z. (1990) 'Modernity and Ambivalence', *Theory, Culture & Society*, 7: 143–69.

Bauman, Z. (1993) *Postmodern Ethics*. Oxford: Oxford University Press.

Bauman, Z. (1998) 'On Postmodern Uses of Sex', *Theory, Culture & Society*, 15 (3/4): 19–33.

Beck, U. (1992) *Risk Society: Towards a New Modernity*. Trans. M. Ritter. London: Sage.

Bell, D. (1973) *The Coming of Post-Industrial Society*. New York: Basic Books.

Bell, D. (1980a) 'The Social Framework of the Information Society', in T. Forrester (ed.), *The Microelectronics Revolution*. Oxford: Basil Blackwell. pp. 500-49.

Bell, D. (1980b) 'Teletext and Technology', *Sociological Journeys: Essays 1960–1980*. London: Heinemann. pp. 275–302.

Bell, E. (1999) 'Changing the "Line of Sight" on Payment Systems: A Study of Shop-floor Workers and Managers within the British Chemical Industry', *The International Journal of Human Resource Management*, 10 (5): 924–40.

Bendelow, G. and Williams S. (eds) (1998) *Emotions in Social Life: Critical Themes and Contemporary Issues*. London: Routledge.

Benhabib, S. (1990) 'Epistemologies of Postmodernism: A Rejoinder to Jean-François Lyotard', in L. Nicholson (ed.), *Feminism/Postmodernism*. London: Routledge. pp. 107–30.

Benhabib, S. (1992) *Situating the Self: Gender, Community and Postmodernism in Contemporary Ethics*. Cambridge: Polity Press.

Benson, J.K. (1977) 'Organizations: A Dialectical View', *Administrative Science Quarterly*, 22 (1): 1–21.

Bentham, J. (1995) *The Panopticon Writings*. Ed. M. Bozovic. London: Verso (first published, 1791).

Berger, P.L. and Luckmann, T. (1967) *The Social Construction of Reality*. Harmondsworth: Penguin.

Bergquist, W. (1993) *The Postmodern Organization: Mastering the Art of Irreversible Change*. San Francisco, CA: Jossey-Bass.

Berman, M. (1983) *All That Is Solid Melts into Air: The Experience of Modernity*. London: Verso.

Bernstein, R.J. (1976) *The Restructuring of Social and Political Theory*. Oxford: Basil Blackwell.

Bertens, H. (1995) *The Idea of the Postmodern: A History*. London: Routledge.

Best, S. and Kellner, D. (1991) *Postmodern Theory: Critical Interrogations*. Basingstoke: Macmillan.

Best, S. and Kellner, D. (1997) *The Postmodern Turn*. London: The Guilford Press.

Bettencourt, L. and Gwinner, K. (1996) 'Customization of the Service Experience: The Role of the Frontline Employee', *International Journal of Service Industry Management*, 7 (2): 3–20.

Bhaskar, R. (1979) *The Possibility of Naturalism: A Philosophical Critique of the Contemporary Human Sciences*. Brighton: Harvester.

Bhaskar, R. (1986) *Scientific Realism and Human Emancipation*. London: Verso.

Blacker, F. (1992) 'Formative Contexts and Activity Systems. Postmodern Approaches to the Management of Change', in M. Reed and M. Hughes (eds), *Rethinking Organization: New Directions in Organization Theory and Analysis*. London: Sage. pp. 273–94.

Blaikie, N. (1993) *Approaches to Social Enquiry*. Cambridge: Polity Press.

Blau, P. and Scott, W.R. (1963) *Formal Organizations: A Comparative Approach*. London: Routledge and Kegan Paul.

Boje, D. (1991) 'The Storytelling Organization: A Study of Storytelling Performance in an Office Supply Firm', *Administrative Science Quarterly*, 36: 106–26.

Boje, D. (1995) 'Stories of the Storytelling Organization: A Postmodern Analysis of Disney as "Tamara-Land"', *Academy of Management Journal*, 38 (4): 997–1035.

Boje, D. (forthcoming) *Spectacles and Festivals of Organization: Towards Ahisma Production and Consumption*. Under review (London: Harwood).

Boje, D. and Dennehy, R.F. (1993) *Managing in the Postmodern World: America's Revolution against Exploitation*. Dubuque, IA: Kendall/Hunt.

Boje, D., Fitzgibbons, D. and Steingard, D. (1996) 'Storytelling at *Administrative Science Quarterly*: Warding off the Postmodern Barbarians', in D.M. Boje, R.P. Gephart Jr and T.J. Thatchenkery (eds), *Postmodern Management and Organization Theory*. Thousand Oaks, CA: Sage. pp. 60–94.

Boje, D.M., Gephart Jr, R.P. and Thatchenkery, T.J. (eds) (1996) *Postmodern Management and Organization Theory*. Thousand Oaks, CA: Sage.

Bologh, R.W. (1990) *Love or Greatness: Max Weber and Masculine Thinking - A Feminist Inquiry*. London: Unwin Hyman.

Bourdieu, P. (1984) *Distinction: A Social Critique of the Judgement of Taste*. London: Routledge and Kegan Paul.

Bowen, D.E., Siehl, C. and Schneider, B. (1989) 'A Framework for Analysing Customer Service Orientations in Manufacturing', *Academy of Management Review*, 14 (1): 75–95.

Boxall, P. (1994) 'Placing HR Strategy at the Heart of Business Success', *Personnel Management*, July: 32–5.

Braverman H. (1974) *Labor and Monopoly Capital: The Degradation of Work in the Twentieth Century*. New York: Monthly Review Press.

Brecher, A. (1970) *The Sex Researchers*. London: Andre Deutsch.

Brenner, R. and Glick, M. (1991) 'The Regulation School and the West's Economic Impasse', *New Left Review*, 188: 45–119.

Brewis, J. (1998) 'What is Wrong with This Picture? Sex and Gender Relations in Disclosure', in J. Hassard and R. Holliday (eds), *Organization Representation: Work and Organizations in Popular Culture*. London: Sage. pp. 80–99.

Brewis, J. and Grey, C. (1994) 'Re-eroticizing the Organization: An Exegesis and Critique', *Gender, Work and Organization*, 1 (2): 67–82.

Brewis, J. and Linstead, S. (2000a) *Sex, Work and Sex Work: Eroticizing Organization*. London: Routledge.

Brewis, J. and Linstead, S. (2000b) 'The Worst Thing is the Screwing' (1): Consumption and the Management of Identity in Sex Work', *Gender, Work and Organization*, 7 (2): 84–97.

Brewis, J., Hampton, M.P. and Linstead, S. (1997) 'Unpacking Priscilla: Subjectivity and Identity in the Organization of Gendered Appearance', *Human Relations*, 50 (10): 1275–304.

Brighton Labour Process Group (1977) 'The Capitalist Labour Process', *Capital and Class*, 1 (1).

Bryant, C. (1985) *Positivism in Social Theory and Research*. London: Macmillan.

Burawoy, M. (1979) *Manufacturing Consent*. Chicago, IL: University of Chicago Press.

Burkitt, I. (1998) 'Sexuality and Gender Identity: From a Discursive to a Relational Analysis', *Sociological Review*, 46 (3): 483–504.

Burrell, G. (1980) 'Radical Organization Theory', in D. Dunkerley and G. Salaman (eds), *The International Yearbook of Organizational Studies*. London: Routledge and Kegan Paul. pp. 90–107.

Burrell, G. (1984) 'Sex and Organizational Analysis', *Organization Studies*, 5 (2): 97–118.

Burrell, G. (1988) 'Modernism, Postmodernism and Organizational Analysis 2: The Contribution of Michel Foucault', *Organization Studies*, 9 (2): 221–35.

Burrell, G. (1992) 'The Organization of Pleasure', in M. Alvesson and H. Willmott (eds), *Critical Management Studies*. London: Sage. pp. 65–89.

Burrell, G. (1994) 'Organizational Analysis 4: The Contribution of Jürgen Habermas', *Organization Studies*, 15 (1): 1–45.

Burrell, G. (1996) 'Normal Science, Paradigms, Metaphors, Discourses and Genealogies of Analysis', in S.R. Clegg, C. Hardy and W.R. Nord (eds), *Handbook of Organization Studies*. London: Sage. pp. 642–58.

Burrell, G. (1997) *Pandemonium: Towards a Retro-Organization Theory*. London: Sage.

Burrell, G. and Hearn, J. (1989) 'The Sexuality of Organization', in J. Hearn, D. Sheppard, P. Tancred-Sheriff and G. Burrell (eds), *The Sexuality of Organization*. London: Sage. pp. 1–28.

Burrell, G. and Morgan, G. (1979) *Sociological Paradigms and Organisational Analysis*. London: Heinemann.

Butler, J. (1988) 'Performative Acts and Gender Constitution: An Essay in Phenomenology and Feminist Theory', *Theater Journal*, 40: 519–31.

Butler, J. (1990a) *Gender Trouble: Feminism and the Subversion of Identity*. London: Routledge.

Butler, J. (1990b) 'Gender Trouble, Feminist Theory and Psychoanalytic Discourse', in L. Nicholson (ed.), *Feminism/Postmodernism*. London: Routledge. pp. 324–40.

Butler, J. (1993) *Bodies That Matter*. New York: Routledge.

Cahoone, L. (ed.) (1996) *From Modernism to Postmodernism: An Anthology*. Oxford: Blackwell.

Cálas, M. and Smircich, L. (1997) 'Post-Culture: Is the Organizational Culture Literature Dominant but Dead?', *Comportamento Organizacional Egestao*, 3 (1): 29–56.

Callinicos, A. (1989) *Against Postmodernism*. Cambridge: Polity Press.

Carabine, J. (1992) 'Constructing Women: Women's Sexuality and Social Policy', *Critical Social Policy*, 34 (1): 23–37.

Carlzon, J. (1987) *Moments of Truth*. New York: Harper and Row.

Carr, A. (1999) ' "It's All a Bunch of Tree-huggin' Hippie Crap": From the Negative to the Positive View of Postmodernism', paper presented to The Business and Economics Society International Conference, Las Palmas, Canary Islands.

Carr, A. and Zanetti, L.A. (1999) 'Rethinking the "Production" of Identity in the Work Context', paper presented to the First International Critical Management Studies Conference, Manchester, UK.

Casey, C. (1995) *Work, Self and Society: After Industrialism*. London: Routledge.

Cassirer, E. (1951) *The Philosophy of the Enlightenment*. Princeton, NJ: Princeton University Press.

Castells, M. (1989) *The Informational City: Information Technology, Economic Restructuring and the Urban Regional Process*. Oxford: Basil Blackwell.

Castells, M. (1996) *The Rise of the Network Society*. Oxford: Blackwell.

Central Statistical Office (CSO) (1998) *Social Trends Pocketbook*. Newport: Central Statistical Office.

Chatman, J.A. (1991) 'Matching People and Organizations: Selection and Socialization in Public Accounting Firms', *Administrative Science Quarterly*, 36: 459–84.

Chemers, M., Oskamp, S. and Costanzo, M. (eds) (1995) *Diversity in Organizations: New Perspectives for a Changing Workplace*. London: Sage.

Chia, R. (1995) 'From Modern to Postmodern Organizational Analysis', *Organization Studies*, 16 (4): 579–604.

Chia, R. (1996) 'The Problem of Reflexivity in Organizational Research: Towards a Postmodern Science of Organization', *Organization*, 3 (1): 31–59.

Child, J. (1985) 'Management Strategies, New Technologies and the Labour Process', in D. Knights, H. Willmott and D. Collinson (eds), *Job Redesign: Critical Perspectives on the Labour Process*. Aldershot: Gower.

Cixous, H. (1986) 'Sorties', in H. Cixous and C. Clement, *The Newly Born Woman*. Manchester: Manchester University Press.

Clarke, S. (1990) 'New Utopia's for Old: Fordist Dreams and Post-Fordist Fantasies', *Capital and Class*, 42: 131–55.

Clegg, S. (1987) 'The Power of Language, the Language of Power', *Organization Studies*, 8 (1): 60–70.

Clegg, S. (1989) *Frameworks of Power*. London: Sage.

Clegg, S. (1990) *Modern Organizations: Organization Studies in the Postmodern World*. London: Sage.

Clegg, S. (1992) 'Modern and Postmodern Organizations', *Sociology Review*, 1 (4): 24–8.

Clegg, S. (1994) 'Weber and Foucault: Social Theory for the Study of Organizations', *Organization*, 1 (1): 149-78.

Clegg, S. and Dunkerley, D. (1980) *Organization, Class and Control*. London: Routledge and Kegan Paul.

Clegg, S. and Hardy, C. (1996) 'Introduction – Organizations, Organization and Organizing', in S.R. Clegg, C. Hardy and W.R. Nord (eds), *Handbook of Organization Studies*. London: Sage. pp. 1–28.

Clegg, S.R., Hardy, C. and Nord, W.R. (eds) (1996) *Handbook of Organization Studies*. London: Sage.

Cockburn, C. (1990) *In the Way of Women: Men's Resistance to Sex Equality in Organizations*. London: Macmillan.

Collins, R. (1981) 'On the Microfoundations of Macrosociology', *American Journal of Sociology*, 86: 984–1014.

Collinson, D. and Collinson, M. (1989) 'Sexuality in the Workplace: The Domination of Men's Sexuality', in J. Hearn, D. Sheppard, P. Tancred-Sheriff and G. Burrell (eds), *The Sexuality of Organization*. London: Sage. pp. 91–109.

Conner, D.R. (1992) *Managing at the Speed of Change: How Resilient Managers Succeed and Prosper Where Others Fall*. New York: Villard Books.

Cooke, P. (1990) *Back to the Future: Modernity, Postmodernity and Locality*. London: Unwin Hyman.

Cooper, R. (1989) 'Modernism, Postmodernism and Organizational Analysis 3: The Contribution of Jacques Derrida', *Organization Studies*, 10 (4): 479–502.

Cooper, R. (1990) 'Organization/Disorganization', in J. Hassard and D. Pym (eds), *The Theory and Philosophy of Organizations: Critical Issues and New Perspectives*. London: Routledge. pp. 167–97.

Cooper, R. (1998) 'Sentimental Value', *People Management*, April: 48–50.

Cooper, R. and Burrell, G. (1988) 'Modernism, Postmodernism and Organizational Analysis: An Introduction', *Organization Studies*, 9 (1): 91–112.

Cooper, R. and Law, J. (1995) 'Organization: Distal and Proximal Views', *Research in the Sociology of Organizations 13*. Greenwich, CT: JAI Press. pp. 237–74.

Cooper, R. and Sawaf, A. (1998) *Executive EQ*. New York: Orion.

Creith, E. (1996) *Undressing Lesbian Sex: Popular Images, Private Acts and Public Consequences*. London: Cassell.

Cressey, P. and McInnes, J. (1980) 'Voting for Ford: Industrial Democracy and the Control of Labour', *Capital and Class*, 11: 5–33.

Crook, S., Pakulski, J. and Waters, M. (1992) *Postmodernization: Change in Advanced Societies*. London: Sage.

Crossley, N. (1996) *Intersubjectivity: The Fabric of Social Becoming*. London: Sage.

Czajka, J. and DeNisi, A. (1988) 'Effects of Emotional Disability and Clear Performance Standards on Performance Ratings', *Academy of Management Journal*, 31 (2): 394–404.

Dandeker, C. (1990) *Surveillance, Power and Modernity*. Oxford: Polity Press.

Dandridge, T.C. (1986) 'Ceremony as an Integration of Work and Play', *Organization Studies*, 7 (2): 159–70.

De Grazia, S. (1962) *Of Time, Work and Leisure*. New York: The Twentieth Century Fund.

De Saussure, F. (1974) *Course in General Linguistics*. London: Fontana.

Deal, T.E. and Kennedy, A.A. (1982) *Corporate Culture: The Rites and Rituals of Corporate Life*. Reading, MA: Addison-Wesley.

Deetz, S. (1992) 'Disciplinary Power in the Modern Corporation', in M. Alvesson and H. Willmott (eds), *Critical Management Studies*. London: Sage. pp. 21–45.

Delanty, G. (1997) *Social Science: Beyond Constructivism and Realism*. Buckingham: Open University Press.

Deleuze, G. and Guattari, F. (1984) *Anti-Oedipus*. London: Athlone Press.

Denison, D. (1990) *Corporate Culture and Organizational Effectiveness*. New York: Wiley.

Dent, M. (1995) 'The New National Health Service: A Case of Postmodernism?', *Organization Studies*, 16 (5): 875–99.

Derrida, J. (1976) *Of Grammatology*. Baltimore, MD: Johns Hopkins University Press.

Derrida, J. (1994) *Specters of Marx: The State of the Debt, the Work of Mourning and the New International*. London: Routledge.

Dews, P. (1987) *Logics of Disintegration: Post-structuralist Thought and the Claims of Critical Theory*. London: Verso.

DiTomaso, N. (1989) 'Sexuality in the Workplace: Discrimination and Harassment', in J. Hearn, D. Sheppard, P. Tancred-Sheriff and G. Burrell (eds), *The Sexuality of Organization*. London: Sage. pp. 71–90.

Donaldson, L. (1976) 'Woodward, Technology, Organizational Structure and Performance – A Critique of Universal Generalization', *Journal of Management Studies*, 13 (3): 255–73.

Donaldson, L. (1996a) *For Positivist Organization Theory: Proving the Hard Core.* London: Sage.

Donaldson, L. (1996b) 'The Normal Science of Structural Contingency Theory', in S.R. Clegg, C. Hardy and W.R. Nord (eds), *Handbook of Organization Studies*. London: Sage. pp. 57–76.

Douglas, M. (1966) *Purity and Danger: An Analysis of Concepts of Pollution and Taboo.* London: Routledge and Kegan Paul.

Drucker, P. (1969) *The Age of Discontinuity.* London: Heinemann.

Du Gay, P. (1996) *Consumption and Identity at Work.* London: Sage.

Du Gay, P. and Salaman, G. (1992) 'The Cult(ure) of the Customer', *Journal of Management Studies*, 29 (5): 615–33.

Dunn, R. (1991) 'Postmodernism: Populism, Mass Culture, and Avant-Garde', *Theory, Culture & Society*, 8: 111–35.

Durkheim, E. (1964) *The Division of Labor in Society.* New York: The Free Press (first published, 1893).

Dutton, J., Dukerich, J. and Harquail, C. (1994) 'Organizational Images and Member Identification', *Administrative Science Quarterly*, 39: 239–63.

Eagleton, T. (1996) *The Illusions of Postmodernism.* Oxford: Blackwell.

Easton, G. and Araujo, L. (1997) 'Management Research and Literary Criticism', *British Journal of Management*, 8: 99–106.

Elger, T. and Smith, C. (eds) (1994) *Global Japanization?* London: Routledge.

Elias, N. (1978) *The Civilizing Process.* Vol. I: *The History of Manners.* Oxford: Blackwell.

Elias, N. (1982) *The Civilizing Process.* Vol. II: *State Formation and Civilization.* Oxford: Blackwell.

Elias, N. (1991) *The Society of Individuals.* Oxford: Blackwell.

Ellis, H. (1913) *Studies in the Psychology of Sex.* Vol. III. London: Macmillan.

Etzioni, A. (1961) *The Comparative Analysis of Complex Organizations.* New York: The Free Press.

Evans, D. (1993) *Sexual Citizenship: The Material Construction of Sexualities.* London: Routledge.

Fayol, H. (1949) *General and Industrial Management.* London: Pitman.

Featherstone, M. (1988) 'In Pursuit of the Postmodern: An Introduction', *Theory Culture & Society*, 5 (2): 195–215.

Featherstone, M. (1991) *Consumer Culture and Postmodernism.* London: Sage.

Ferguson, K.E. (1984) *The Feminist Case against Bureaucracy.* Philadelphia, PA: Temple University Press.

Filby, M. (1992) 'The Figures, the Personality and the Bums: Service Work and Sexuality', *Work, Employment and Society*, 6 (1): 23–42.

Fineman, S. (ed.) (1993) *Emotion in Organizations.* London: Sage.

Fineman, S. (1994) 'Organizing and Emotion: Towards a Social Construction', in J. Hassard and M. Parker (eds), *Towards a New Theory of Organizations.* London: Routledge. pp. 75–86.

Fiske, J. (1989) *Understanding Popular Culture.* London: Routledge.

Folgero, I. and Fjeldstad, I. (1995) 'On Duty–Off Guard: Cultural Norms and Sexual Harassment in Service Organizations', *Organization Studies*, 16 (2): 299–313.

Forester, J. (1992) 'Critical Ethnography: On Fieldwork in a Habermasian Way', in M. Alvesson and H. Willmott (eds), *Critical Management Studies.* London: Sage. pp. 46–65.

Forester, J. (1993) *Critical Theory, Public Policy, and Planning Practice: Towards a Critical Pragmatism.* Albany, NY: State University of New York Press.

Foucault, M. (1970) *The Order of Things: An Archaeology of the Human Sciences*. London: Routledge.

Foucault, M. (1977a) *Discipline and Punish: The Birth of the Prison*. London: Penguin.

Foucault, M. (1977b) *The Archaeology of Knowledge*. London: Tavistock.

Foucault, M. (1979) *The History of Sexuality*. Vol. I: *An Introduction*. Trans. R. Hurley. London: Allen Lane.

Foucault, M. (1980) *Michel Foucault: Power/Knowledge*. Ed. C. Gordon. Hemel Hempstead: Harvester Wheatsheaf.

Foucault, M. (1985) *The History of Sexuality*. Vol. II: *The Use of Pleasure*. London: Penguin.

Foucault, M. (1986) *The History of Sexuality*. Vol. III: *The Case of the Self*. London: Penguin.

Foucault, M. (1991) 'Governmentality', Trans. R. Braidotti, *Ideology and Consciousness*, 6: 5–21.

Foulkes, F.K. (ed.) (1986) *Strategic Human Resource Management: A Guide for Effective Practice*. Englewood Cliffs, NJ: Prentice-Hall.

Fournier, V. and Grey, C. (1998) 'At the Critical Moment: Conditions and Prospects for Critical Management Studies', paper presented at the 16th annual International Labour Process Conference, Manchester, UK.

Fox, A. (1974) *Beyond Contract: Work, Power and Trust Relations*. London: Faber and Faber.

Frank, A. (1992) 'Only by Daylight: Habermas's Postmodern Modernism', *Theory, Culture & Society*, 9: 149–65.

Frankel, B. (1987) *The Post-Industrial Utopians*. Cambridge: Polity Press.

Fraser, N. (1989) *Unruly Practices: Power, Discourse and Gender in Contemporary Social Theory*. Cambridge: Polity Press.

Friedan, B. (1963) 'The Sexual Sell', in *The Feminine Mystique*. Harmondsworth: Penguin. pp. 181–204.

Frost, P.J., Moore, L.F., Louis, M.R., Lundberg, C.C. and Martin, J. (eds) (1985) *Oragnizational Culture*. Beverly Hills, CA: Sage.

Frug, G.E. (1984) 'The Ideology of Bureacracy in American Law', *Harvard Law Review*, 97 (6): 1276–388.

Gadamer, H.G. (1971) *Hegel's Dialectic: Five Hermeneutical Studies*. Trans. P. Christopher Smith. London: Yale University Press.

Gagliardi, P. (1986) 'The Creation and Change of Organizational Cultures: A Conceptual Framework, *Organization Studies*, 7 (2): 117–34.

Gagliardi, P. (ed.) (1990) *Symbols and Artifacts: Views of the Corporate Landscape*. Berlin: de Gruyter.

Gagnon, J. and Simon, W. (1973) *Sexual Conduct: The Social Sources of Human Sexuality*. Chicago, IL: Aldine.

Gaines, J. and Jermier, J. (1983) 'Emotional Exhaustion in a High Stress Organization', *Academy of Management Journal*, 26 (4): 567–86.

Garfinkel, H. (1967) *Studies in Ethnomethodology*. Englewood Cliffs, NJ: Prentice-Hall.

Geertz, C. (1973) *The Interpretation of Cultures*. New York: Basic Books.

Gellner, E. (1992) *Postmodernism, Reason and Religion*. London: Routledge.

Gephart Jr, R.P., Thatchenkery, T.J. and Boje, D.M. (1996) 'Conclusion: Reconstructing Organizations for Future Survival', in D.M. Boje, R.P. Gephart Jr and T.J. Thatchenkery (eds), *Postmodern Management and Organization Theory*. Thousand Oaks, CA: Sage. pp. 358–64.

Gergen, K. (1991) *The Saturated Self: Dilemmas of Identity in Contemporary Life*. New York: Basic Books.

Gergen, K. (1992) 'Organization Theory in the Postmodern Era', in M. Reed and M. Hughes (eds), *Rethinking Organization: New Directions in Organization Theory and Analysis*. London: Sage. pp. 207–26.

Gherardi, S. (1995) *Gender, Symbolism and Organizational Cultures*. London: Sage.

Giddens, A. (1990) *The Consequences of Modernity*. Cambridge: Polity Press.

Goffman, E. (1959) *The Presentation of Self in Everyday Life*. Harmondsworth: Penguin.

Golden, K. (1992) 'The Individual and Organizational Culture: Strategies for Action in Highly-ordered Contexts', *Journal of Management Studies*, 29 (1): 1–21.

Goleman, D. (1996) *Emotional Intelligence: Why It Can Matter More Than IQ*. London: Bloomsbury.

Goleman, D. (1999) *Working with Emotional Intelligence*. London: Bloomsbury.

Goodall, H. (1994) *Casing a Promised Land: The Autobiography of an Organizational Detective as Cultural Ethnographer*. Carbondale, IL.: Southern Illinois University Press.

Gordon, G. (1992) 'Predicting Corporate Performance from Organizational Culture', *Journal of Management Studies*, 29 (6): 783–98.

Gorz, A. (1982) *Farewell to the Working Class: An Essay on Post-Industrial Socialism*. London: Pluto Press.

Gramsci, A. (1971) 'Americanism and Fordism', in Q. Hoare and G. Nowell-Smith (eds), *Selections from the Prison Notebooks of Antonio Gramsci*. London: Lawrence and Wishart. pp. 277–318.

Greenberg, D. (1988) *The Construction of Homosexuality*. Chicago, IL: University of Chicago Press.

Greensdale, M. (1991) 'Managing Diversity. Lessons from the United States', *Personnel Management*, December: 28–33.

Grey, C. (1994) 'Career as a Project of the Self and Labour Process Discipline', *Sociology*, 28 (2): 479–97.

Gutek, B. (1985) *Sex and the Workplace*. San Francisco, CA: Jossey-Bass.

Gutek, B., Cohen, A. and Conrad, A. (1990) 'Predicting Social-Sexual Behavior at Work: A Contact Hypothesis', *Academy of Management Journal*, 33 (3): 565–77.

Habermas, J. (1972) *Knowledge and Human Interests*. Trans. J.J. Shapiro. London: Heinemann.

Habermas, J. (1984) *The Theory of Communicative Action*. Vol. I: *Reason and the Rationalization of Society*. Trans. T. McCarthy. Cambridge: Polity Press.

Habermas, J. (1986) *Theory and Practice*. Trans. J. Viertel. Cambridge: Polity Press (first published, 1973).

Habermas, J. (1987a) *The Philosophical Discourse of Modernity: Twelve Lectures*. Trans. F. Lawrence. Cambridge, MA: The MIT Press (first published, 1985).

Habermas, J. (1987b) *Towards a Rational Society: Student Protest, Science and Politics*. Trans. J.J. Shapiro. Cambridge: Polity Press (first published, 1969).

Habermas, J. (1989) *The New Conservatism: Cultural Criticism and the Historians' Debate*. Trans. S.W. Nicholsen. Cambridge: Polity Press.

Habermas, J. (1993) 'Modernity – An Incomplete Project', in T. Docherty (ed.), *Postmodernism: A Reader*. Hemel Hempstead: Harvester Wheatsheaf. pp. 98–109 (first published, 1981).

Hall, E.J. (1993) 'Waitering/Waitressing: Engendering the Work of Table Servers', *Gender and Society*, 17 (3): 329–46.

Hall, M. (1989) 'Private Experiences in the Public Domain: Lesbians in Organizations', in J. Hearn, D. Sheppard, P. Tancred-Sheriff and G. Burrell (eds), *The Sexuality of Organization*. London: Sage. pp. 125–38.

Hall, S. and Jacques, M. (1989) *New Times: The Changing Face of Politics in the 1990s*. London: Lawrence and Wishart.

Halmos, P. (1970) *The Personal Service Society*. London: Constable.

Hammer, M. and Champy, J. (1993) *Reengineering the Corporation*. London: Nicholas Brealey.

Hancock, P. (1997) 'Citizenship or Vassalage? Organizational Membership in the Age of Unreason', *Organization*, 4 (1): 93–111.

Hancock, P. (1999) 'Baudrillard and the Metaphysics of Motivation: A Reappraisal of Corporate Culturalism in the Light of the Work and Ideas of Jean Baudrillard', *Journal of Management Studies*, 36 (2): 155–75.

Hancock, P. and Tyler, M. (2000) 'The Look of Love', in J. Hassard, R. Holliday and H. Willmott (eds), *Body and Organization*. London: Sage. pp. 108–29.

Hardy, C. and Clegg, S. (1996) 'Some Dare Call It Power', in S.R. Clegg, C. Hardy and W.R. Nord (eds), *Handbook of Organization Studies*. London: Sage. pp. 622–41.

Harlow, E. and Hearn, J. (1995) 'Cultural Constructions: Contrasting Theories of Organizational Culture and Gender Construction', *Gender, Work and Organization*, 2 (4): 180–91.

Harris, J. (1996) *Getting Employees To Fall in Love with Your Company*. New York: Amacom.

Harvey, D. (1989) *The Condition of Postmodernity*. Oxford: Basil Blackwell.

Hassard, J. (1993a) 'Postmodernism and Organizational Analysis: An Overview', in J. Hassard and M. Parker (eds), *Postmodernism and Organization*. London: Sage. pp. 1–23.

Hassard, J. (1993b) *Sociology and Organization Theory: Positivism, Paradigms and Postmodernity*. Cambridge: Cambridge University Press.

Hassard, J. (1996) 'Exploring the Terrain of Modernism and Postmodernism in Organization Theory', in D.M. Boje, R.P. Gephart Jr and T.J. Thatchenkery (eds), *Postmodern Management and Organization Theory*. Thousand Oaks, CA: Sage. pp. 45–59.

Hassard, J. and Parker, M. (eds) (1993) *Postmodernism and Organization*. London: Sage.

Hatch, M.J. (1997) *Organization Theory: Modern, Symbolic and Postmodern Perspectives*. London: Oxford University Press.

Hatcher, C. (1999) 'Practices of the Heart: Constituting the Identities of Managers', paper presented at the First International Critical Management Studies Conference, Manchester, UK.

Hawkes, G. (1996) *A Sociology of Sex and Sexuality*. Milton Keynes: Open University Press.

Hearn, J. (1992) *Men in the Public Eye: The Construction and Deconstruction of Public Men and Public Patriarchies*. London: Routledge.

Hearn, J. (1993) 'Emotive Subjects: Organizational Men, Organizational Masculinities and the (De)construction of "Emotions"', in S. Fineman (ed.), *Emotion in Organizations*. London: Sage. pp. 142–66.

Hearn, J. and Parkin, W. (1987) *'Sex' at 'Work': The Power and Paradox of Organisation Sexuality*. Hemel Hempstead: Prentice-Hall.

Hearn, J., Sheppard, D., Tancred-Sheriff, P. and Burrell, G. (eds) (1989) *The Sexuality of Organization*. London: Sage.

Hebdige, D. (1979) *Subculture: The Meaning of Style*. London: Methuen.

Heckscher, C. (1994) 'Defining the Post-Bureaucratic Type', in C. Heckscher and A. Donnallon (eds), *The Post-Bureaucratic Organization: New Perspectives of Organizational Change*. Thousand Oaks, CA: Sage. pp. 14–62.

Hegel, G.W.F. (1967) *Philosophy of Right*. Trans. H.B. Nisbet. Oxford: Oxford University Press (first published, 1821).

Hegel, G.W.F. (1977) *Phenomenology of Spirit*. Trans. A.V. Miller. Oxford: Clarendon Press (first published, 1807).

Herzberg, F. (1974) *Work and the Nature of Man*. London: Crosby Lockwood Staples.

Heydebrand, W.V. (1989) 'New Organizational Forms', *Work and Occupations*, 16 (3): 323–57.

Hite, S. (2000) *Sex & Business*. London: Financial Times and Prentice-Hall.

Hochschild, A.R. (1979) 'Emotion Work, Feeling Rules and Social Structure', *American Journal of Sociology*, 85 (3): 551–75.

Hochschild, A.R. (1983) *The Managed Heart: Commercialization of Human Feeling*. Berkeley, CA: University of California Press.

Hochschild, A.R. (1993) 'Preface', in S. Fineman (ed.), *Emotion in Organizations*. London: Sage. pp. ix–xiii.

Hochschild, A.R. (1997) *The Time Bind: When Work Becomes Home and Home Becomes Work*. New York: Metropolitan Books.

Hochschild, A.R. (1998) 'The Sociology of Emotion as a Way of Seeing', in G. Bendelow and S. Williams (eds), *Emotions in Social Life: Critical Themes and Contemporary Issues*. London: Routledge. pp. 3–15.

Holliday, R. (1998) 'Philadelphia: AIDS, Organization, Representation', in J. Hassard and R. Holliday (eds), *Organization Representation: Work and Organizations in Popular Culture*. London: Sage. pp. 100–16.

Hollinger, R. (1994) *Postmodernism and the Social Sciences: A Thematic Approach*. Thousand Oaks, CA: Sage.

Hollway, W. (1991) *Work Psychology and Organizational Behaviour*. London: Sage.

Horkheimer, M. (1989) 'The State of Contemporary Social Philosophy and the Tasks of an Institute for Social Research', trans. P. Wagner, in S. Bronner and D. Kellner (eds), *Critical Theory and Society: A Reader*. London: Routledge. pp. 25–36.

Horkheimer, M. (1994) *Critique of Instrumental Reason: Lectures and Essays since the End of World War II*. Trans. M.J. O'Connell et al. New York: Continuum (first edition, 1974).

Hosking, D. and Fineman, S. (1990) 'Organizing Processes', *Journal of Management Studies*, 27 (6): 583–604.

Hughes, B. (1996) 'Nietzsche: Philosophizing with the Body', *Body & Society*, 2 (1): 31–44.

Humphrey, J. (1999) 'Organizing Sexualities, Organized Inequalities: Lesbians and Gay Men in Public Service Occupations', *Gender, Work and Organization*, 6 (3): 134–51.

Hutchins, D. (1988) *Just in Time*. Aldershot: Gower.

Huws, U., Werner, B.K. and Robinson, S. (1990) *Telework: Towards the Elusive Office*. Chichester: John Wiley.

Irigaray, L. (1985) *This Sex Which is Not One*. Ithaca, NY: Cornell University Press.

Irigaray, L. (1990) *Je, Tu, Nous: Toward a Culture of Difference*. Trans. A. Martin. London: Routledge.

Isaack, T. (1978) 'Intuition: An Ignored Dimension of Management', *Academy of Management Review*, 3 (4): 917–21.

Jackson, M. (1987) '"Facts of Life" or the Eroticization of Women's Oppression? Sexology and the Social Construction of Heterosexuality', in P. Caplan (ed.), *The Cultural Construction of Sexuality*. London: Tavistock. pp. 52–81.

Jackson, N. and Carter, P. (1985) 'The Ergonomics of Desire', *Personnel Review*, 14 (3): 20–8.

Jackson, N. and Carter, P. (1986) 'Desire Versus Interest', *Dragon*, 1 (3): 48–60.

Jackson, N. and Carter, P. (1998) 'Labour as Dressage', in A. McKinlay and K. Starkey (eds), *Foucault, Management and Organization Theory*. London: Sage. pp. 49–64.

Jackson, S. (1993) 'Even Sociologists Fall in Love: An Exploration in the Sociology of Emotions', *Sociology*, 27: 201–20.

Jackson, S. and Scott, S. (1997) 'Gut Reactions to Matters of the Heart: Reflections on Rationality, Irrationality and Sexuality', *Sociological Review*, 45 (4): 551–75.

Jaggar, A. (1989) 'Love and Knowledge: Emotion in Feminist Epistemology', in A. Jaggar and S. Bordo (eds), *Gender/Body/Knowledge: Feminist Reconstructions of Being and Knowing*. New Brunswick, NJ: Rutgers University Press. pp. 145–71.

Jameson, F. (1991) *Postmodernism or, the Cultural Logic of Late Capitalism*. London: Verso.

Jaques, E. (1951) *The Changing Culture of a Factory*. London: Tavistock.

Jeffcutt, P. (1993) 'From Interpretation to Representation', in J. Hassard and M. Parker (eds), *Postmodernism and Organizations*. London: Sage. pp. 25–48.

Jeffcutt, P. (1994) 'From Interpretation to Representation in Organization Analysis: Postmodernism, Ethnography and Organizational Symbolism', *Organization Studies*, 15 (2): 241–74.

Jencks, C. (1996) 'The Death of Modern Architecture', in L. Cahoone (ed.), *From Modernism to Postmodernism: An Anthology*. Oxford: Blackwell. pp. 469–80.

Jessop, B. (1994) 'Post-Fordism and the State', in A. Amin (ed.), *Post-Fordism: A Reader*. Oxford: Blackwell. pp. 251–79.

Jones, M.O. (1996) *Studying Organizational Symbolism*. Thousand Oaks, CA: Sage.

Kandola, R. and Fullerton, J. (1995) *Managing the Mosaic: Diversity in Action*. London: Institute of Personnel and Development.

Kant, I. (1991) *An Answer to the Question: 'What is Enlightenment?'*. Cambridge: Cambridge University Press (first published, 1784).

Kanter, R.M. (1977) *Men and Women of the Corporation*. New York: Basic Books.

Kanter, R.M. (1989) *When Giants Learn to Dance*. New York: Simon and Schuster.

Keenoy, T. and Anthony, P. (1992) 'HRM: Metaphor, Meaning and Morality', in P. Turnbull and P. Blyton (eds), *Reassessing Human Resource Management*. London: Sage. pp. 233–55.

Kellner, D. (1995) *Media Culture*. London: Routledge.

Kenney, M. and Florida, R. (1989) 'Japan's Role in a Post-Fordist Age', *Futures*, April: 136–51.

Kern, H. and Schumann, M. (1987) 'Limits of the Division of Labour: New Production and Employment Concepts in West German Industry', *Economic and Industrial Democracy*, 5: 151–71.

Kern, H. and Schumann, M. (1989) 'New Concepts of Production in West German Plants', in P.J. Katzenstein (ed.), *Industry and Politics in West Germany: Toward the Third Republic*. Ithaca, NY: Cornell University Press.

Kilduff, M. (1993) 'Deconstructing Organizations', *The Academy of Management Review*, 18 (1): 13–31.

Kilduff, M. and Mehra, A. (1997) 'Postmodernism and Organizational Research', *Academy of Management Review*, 22 (2): 453–81.

Kilmann, R.H., Saxton, M.J., Serpa, R. and Associates (eds) (1985) *Gaining Control of the Corporate Culture*. San Francisco, CA: Jossey-Bass.

Kinsey, A., Pomeroy, W. and Martin, C. (1948) *Sexual Behaviour in the Human Male*. London: W.B. Saunders.

Kinsey, A., Pomeroy, W. and Martin, C. (1953) *Sexual Behaviour in the Human Female*. London: W.B. Saunders.

Knights, D. (1990) 'Subjectivity, Power and the Labour Process', in D. Knights and H. Willmott (eds), *Labour Process Theory*. Basingstoke: Macmillan. pp. 297–356.

Knights, D. (1992) 'Changing Spaces: The Disruptive Power of Epistemological Location for the Management and Organizational Sciences', *Academy of Management Review*, 17 (3): 513–36.

Knights, D. (1995) 'Hanging Out the Dirty Washing: Labour Process Theory in the Age of Deconstruction', paper presented to the 13th annual International Labour Process Conference, Blackpool, UK.

Knights, D. (1997) 'Organization Theory in the Age of Deconstruction: Dualism, Gender and Postmodernism Revisited', *Organization Studies*, 18 (1): 1–19.

Knights, D. and McCabe, D. (1994) 'Total Quality Management and Organizational "Grey" Matter', paper presented at the Work, Employment and Society conference, Canterbury, UK.

Knights, D. and Morgan, G. (1991) 'Corporate Strategy, Organizations and Subjectivity: A Critique', *Organization Studies*, 12 (2): 251–73.

Knights, D. and Vurdubakis, T. (1994) 'Foucault, Power, Resistance and All That', in J. Jermier, D. Knights and W. Nord (eds), *Resistance and Power in Organisations*. London: Routledge. pp. 167–98.

Knights, D. and Willmott, H. (eds) (1986) *Managing the Labour Process*. Aldershot: Gower.

Knights, D. and Willmott, H. (1989) 'Power and Subjectivity at Work: From Degradation to Subjugation in Social Relations', *Sociology*, 23 (4): 535–58

Knights, D. and Willmott, H. (eds) (1990) *Labour Process Theory*. Basingstoke: Macmillan.

Kristeva, J. (1980) *Desire in Language*. Oxford: Blackwell.

Kroll, L. (1987) *An Architecture of Complexity*. Cambridge, MA: The MIT Press.

Kuhn, T. (1962) *The Structure of Scientific Revolutions*. Chicago, IL: University of Chicago Press.

Kumar, K. (1978) *Prophecy and Progress: The Sociology of Industrial and Post-industrial Society*. Harmondsworth: Penguin.

Kumar, K. (1995) *From Post-Industrial to Post-Modern Society: New Theories of the Contemporary World*. Oxford: Blackwell.

Kunda, G. (1991) *Engineering Culture: Control and Commitment in a High-Tech Corporation*. Philadelphia, PA: Temple University Press.

Laclau, E. (1990) *New Reflections on the Revolution of Our Time*. London: Verso.

Laclau, E. and Mouffe, C. (1985) *Hegemony and Socialist Strategy: Towards a Radical Democratic Politics*. London: Verso.

Laing, R.D. (1970) *The Divided Self*. New York: Pantheon.

Lash, S. (1988) 'Postmodernism as a Regime of Signification', *Theory, Culture & Society*, 5 (2–3): 311–36.

Lash, S. (1990) *Sociology of Postmodernism*. London: Routledge.

Lash, S. and Urry, J. (1987) *The End of Organized Capitalism*. Cambridge: Polity Press.

Latour, B. (1987) *Science in Action*. Milton Keynes: Open University Press.

Latour, B. (1993) *We Have Never Been Modern*. New York: Harvester Wheatsheaf.

Lawrence, D.H. (1960) *Lady Chatterley's Lover*. Harmondsworth: Penguin (first published, 1928).

Legge, K. (1995) *Human Resource Management: Rhetorics and Realities*. Basingstoke: Macmillan Business.

Leidner, R. (1993) *Fast Food, Fast Talk: Service Work and the Routinization of Everyday Life*. Berkeley, CA: University of California Press.

Leidner, R. (1999) 'Emotional Labour in Service Work', *Annals of the American Academy of Political and Social Sciences*, 561: 81–95.

Liff, S. and Wajcman, J. (1996) 'Sameness and Difference Revisited: Which Way Forward for Equal Opportunity Initiatives?', *Journal of Management Studies*, 33 (1): 79–94.

Liljander, V. and Strandvik, T. (1997) 'Emotions in Service Satisfaction', *International Journal of Service Industry Management*, 8 (2): 148–69.

Linstead, S. (1993) 'Deconstruction in the Study of Organizations', in J. Hassard and M. Parker (eds), *Postmodernism and Organizations*. London: Sage. pp. 49–70.

Linstead, S. and Grafton-Small, R. (1992) 'On Reading Organizational Culture', *Organization Studies*, 31 (3): 331–56.

Lipset, S.M. and Bendix, R. (1959) *Social Mobility in Industrial Society*. Berkeley, CA: University of California Press.

Littler, C. (1982) *The Development of the Labour Process in Capitalist Societies*. London: Heinemann.

Lofstrom, J. (1997) 'The Birth of the Queen/the Modern Homosexual: Historical Explanations Revisited', *The Sociological Review*, 45 (1): 24–41.

Lont, C.M. (1988) 'Redwood Records: Principles and Profit in Women's Music', in B. Bate and A. Taylor (eds), *Women Communicating: Studies of Women's Talk*. Norwood, NJ: Ablex. pp. 233–50.

Lyon, D. (1993) 'An Electronic Panopticon? A Sociological Critique of Surveillance Theory', *Sociological Review*, 41 (4): 653–78.

Lyotard, J.-F. (1984) *The Postmodern Condition: A Report on Knowledge*. Manchester: Manchester University Press.

Lyotard, J,-F. (1988) *The Differend: Phrases in Dispute*. Manchester: Manchester University Press.

Lyotard, J.-F. and Thebaud, J.-L. (1986) *Just Gaming*. Manchester: Manchester University Press.

Maddock, S. (1999) *Challenging Women: Gender, Culture and Organization*. London: Sage.

Mandel, E. (1978) *Late Capitalism*. London: Verso.

Manning, P. (1992) *Organizational Communication*. New York: de Gruyter.

March, J. and Simon, H. (1958) *Organizations*. New York: John Wiley.

Marcuse, H. (1972) *Eros and Civilization: A Philsophical Inquiry into Freud*. London: Abacus (first published, 1955).

Marcuse, H. (1983) *Reason and Revolution: Hegel and the Rise of Social Theory*. Atlantic Highlands, NJ: Humanities Press (first published, 1941).

Marcuse, H. (1986) *One Dimensional Man: Studies in the Ideology of Advanced Industrial Society*. London: Ark Paperbacks (first published, 1964).

Marshall, J. (1989) 'Re-visioning Career Concepts: A Feminist Invitation', in M.B. Arthur, D.T. Hall and B.S. Lawrence (eds), *Handbook of Career Theory*. Cambridge: Cambridge University Press. pp. 275–91.

Martin, J. (1990) 'Deconstructing Organizational Taboos: The Suppression of Gender Conflict in Organizations', *Organization Science*, 1 (4): 339–59.

Martin, J. (1992) *Cultures in Organizations: Three Perspectives*. New York: Oxford University Press.

Martin, J., Knopoff, K. and Beckman, C. (1998) 'An Alternative to Bureaucratic Impersonality and Emotional Labour: Bounded Emotionality at The Body Shop', *Administrative Science Quarterly*, 43 (2): 429–69.

Marx, K. (1970) *Capital: Volume One*. London: Lawrence and Wishart (first published, 1864).

Marx, K. and Engels, F. (1986) *Manifesto of the Communist Party*. Moscow: Progress Publishers (first published, 1848).

Maslow, A.H. (1943) 'A Theory of Human Motivation', *Psychological Review*, 50: 372–96.

Masters, W. and Johnson, V. (1966) *Human Sexual Response*. Boston, MA: Little, Brown.

Mayer, J.P. (1956) *Max Weber and German Politics*. London: Faber and Faber.

Mayo, E. (1933) *The Human Problems of Industrial Civilization*. New York: Macmillan.

McKeganey, N. and Barnard, M. (1996) *Sex Work on the Streets: Prostitutes and their Clients*. Buckingham: Open University Press.

McKinlay, A. and Starkey, K. (eds) (1998) *Foucault, Management and Organization Theory*. London: Sage.

McRobbie, A. (1994) *Postmodernism and Popular Culture*. London: Routledge.

Meek, V.L. (1989) 'Organizational Culture: Origins and Weaknesses', *Organization Studies*, 9 (4): 453–73.

Merton, R. (1949) *Social Theory and Social Structure*. New York: Collier Macmillan.

Meštrović, S. (1997) *Postemotional Society*. London: Sage.

Meyer, M. (1994) *The Politics and Poetics of Camp*. London: Routledge.

Miller, E.J. and Rice, A.K. (1967) *Systems of Organizations*. London: Tavistock.

Mills, A.J. (1989) 'Gender, Sexuality and Organization Theory', in J. Hearn, D. Sheppard, P. Tancred-Sheriff and G. Burrell (eds), *The Sexuality of Organization*. London: Sage. pp. 29–44.

Mills, A.J. (1994) 'Duelling Discourses: Desexualization versus Eroticism in the Corporate Framing of Female Sexuality, Images of British Airways 1945–1960', paper presented to the annual conference of the British Sociological Association, Preston, UK.

Moore, S. (1988) 'Getting a Bit of the Other – the Pimps of Postmodernism', in J. Chapman and R. Rutherford (eds), *Male Order: Unwrapping Masculinity*. London: Lawrence and Wishart. pp. 165–92.

Morgan, G. (1993) *Imaginization: The Art of Creative Management*. Newbury Park, CA: Sage.

Morgan, G. (1997) *Images of Organization* (2nd edn). Thousand Oaks, CA: Sage (first edition, 1986).

Morris, J. and Feldman, D. (1996) 'The Dimension, Antecedents, and Consequences of Emotional Labour', *Academy of Management Review*, 21 (4): 986–1010.

Morrow, R. and Brown, D.D. (1994) *Critical Theory and Methodology*. Thousand Oaks, CA: Sage.

Mort, F. (1987) *Dangerous Sexualities: Medico-Moral Politics in England since 1830*. London. Routledge and Kegan Paul.

Mulgan, G. (1989) 'The Power of the Weak', in S. Hall and M. Jacques (eds), *New Times: The Changing Face of Politics in the 1990s*. London: Lawrence and Wishart. pp. 347–63.

Mumby, D. and Putnam, L. (1992) 'The Politics of Emotion: A Feminist Reading of Bounded Rationality', *The Academy of Management Review*, 17 (3): 465–86.

Murray, R. (1989a) 'Fordism and Post-Fordism', in S. Hall and M. Jacques (eds), *New Times: The Changing Face of Politics in the 1990s*. London: Lawrence and Wishart. pp. 38–53.

Murray, R. (1989b) 'Benetton Britain: The Economic Order', in S. Hall and M. Jacques (eds), *New Times: The Changing Face of Politics in the 1990s*. London: Lawrence and Wishart. pp. 54–64.

Naisbitt, J. (1984) *Megatrends: Ten New Directions Transforming Our Lives*. New York: Warner Brothers.

Newton, T. (1996) 'Postmodernism and Action', *Organization*, 3 (1): 7–29.

Newton, T. (1998) 'Theorizing Subjectivity in Organizations: The Failure of Foucauldian Studies?', *Organization Studies*, 19 (3): 415–47.

Newton, T. (1999) 'Power, Subjectivity and British Industrial and Organizational Sociology: The Relevance of the Work of Norbert Elias', *Sociology*, 33 (2): 411–40.

Nietzsche, F. (1989) *On the Genealogy of Morals*. Trans. W. Kaufmann and R.J. Hollingdale. New York: Vintage Books (first published, 1887).

Nietzsche, F. (1990a) *Beyond Good and Evil*. Trans. R.J. Hollingdale. London: Penguin (first published, 1886).

Nietzsche, F. (1990b) *The Anti-Christ*. Tr. R.J. Hollingdale. London: Penguin (first published, 1895).

Nightingale Multimedia (1999) *The Best 100 Companies to Work for in the UK: Millennium Edition* (2nd edn). London: Hodder and Stoughton (first edition, 1997).

Noon, M. and Blyton, P. (1997) 'Emotion Work', in *The Realities of Work*. London: Macmillan Business. pp. 121–39.

Nottingham, C. (1998) 'An Intellectual Titan of Our Modern Renaissance: Havelock Ellis and the Progressive Tradition', *Amsterdams Sociologisch Tijdschrift*, 25 (3): 407–28.

O'Connell-Davidson, J. (1995) 'The Anatomy of "Free Choice" Prostitution', *Gender, Work and Organization*, 2 (1): 1–10.

Offe, C. (1985) *Disorganized Capitalism: Contemporary Transformations of Work and Politics*. Cambridge: Polity Press.

Ostell, A. (1996) 'Managing Dysfuntional Emotions in Organizations', *Journal of Management Studies*, 33 (4): 22–8.

Ouchi, W.G. (1981) *Theory Z: How American Business Can Meet the Japanese Challenge*. New York: Addison-Wesley.

Parker, M. (1992) 'Post-Modern Organizations or Postmodern Organization Theory?', *Organization Studies*, 13 (1): 1–17.

Parker, M. (1993) 'Life after Jean-François', in J. Hassard and M. Parker (eds), *Postmodernism and Organizations*. London: Sage. pp. 204–12.

Parker, M. (1995) 'Critique in the Name of What? Postmodernism and Critical Approaches to Organization', *Organization Studies*, 16 (4): 553–64.

Parker, M. (1998) 'Organisation, Community, Utopia', *Studies in Cultures, Organizations and Societies*, (4): 71–91.

Parker, M. (1999) 'Fucking Management: Queering Theory', paper presented at the annual conference of the Standing Conference on Organizational Symbolism (SCOS), Edinburgh, UK.

Parker, M. (2000a) *Organizational Culture and Identity*. London: Sage.

Parker, M. (2000b) 'The Sociology of Organizations and the Organization of Sociology: Some Reflections on the Making of a Division of Labour', *The Sociological Review*, 48 (1): 124–146.

Parsons, T. (1966) *Societies: Evolutionary and Comparative Perspectives*. New York: Englewood Cliffs, NJ: Prentice-Hall.

Parsons, T. (1991) *The Social System* (2nd edn). London: Routledge (first edition, 1951).

Pascale, R.T. and Athos, A.G. (1981) *The Art of Japanese Management: Applications for American Executives*. Harmondsworth: Penguin.

Pateman, C. (1988) *The Sexual Contract*. Cambridge: Polity Press.

Payne, R. (1991) 'Taking Stock of Corporate Culture', *Personnel Management*, July: 26–9.

Peppard, J. and Rowland, P. (1995) *The Essence of Business Process Re-engineering*. London: Prentice-Hall.

Peters, T. (1989) *Thriving on Chaos*. London: Pan Books.

Peters, T. and Austin, N. (1985) *A Passion for Excellence*. New York: Random House.

Peters, T. and Waterman, R. (1982) *In Search of Excellence*. New York: Harper and Row.

Pettigrew, A. (1979) 'On Studying Organizational Cultures', *Administrative Science Quarterly*, 24 (4): 570–81.

Pheysey, D.C. (1993) *Organizational Cultures: Types and Transformations*. London: Routledge.

Phillips, N. (1995) 'Telling Organizational Tales: On the Role of Narrative Fiction in the Study of Organizations', *Organization Studies*, 16 (4): 625–49.

Piore, M. and Sabel, C. (1984) *The Second Industrial Divide: Possibilities for Prosperity*. New York: Basic Books.

Plummer, K. (1995) *Telling Sexual Stories: Power, Change and Social Worlds*. London: Routledge.

Plummer, K. (1996) 'Foreword: Symbols of Change', in W. Simon (ed.), *Postmodern Sexualities*. London: Routledge. pp. ix–xvi.

Pollert, A. (1988a) '"The Flexible Firm": Fixation or Fact?', *Work Employment and Society*, 2 (3): 281–316.

Pollert, A. (1988b) 'Dismantling Flexibility', *Capital and Class*, 34: 42–75.

Pondy, L.R., Frost, P.J., Morgan, G. and Dandridge, T.C. (eds) (1983) *Organizational Symbolism*. Greenwich, CT: JAI Press.

Poole, M. and Mansfield, R. (1992) 'Managers' Attitudes to Human Resource Management: Rhetoric and Reality', in P. Blyton and P. Turnbull (eds), *Reassessing Human Resource Management*. London: Sage. pp. 200–14.

Price, L. and Arnould, E. (1995) 'Consumers' Emotional Responses to Service Encounters: The Influence of the Service Provider', *International Journal of Service Industry Management*, 6 (3): 34–63.

Pringle, R. (1989a) *Secretaries Talk: Sexuality, Power and Work*. London: Verso.

Pringle, R. (1989b) 'Bureaucracy, Rationality and Sexuality: The Case of Secretaries', in J. Hearn, D. Sheppard, P. Tancred-Sheriff and G. Burrell (eds), *The Sexuality of Organization*. London: Sage. pp. 158–77.

Pugh, D. and Hickson, D. (eds) (1976) *Organizational Structure in its Context: The Aston Programme I*. Farnborough, Hants: Saxon House.

Putnam, L. and Mumby, D. (1993) 'Organizations, Emotion and the Myth of Rationality', in S. Fineman (ed.), *Emotion in Organizations*. London: Sage. pp. 36–57.

Rafaeli, A. and Sutton, R. (1987) 'Expression of Emotion as Part of the Work Role', *Academy of Management Review*, 12 (1): 23–37.

Ray, C.A. (1986) 'Corporate Culture: The Last Frontier of Control?', *Journal of Management Studies*, 23 (3): 287–97.

Reed, M. (1992) *The Sociology of Organizations: Themes, Perspectives and Prospects*. Hemel Hempstead: Harvester Wheatsheaf.

Reed, M. (1993) 'Organizations and Modernity: Continuity and Discontinuity in Organization Theory', in J. Hassard and M. Parker (eds), *Postmodernism and Organizations*. London: Sage. pp. 163–82.

Reed, M. (1996a) 'Organizational Theorizing: A Historically Contested Terrain', in S.R. Clegg, C. Hardy and W.R. Nord (eds), *Handbook of Organization Studies*. London: Sage. pp. 31–56.

Reed, M. (1996b) 'Rediscovering Hegel: The "New Historicism" in Organization and Management Studies', *Journal of Management Studies*, 33 (2): 139–58.

Reed, M. (1997) 'In Praise of Duality and Dualism: Rethinking Agency and Structure in Organizational Analysis', *Organization Studies*, 18 (1): 21–42.

Reich, W. (1962) *The Function of the Orgasm*. London: Panther.

Revenaugh, D.L. (1994) 'Implementing Major Organizational Change: Can We Really Do It?', *The TQM Magazine*, 6 (6): 38–48.

Ritzer, G. (1993) *The McDonaldization of Society: An Investigation into the Changing Character of Contemporary Social Life*. Newbury Park, CA: Pine Forge Press.

Ritzer, G. (1996) *The McDonaldization of Society: An Investigation into the Changing Character of Contemporary Social Life* (revised edn). Thousand Oaks, CA: Pine Forge Press (first edition, 1993).

Ritzer, G. (1997) *The McDonaldization Thesis*. London: Sage.

Ritzer, G. (1999) *Enchanting a Disenchanted World*. Newbury Park, CA: Pine Forge Press.

Robinson, P. (1976) *The Modernization of Sex*. New York: Harper and Row.

Rodgers, D. (1978) *The Work Ethic in Industrial America: 1850–1920*. Chicago, IL: University of Chicago Press.

Roethlisberger, F.J. and Dickson, W.J. (1939) *Management and the Worker*. Cambridge, MA: Harvard University Press.

Rorty, R. (1989) *Contingency, Irony and Solidarity*. Cambridge: Cambridge University Press.

Rose, G. (1981) *Hegel Contra Sociology*. London: Athlone Press.

Rose, N. (1990) *Governing the Soul: The Shaping of the Private Self*. London: Routledge.

Rosenau, P.M. (1992) *Post-Modernism and the Social Sciences: Insights, Inroads, and Intrusions*. Princeton, NJ: Princeton University Press.

Rustin, M. (1989) 'The Politics of Post-Fordism: or, the Trouble with "New Times"', *New Left Review*, 175: 54–77.

Rustin, M. (1994) 'Flexibility in Higher Education', in R. Burrows and B. Loader (eds), *Towards a Post-Fordist Welfare State*. London: Routledge. pp. 177–202.

Sabel, C. (1982) *Work and Politics: The Division of Labour in Industry*. Cambridge: Cambridge University Press.

Sabel, C.F. (1994) 'Flexible Specialisation and the Re-emergence of Regional Economies', in A. Amin (ed.), *Post-Fordism: A Reader*. Oxford: Blackwell. pp. 101–56.

Saffold, G. (1988) 'Culture Traits, Strength and Organizational Performance: Moving Beyond "Strong" Culture', *Academy of Management Review*, 13 (4): 546–58.

Sampson, A. (1996) *Company Man: The Rise and Fall of Corporate Life*. London: HarperCollins.

Sardar, Z. (1998) 'The Dangerous Illusion', *The Herald*, Saturday 21 February.

Sartre, J.-P. (1990) *In Camera and Other Plays*. Harmondsworth: Penguin (first edition, 1944).

Sarup, M. (1993) *An Introductory Guide to Post-Structuralism and Postmodernism* (2nd edn). London: Harvester Wheatsheaf (first edition, 1988).

Savage, M. (1998) 'Discipline, Surveillance and the "Career": Employment on the Great Western Railway', in A. McKinlay and K.Starkey (eds), *Foucault, Management and Organization Theory*. London: Sage. pp. 65–92.

Sayer, D. (1991) *Capitalism and Modernity*. London: Routledge.

Scambler, G. and Scambler, A. (1997) *Rethinking Prostitution: Purchasing Sex in the 1990s*. London: Routledge.

Schein, E. (1985) *Organizational Culture and Leadership*. San Francisco, CA: Jossey-Bass.

Schneider, B. (1987) 'The People Make the Place', *Personnel Psychology*, 40: 437–53.

Schumann, M. (1987) 'The Future of Work, Training and Innovation', in W. Wobbe (ed.), *Flexible Manufacturing in Europe: State of the Approaches and Diffusion Patterns* (FAST Occasional Papers No. 155). Brussels: European Commission.

Schutz, A. (1967) *The Phenomenology of the Social World*. Evanston, IL: Northwestern University Press.

Seidman, S. (1998) *Contested Knowledge: Social Theory in the Postmodern Era*. Oxford: Blackwell.

Sewell, G. and Wilkinson, B. (1992a) '"Someone To Watch Over Me": Surveillance, Discipline and the Just-In-Time Labour Process', *Sociology*, 26 (2): 271–89.

Sewell, G. and Wilkinson, B. (1992b) 'Empowerment or Emasculation? Shopfloor Surveillance in a Total Quality Organization', in P. Blyton and P. Turnbull (eds), *Reassessing Human Resource Management*. London: Sage. pp. 97–115.

Sheppard, D. (1989) 'Organizations, Power and Sexuality: The Image and Self-Image of Women Managers', in J. Hearn, D. Sheppard, P. Tancred-Sheriff and G. Burrell (eds), *The Sexuality of Organization*. London: Sage. pp. 139–57.

Sheridan, J. (1992) 'Organizational Culture and Employee Retention', *Academy of Management Journal*, 35 (5): 1036–56.

Silverman, D. (1970) *The Theory of Organizations*. London: Heinemann.

Silverman, D. and Jones, J. (1973) 'Getting-in', in J. Child (ed.), *Man and Organization*. London: Allen and Unwin.

Silverman, D. and Jones, J. (1976) *Organizational Work*. London: Collier-Macmillan.

Simon, H. (1976) *Administrative Behaviour*. New York: The Free Press.

Simon, H. (1989) 'Making Management Decisions: The Role of Intuition and Emotion', in W. Agor (ed.), *Intuition in Organizations*. Newbury Park, CA: Sage. pp. 23–39.

Simon, W. (1996) *Postmodern Sexualities*. London: Routledge.

Simpson, L. (1999) *Working from the Heart: A Practical Guide to Loving What You Do for a Living*. London: Vermillion.

Sims, D., Fineman, S. and Gabriel, Y. (1993) *Organizing and Organizations: An Introduction*. London: Sage.

Smart, B. (1992) *Modern Conditions, Postmodern Controversies*. London: Routledge.

Smircich, L. (1983) 'Concepts of Culture and Organizational Analysis', *Administrative Science Quarterly*, 28: 339–58.

Snyder, M. (1987) *Public Appearances, Private Realities*. New York: Freeman.

Sonnenstuhl, W. (1986) *Inside an Emotional Health Program: A Field Study of Workplace Assistance for Troubled Employees*. Ithaca, NY: Cornell University Press.

Sontag, S. (1966) *Against Interpretation*. New York: Farrar, Straus & Giroux.

Sotirin, P. and Tyrell, S.J. (1998) 'Wondering about Critical Management Studies', *Management Communication Quarterly*, 12 (2): 303–36.

Stablein, R. and Nord, W. (1985) 'Practical and Emancipatory Interests in Organizational Symbolism', *Journal of Management*, 11 (2): 13–28.

Starkey, K. (1998) 'Durkheim and the Limits of Corporate Culture: Whose Culture? Which Durkheim?', *Journal of Management Studies*, 35 (2): 125–36.

Steffy, B. and Grimes, A. (1986) 'A Critical Theory of Organizational Science', *Academy of Management Review*, 11 (2): 322–36.

Stein, A. and Plummer, K. (1996) '"I Can't Even Think Straight": "Queer" Theory and the Missing Sexual Revolution in Sociology', in S. Seidman (ed.), *Queer Theory/Sociology*. Oxford: Blackwell.

Steingard, D.S. and Fitzgibbons, D.E. (1993) 'A Postmodern Deconstruction of Total Quality Management (TQM)', *Journal of Organizational Change Management*, 6 (5): 27–42.

Stonier, T. (1983) *The Wealth of Information. A Profile of the Post-Industrial Economy*. London: Thames Methuen.

Storey, J. (1983) *Managerial Prerogative and the Question of Control*. London: Routledge.

Strati, A. (1999) *Organization and Aesthetics*. London: Sage.

Sutton, R.I. (1991) 'Maintaining Norms about Expressed Emotions: The Case of Bill Collectors', *Administrative Science Quarterly*, 36: 245–68.

Tancred-Sheriff, P. (1989) 'Gender, Sexuality and the Labour Process', in J. Hearn, D. Sheppard, P. Tancred-Sheriff and G. Burrell (eds), *The Sexuality of Organization*. London: Sage. pp. 45–55.

Taska, L. (1992) 'Scientific Management: Technique or Cultural Ideology?', *Journal of Industrial Relations*, 34 (3): 365–97.

Taylor, F.W. (1911) *Principles of Scientific Management*. New York: Harper and Row.

Thompson, P. (1989) *The Nature of Work* (2nd edn). London: Macmillan (first edition, 1983).

Thompson, P. (1990) 'Crawling from the Wreckage: The Labour Process and the Politics of Production', in D. Knights and H. Willmott (eds), *Labour Process Theory*. Basingstoke: Macmillan. pp. 95–124.

Thompson, P. (1993) 'Postmodernism: Fatal Distraction', in J. Hassard and M. Parker (eds), *Postmodernism and Organizations*. London: Sage. pp. 181–203.

Thompson, P. and Ackroyd, S. (1995) 'All Quiet on the Workplace Front? A Critique of Recent Trends in British Industrial Sociology', *Sociology*, 29 (4): 615–63.

Thompson, P. and Findlay, P. (1996) 'The Mystery of the Missing Subject', paper presented to the 14th annual International Labour Process Conference, Aston, UK.

Thompson, P. and Warhurst, C. (1998) *Workplaces of the Future*. Basingstoke: Macmillan Business.

Thompson, V.A. (1976) *Bureaucracy and the Modern World*. Morristown, NJ: General Learning Press.

Thomson, K. (1997) *Emotional Capital: Capturing Hearts and Minds to Create Lasting Business Success*. London: Carstone.

Toffler, A. (1970) *Future Shock*. New York: Random House.

Toffler, A. (1981) *The Third Wave*. New York: Bantam Books.

Tomaney, J. (1990) 'The Reality of Workplace Flexibility', *Capital and Class*, 40: 29–60.

Tomaney, J. (1994) 'A New Paradigm of Work Organization and Technology', in A. Amin (ed.), *Post-Fordism: A Reader*. Oxford: Blackwell. pp. 157–94.

Torrington, D. and Hall, L. (1987) *Personnel Management: A New Approach*. London: Prentice-Hall.

Touraine, A. (1974) *The Post-Industrial Society*. London: Wildwood House.

Townley, B. (1993) 'Foucault, Power/Knowledge, and its Relevance for Human Resource Management', *The Academy of Management Review*, 18 (3): 518–45.

Townley, B. (1994) *Reframing Human Resource Management*. London: Sage.

Trethewey, A. (1999) 'Disciplined Bodies: Women's Embodied Identities at Work', *Organization Studies*, 20 (3): 423–50.

Tsoukas, H. (1992) 'Postmodernism, Reflexive Rationalism and Organizational Studies: A Reply to Martin Parker', *Organization Studies*, 13 (4): 643–9.

Tuckman, A. (1994) 'The Yellow Brick Road: Total Quality Management and the Restructuring of Organizational Culture', *Organization Studies*, 15 (5): 727–51.

Turner, B.A. (1986) 'Sociological Aspects of Organizational Symbolism', *Organizational Studies*, 7: 101–15.

Turner, B.A. (ed.) (1990) *Organizational Symbolism*. Berlin: de Gruyter.

Turner, B.A. (1992) 'The Symbolic Understanding of Organizations', in M. Reed and M. Hughes (eds), *Rethinking Organization: New Directions in Organization Theory and Analysis*. London: Sage. pp. 46–66.

Tyler, M. (1997) 'Women's Work as the Labour of Sexual Difference: Female Employment in the Contemporary Airline Industry', unpublished doctoral dissertation, University of Derby.

Tyler, M. (1999) 'Generation Sex? The Management of Sexuality in Everyday Life', paper presented to the First International Critical Management Studies Conference, Manchester, UK.

Tyler, M. (2000) 'Carry on Organizing? Towards a Queer Organization Theory', paper presented to the School of Social Sciences research seminar series, Glasgow Caledonian University, UK.

Tyler, M. and Abbott, P. (1998) 'Chocs Away: Weight Watching in the Contemporary Airline Industry', *Sociology*, 32 (3): 433–50.

Van Maanen, J. (1986) 'Power in the Bottle', in S. Srivasta (ed.), *Executive Power*. San Francisco, CA: Jossey-Bass.

Van Maanen, J. and Kunda, G. (1989) '"Real Feelings": Emotional Expression and Organizational Culture', in L.L. Cummings and B.M. Straw (eds), *Research in Organizational Behaviour*. Volume 11. Greenwich, CT: JAI Press. pp. 43–104.

Vattimo, G. (1992) *The Transparent Society*. Cambridge: Polity Press.

Wagner, P. (1994) *A Sociology of Modernity: Liberty and Discipline*. London: Routledge.

Walby, S. (1989) *Patriarchy at Work*. Cambridge: Polity Press.

Walton, R.E. (1985) 'From Control to Commitment in the Workplace', *Harvard Business Review*, 63 (2): 77–84.

Warhurst, C. and Thompson, P. (1998) 'Hands, Hearts and Minds: Changing Work and Workers at the End of the Century', in P. Thompson and C. Warhurst (eds), *Workplaces of the Future*. Basingstoke: Macmillan Business.

Watson, T.J. (1995a) 'In Search of HRM: Beyond the Rhetoric and Reality Distinction', *Personnel Review*, 24 (6): 6–16.

Watson, T.J. (1995b) 'Speaking Professionally – Soft Postmodernist Thoughts on Some Late Modernist Questions about Work, Occupations and Markets', paper presented to the Cardiff Business School/ESRC 'Professionals in Late Modernity' seminar series, Warwick Business School.

Weber, M. (1964) *The Theory of Social and Economic Organization*. Ed. T. Parsons. New York: The Free Press (first published, 1925).

Weber, M. (1978) *Economy and Society*. Trans. G. Roth and C. Wittich. Berkeley, CA: University of California Press (first published, 1921).

Weber, M. (1989) *The Protestant Ethic and the Spirit of Capitalism*. London: Unwin Hyman (first published, 1904).

Webster, F. and Robbins, K. (1989) 'Plan and Control: Towards a Cultural History of the Information Society', *Theory and Society*, 18: 323–51.

Weedon, C. (1987) *Feminist Practice and Poststructuralist Theory*. Oxford: Blackwell.

Weeks, J. (1985) *Sexuality and Its Discontents: Meanings, Myths and Modern Sexualities*. London: Routledge and Kegan Paul.

Weeks, J. (1986) *Sexuality*. London: Tavistock.

Weeks, J. (1989) *Sex, Politics and Society: The Regulation of Sexuality since 1800.* London: Longman.

Weick, K. (1969) *The Social Psychology of Organizing.* Reading, MA: Addison-Wesley.

Weisinger, H. (1998) *Emotional Intelligence at Work.* San Francisco, CA: Jossey-Bass.

Weiskopf, R. and Willmott, H. (1997) 'Turning the Given into a Question: A Critical Discussion of Chia's Organizational Analysis as Deconstructive Practice', *Electronic Journal of Radical Organization Theory,* 3 (2): 1–8.

Whitaker, A. (1992) 'The Transformation in Work: Post-Fordism Revisited', in M. Reed and M. Hughes (eds), *Rethinking Organization: New Directions in Organizational Theory and Analysis.* London: Sage. pp. 184–206.

Wibberley, M. (1993) 'Does "Lean" Necessarily Equal "Mean"?', *Personnel Management,* July: 32–3.

Wiggershaus, R. (1994) *The Frankfurt School: Its History, Theories and Political Significance.* Trans. M. Robertson. Cambridge: Polity Press (first published, 1986).

Wilkinson, A. and Willmott, H. (eds) (1995) *Making Quality Critical: New Perspectives on Organizational Change.* London: Routledge.

Williams, K., Haslam, C. and Williams, J. (1992) 'Ford Versus "Fordism": The Beginning of Mass Production?', *Work, Employment and Society,* 6 (4): 517–55.

Williams, R. (1976) *Keywords.* London: Fontana.

Williams, S. (1998) 'Modernity and the Emotions: Corporeal Reflections on the (Ir)Rational', *Sociology,* 32 (4): 747–69.

Williamson, O. (1975) *Markets and Hierarchies.* New York: The Free Press.

Willmott, H. (1990a) 'Beyond Paradigmatic Closure in Organizational Enquiry', in J. Hassard and D. Pym (eds), *The Theory and Philosophy of Organizations: Critical Issues and New Perspectives.* London: Routledge. pp. 44–60.

Willmott, H. (1990b) 'Subjectivity and the Dialectics of Praxis: Opening Up the Core of Labour Process Analysis', in D. Knights and H. Willmott (eds), *Labour Process Theory.* Basingstoke: Macmillan. pp. 336–78.

Willmott, H. (1992) 'Postmodernism and Excellence: The De-Differentiation of Economy and Culture', *Journal of Organizational Change Management,* 5 (3): 58–68.

Willmott, H. (1993) 'Strength is Ignorance, Slavery is Freedom: Managing Culture in Modern Organizations', *Journal of Management Studies,* 30 (4): 515–52.

Willmott, H. (1994) 'Bringing Agency (Back) into Organizational Analysis: Responding to the Crisis of (Post) Modernity', in J. Hassard and M. Parker (eds), *Towards a New Theory of Organizations.* London: Routledge. pp. 87–130.

Willmott, H. (1995a) 'What Has Been Happening in Organization Theory and Does it Matter?', *Personnel Review,* 24 (8): 33–53.

Willmott, H. (1995b) 'From Bravermania to Schizophrenia: The Dec(is-)eased Condition of Subjectivity in Labour Process Theory', paper presented at the 13th annual International Labour Process Conference, Blackpool, UK.

Willmott, H. (1997a) '"Outing" Organizational Analysts: Some Reflections upon Parker's Tantrum', *Organization,* 4 (2): 255–68.

Willmott, H. (1997b) 'Management and Organization Studies as Science?', *Organization,* 4 (3): 309–44.

Willmott, H. (1998) 'Re-cognizing the Other: Reflections on a "New Sensibility" in Social and Organization Studies', in R. Chia (ed.), *In the Realm of Organization: Essays for Robert Cooper.* London: Routledge. pp. 213–41.

Wittgenstein, L. (1958) *Philosophical Investigations.* Oxford: Basil Blackwell.

Witz, A. and Savage, M. (1992) 'The Gender of Organizations', in A. Witz and M. Savage (eds), *Gender and Bureaucracy.* Oxford: Blackwell. pp. 3–61.

Wolin, S. (1961) *Politics and Vision.* London: Allen and Unwin.

Woodward, J. (1970) *Industrial Organization: Behaviour and Control.* Oxford: Oxford University Press.

Wouters, C. (1989) 'The Sociology of Emotions and Flight Attendants: Hochschild's Managed Heart', *Theory, Culture & Society,* 6 (1): 95–123.

Wouters, C. (1998) 'Balancing Sex and Love since the 1960s' Sexual Revolution', *Theory, Culture & Society*, 15 (3–4): 187–214.

Wyatt, N. (1988) 'Shared Leadership in the Weavers Guild', in B. Bate and A. Taylor (eds), *Women Communicating: Studies of Women's Talk*. Norwood, NJ: Ablex. pp. 147–75.

York, K. (1989) 'Defining Sexual Harassment in Workplaces: A Policy-capturing Approach', *Academy of Management Journal*, 32 (4): 830–50.

Zimmerman, D. (1971) 'Record-keeping and the Intake Process in a Public Welfare Bureaucracy', in S. Wheeler (ed.), *On Record*. New York: Russell Sage.

Zimmerman, D. (1973) 'The Practicalities of Rule Use', in G. Salaman and K. Thompson (eds), *People and Organizations*. London: Routledge and Kegan Paul.

Zuboff, S. (1988) *In the Age of the Smart Machine: The Future of Work and Power*. Oxford: Heinemann.

Index